*A Wholly Different Way
of Living*

By the same author:

THE FIRST AND LAST FREEDOM
EDUCATION AND THE SIGNIFICANCE OF LIFE
COMMENTARIES ON LIVING: FIRST SERIES
COMMENTARIES ON LIVING: SECOND SERIES
COMMENTARIES ON LIVING: THIRD SERIES
LIFE AHEAD
THIS MATTER OF CULTURE
FREEDOM FROM THE KNOWN
THE ONLY REVOLUTION
THE URGENCY OF CHANGE
THE IMPOSSIBLE QUESTION
BEYOND VIOLENCE
THE AWAKENING OF INTELLIGENCE
BEGINNINGS OF LEARNING
KRISHNAMURTI'S NOTEBOOK
TRUTH AND ACTUALITY
THE WHOLENESS OF LIFE
EXPLORATION INTO INSIGHT
MEDITATIONS
POEMS AND PARABLES
KRISHNAMURTI'S JOURNAL
THE ENDING OF TIME
(with Dr David Bohm)
LAST TALKS AT SAANEN 1985
(illustrated with photographs)
KRISHNAMURTI TO HIMSELF
THE FUTURE IS NOW

A Wholly Different Way of Living

KRISHNAMURTI

In Dialogue with
Professor Allan W Anderson

LONDON
VICTOR GOLLANCZ LTD
1991

First published in Great Britain 1991
by Victor Gollancz Ltd,
14 Henrietta Street, London WC2E 8QJ

Copyright © 1991 by Krishnamurti Foundation Trust Ltd

The dialogues reproduced in an edited and slightly abridged version in this book took place at San Diego State University from February 18 to 28 1974. They were professionally videotape-recorded for Krishnamurti Foundation of America and videocassettes of the dialogues are available from KFA by writing to P O Box 1560, Ojai CA93024, USA or by writing to the Krishnamurti Foundation Trust, Brockwood Park, Bramdean, Hampshire SO24 OLQ, England.

A catalogue record for this book is
available from the British Library

ISBN 0 575 05166 3

Typeset by CentraCet, Cambridge
and printed in Great Britain by St Edmundsbury Press Ltd
Bury St Edmunds, Suffolk

CONTENTS

Dialogue   *page*

I	Knowledge and the Transformation of Man	7
II	Knowledge and Conflict in Human Relationships	24
III	What Is Communication with Others?	40
IV	What Is a Responsible Human Being?	54
V	Order Comes from the Understanding of Our Disorder	67
VI	The Nature and Total Eradication of Fear	82
VII	Understanding, Not Controlling, Desire	96
VIII	Does Pleasure Bring Happiness?	110
IX	Sorrow, Passion and Beauty	124
X	The Art of Listening	135
XI	Being Hurt and Hurting Others	148
XII	Love, Sex and Pleasure	163
XIII	A Different Way of Living	178
XIV	Death, Life and Love Are Indivisible – the Nature of Immortality	193
XV	Religion, Authority and Education – Part 1	209
XVI	Religion, Authority and Education – Part 2	223
XVII	Meditation, a Quality of Attention that Pervades All of One's Life	238
XVIII	Meditation and the Sacred Mind	255

DIALOGUE I

Knowledge and the Transformation of Man

DR ANDERSON: Mr Krishnamurti, I was very taken with a recent statement of yours in which you said that each human being is responsible for bringing about his own transformation, which is not dependent on knowledge or time. And if it's agreeable to you, I thought it would be a splendid thing if we explored together the general area of transformation itself, and after that perhaps the other related areas would begin to fall into place and we could discuss the relationship between them.

KRISHNAMURTI: Don't you think, sir, considering what's happening in the world, in India, in Europe and in America, the general degeneration, in literature, in art, and especially in the deep cultural sense, in religion, that there is a traditional approach, a mere acceptance of authority, of belief, which is not really the religious spirit? Seeing all this, the confusion, the great misery, the sense of infinite sorrow, any observant and serious person would say that this society can be changed only when the individual human being really transforms himself radically, that is, regenerates himself fundamentally. And the responsibility for that depends on the human being, not on the mass or on the priests or on a church, a temple, but on a human being who is aware of this enormous confusion, politically, religiously and economically; in every direction there is such misery, such unhappiness. And when you see that, it is a very serious thing to ask oneself whether a human being like oneself or another can really deeply undergo a radical transformation. And when that question is put, and when one sees one's responsibility in relation to the whole, then perhaps we can discuss what relationship knowledge and time have to the transformation of man.

A: I quite follow. We need to lay some groundwork.

K: Yes. Because most people are not seriously concerned with the events, with the chaos, with the mess in the world at present. They are concerned only with the problems of energy, of pollution and so on – such superficial things. They are not really deeply concerned with the human mind – the mind that is destroying the world.

A: Yes, I quite follow. What you have said places radical responsibility on the individual as such.

K: Yes.

A: There are no five-year plans that we can expect to help us out!

K: You see, the word 'individual' is really not a correct one because the term, as you know, sir, means undivided, indivisible, in himself. But human beings are totally fragmented, therefore they are not individuals. They may have a bank account, a name, a house, but they are not really individuals in the sense of being total, complete, harmonious, whole, unfragmented, which is really what it means to be an individual.

A: Well, would you say then to move or make passage or, perhaps, a better word would simply be to change, since we are not talking about time, from this fragmented state to one of wholeness could be regarded as a change in the level of the being of the person. Could we say that?

K: Yes, but you see the word 'whole' implies not only sanity, health but also holy. All that's implied in that one word 'whole'. And human beings are never whole. They are fragmented, contradictory, they are torn apart by various desires. So when we talk of an individual, the individual is really a human being who is totally, completely whole, sane, healthy and therefore holy. And to bring about such a human being is our responsibility educationally, politically, religiously, in every way. And therefore it is the responsibility of the educator, of everybody, not just myself; it is your responsibility as well as mine, as well as his.

A: It's everyone's responsibility.

K: Absolutely – because *we* have created this awful mess in the world.

A: But the individual is the one who must make the start.

K: It's the business of the human being, each human being – it does not matter whether he is a politician or a businessman or just an ordinary person like me in the street – to realize the enormous suffering, misery, confusion there is in the world. And it's our responsibility to change all that.

A: It is the responsibility of each human person.

K: Yes, whether he is in India or England or America or wherever he is.

A: If the change is going to start at all, it's going to be with each one of us.

K: Yes, sir, with each human being. Therefore the question arises from that, does a human being realize with all seriousness his responsibility not only to himself but to the whole of mankind?

A: It wouldn't appear so from the way things go on.

K: Obviously not; each one is concerned with his own petty little selfish desires. So responsibility implies tremendous attention, care, diligence – not negligence as is the case now.

A: Yes, I do follow that. The word 'we' used in relation to each brings about the suggestion of a relationship which we could perhaps pursue here a moment. There seems to be an indivisible relation between each of us and what we call the whole, which the individual doesn't sense.

K: Sir, as you know, I have been all over the world, except behind the Iron Curtain and to China, the Bamboo Curtain. I have talked to and seen thousands and thousands of people. I have been doing this for fifty years and more. Human beings wherever they live are more or less the same. They have their problems of sorrow, problems of fear, problems of livelihood, problems of personal relationship, problems of survival, over-population and the enormous problem of death – it is a problem common to all of us. There is no Eastern problem or Western problem. The West has its particular civilization and the East has its own. But all human beings are caught in this trap.

A: Yes, I follow that.

K: They don't seem to be able to get out of it. They have been going on and on in it now for millennia.

A: Therefore the question is, how does one bring this about? The word 'individual', as you have just described it, seems to me to have a relationship to the word 'transform' in itself. It seems that many people have the notion that to transform a thing means to change it utterly without any relationship whatsoever to what it is as such. That would seem to ignore that we are talking about form that undergoes a change, while form still abides.

K: Yes, sir, I understand.

A: Otherwise the change would involve a loss, a total loss.

K: So are we asking this question, sir: what place has knowledge in the regeneration of man, in the transformation of man, in a fundamental, radical movement in man? What place has knowledge and therefore time? Is that what you are asking?

A: Yes, I am. Because either we accept that a change which is a genuine change means the annihilation of what preceded it, or we are talking about a total transformation of something that abides.

K: Yes. So let us look at that word for a minute. Revolution in the ordinary sense of that word does not mean a gradual evolution, does it.

A: I agree.

K: Now, revolution is either bloody, overthrowing the government, or there is a revolution in the psyche. Outer or inner.

A: Yes, outer or inner.

K: The outer *is* the inner. The inner *is* the outer. There is no difference between the outer and the inner; they are totally related to each other.

A: Then this goes back to what you mentioned earlier. There is no division, even though intellectually you make a distinction, between the 'I' and the 'we'.

K: That's right. So, when we talk about change, we mean not a mere bloody physical revolution, but rather a revolution in the makeup of the mind of the human being, the way he thinks, the way he behaves, the way he conducts himself, the way he operates, functions, the whole of that. Now, in that psychological revolution – not evolution in the sense of gradualness – what place has knowledge in that? In the regeneration of man, which is the inward revolution which will affect the outer.

A: And which is not a gradual progress.

K: Gradual progress is endless.

A: Exactly. So we are talking of an instant qualitative change.

K: Again when you use the word 'instant', it seems as though it is to happen suddenly. That's why I am rather hesitant about using the word 'instant'. We will go into it in a minute. First of all, sir, let's be clear what you and I are talking about, if we may. We see objectively the appalling mess the world is in, right? The misery, the confusion, the deep sorrow of man.

A: Yes.

K: I can't tell you what I feel when I go round the world. The pettiness, the shallowness, the emptiness of all this, of the so-called Western civilization, if I may use that word – and which Eastern civilization too is being dragged into. And all the time we are just scratching on the surface and we think that mere change on the surface – change in the structure – is going to do something enormous to all human beings. On the contrary it has done nothing. It polishes things a little bit here and there but deeply and fundamentally it does not change man. So, when we are discussing change we must I think be fairly clear that we mean change in the psyche, in the very being of human beings. That is, in the very structure and nature of his thought.

A: A change at the root.

K: At the root. And therefore when there is that change he will naturally bring about a change in society. It isn't society first, or the individual first, it is human change which will transform society. They are not two separate things.

A: Now I must be very careful that I understand this exactly.

K: After all human beings have created this society. By their greed, by their anger, by their violence, by their brutality, by their pettiness, they have created this society.

A: Precisely.

K: And they think by changing the structure they are going to change the human being. This has been the Communist problem, this has been the eternal problem: that if we change the environment we change man. They have tried that in ten different ways and they haven't succeeded in changing man. On the contrary man conquers the environment as such.

So, let us be clear that the outer is the inner – the inner is the outer – that there is not the division, society and the individual, the collective and the separate human being, but that the human being is the whole, he is society, he is the separate human individual, he is the factor which brings about this chaos.

A: Yes, I am following this very closely.

K: Therefore he is the world and the world is him.

A: Yes. Therefore if he changes everything changes. If he doesn't change nothing changes.

K: I think this is very important because we don't realize, I think, this basic factor that we are the world and the world is us, that the world is not something separate from me nor the me separate from the world. Whatever culture you are born in, you are the result of that culture. And that culture has produced this world. The materialistic world of the West, if one can call it that, which is spreading over the whole globe – everything is being swept aside in the wake of Western culture, and this culture has produced this human being, and the human being has created this culture.

A: Exactly.

K: He has created the paintings, the marvellous cathedrals, the marvellous technological things, going to the moon and so on, human beings have produced all that. But it is human beings who have also created the rotten society in which we live. The immoral society in which we live has been created by human beings.

A: Yes, there is no doubt about that.

K: And therefore the world is you, you are the world, there is no other. If you accept that, if you see that, not intellectually, but feel it in your heart, in your mind, in your blood, then the question is: is it possible for a human being to transform himself inwardly and therefore outwardly?

A: I am very concerned to see this as clearly as I can in terms of two texts that come to mind. I am thinking of that wonderful text in the third chapter of St John's gospel, which says (and I will try to translate this as the Greek has it), 'The one who is doing the truth is coming to the light'. It isn't that he does the truth and then later comes to the light. And it isn't that we could say from the pulpit, I will tell you what the truth is, if you do it then you will see the light. Because we are back again to what you mentioned earlier, the non-temporal relationship between the action which itself is the transformation ...

K: Quite.

A: ... and the marvellous vista of understanding, which is not an 'if then' thing, but is truly concurrent. And the other one that I thought of, and I was hoping you might agree with, is saying the same thing, if I understand it well in terms of what you have said – and again I will try to translate it as literally as I can: 'God is love and the one abiding in love is abiding in God and God is abiding in him.'

K: Quite, quite.

A: I put the '-ing' on all those words because of the character of the language itself. And this 'inging' gives the feeling that there is an activity here that is not bound temporally.

K: It isn't a static state. It isn't something you accept intellectually and leave like that. Then it is death, there is nothing in it.

A: Yes.

K: That's why, you see, we have divided the physical world as the East and the West. We have divided ourselves into different religions, and we have divided the world into nationalities, capitalists and socialists, communists, and the others and so on. We have divided ourselves into fragments, opposing each other; and where there is a division there is conflict.

A: Precisely.

K: I think that is a basic law.

A: Where there is a division there is conflict. But in terms of that word 'knowledge' it appears that people believe to start with that the division is there, and they operate on that radical belief.

K: That's why I am saying it's so important to understand from the beginning of our talks that the world is not different from me and that I am the world. This may sound rather simplistic, but it has got very deep fundamental meaning if you realize what it means, not intellectually, but the understanding of it inwardly and therefore there is no division. The moment I realize that I am the world and the world is me, then I am not a Christian, nor a Hindu, nor a Buddhist – nothing, I am a human being.

A: I was just thinking, when you were saying that, how certain kinds of philosophical analysis would approach this, because on the one hand, as you said, it might sound simplistic. Some would say it is, therefore we don't have to pay attention to it; others would say, well, it's probably so lacking in clarity, even though it's profound, that it is some kind of mysticism. And so we are back and forth, with the division again.

K: I know, I know.

A: So I do follow you.

K: So if that is clear, that the human mind has divided the world in order to find its own security, which brings about its own insecurity, then one must inwardly as well as outwardly deny this division, as we and they, I and you, the Indian and the European and the Capitalist and the Communist. You cut at the very root of this division. Therefore from that arises the question: can the human mind which has been so conditioned for millennia, which has acquired so much knowledge in so many directions – can that human mind change, bring about a regeneration in itself and be free to reincarnate now?

A: Now.

K: That is the question.

A: That is the question – exactly – reincarnate now. It would appear from what you have said that one could say that the vast amount of accumulated knowledge, the accretion of centuries, is a discussion we have been having with ourselves, regardless of which culture we are speaking about, as a commentary on this division.

K: Absolutely.

A: Without really grasping the division itself. And of course since the division is infinitely divisible . . .

K: Of course.

A: Then we can have tome after tome after tome, libraries after libraries, mausoleums of books without end because we are continually dividing the division. Yes, I follow you.

K: And you see that's why culture is different from civilization. Culture implies growth.

A: Oh yes.

K: Growth in the flowering of goodness.

A: A lovely phrase.

K: That is culture – real culture – the flowering of goodness, and that doesn't exist. We have civilization – you can travel from India to America in a few hours – you have better bathrooms, better this and better that and so on with all the complications that involves. That has been the Western culture, which is now absorbing the East. So goodness is the very essence of culture. Religion *is* the transformation of man. Not all the beliefs, churches and the idolatry of the Christians, Hindus and so on. That's not religion.

So we come back to the point. If one sees all this in the world – observes it, not condemning it or justifying it – just observing it, then from that one asks: man has collected such enormous information, knowledge, and has that knowledge changed him into goodness? You follow, sir – into a culture that will make him flower in the beauty of goodness. It has not.

A: No, it has not.

K: Therefore it has no meaning.

A: Excursions into defining goodness are not going to help us.

K: You can give explanations, definitions, but definitions are not the reality.

A: Of course not.

K: The word isn't the thing, the description isn't the described.

A: Precisely.

K: So we come back to the same point again. Because personally I am tremendously concerned with this question: how to change man. I go to India every year for three months or five months and I see what is happening there, and I see what is happening in Europe, and I see what is happening in this country, in America, and I can't tell you what a shock it gives me each time I come to these countries – the degeneration, the superficiality, the intellectual concepts galore without any substance, without any basis or ground in which the beauty of goodness, of reality can grow. So saying all that, what place has knowledge in the regeneration of man? That is the basic question.

A: That's our point of departure. Good. And the knowledge we have pointed to so far in our discussion is a knowledge which in itself has no power to effect this transformation.

K: No, sir, but knowledge has a place.

A: Yes, I didn't mean to deny that. I mean what is expected of this knowledge that is accumulated in libraries and so forth, is an expectation which it cannot in itself fulfil.

K: No. I must go back to that word again – the word 'knowledge', what does it mean 'to know'?

A: Well, I have understood the word in a strict sense this way: knowledge is the apprehension of 'what is', but what passes for knowledge might not be that.

K: No, what is generally accepted as knowledge is experience.

A: Yes, that is what is generally accepted.

K: We will begin with that because it's generally accepted – the experience which yields or leaves a mark which is knowledge. That accumulated knowledge, whether in the scientific world or in the biological world or in the business world or in the world of the mind, the being, is the known. The known is the past, therefore knowledge is the past. Knowledge cannot be in the present. I can *use* knowledge in the present.

A: But it's founded on the past.

K: Yes. It has its roots in the past. I personally don't read any of these books, the Bhagavad Gita or the Upanishads, none of the psychological books, nothing. I am not a reader. I have *observed tremendously* all my life. Now, knowledge has its place.

A: Oh, yes.

K: Let's be clear on this. In practical, technological matters I must know where I am going, physically, and so on. Now, what place has that human experience as well as scientific knowledge in changing the quality of a mind that has become brutal, violent, petty, selfish, greedy, ambitious and all the rest of it? What place has knowledge in that?

A: We are going back to the statement we began with, namely that this transformation is not dependent on knowledge; then the answer would have to be, it doesn't have a place.

K: Therefore let's find out what the limits of knowledge are.

A: Yes, of course.

K: Where is the demarcation, freedom from the known — where does that freedom begin?

A: Yes, now I know precisely the point which we are going to move from. Where does that freedom begin, which is not dependent on this funded accretion from the past?

K: That's right. So, the human mind is constructed on knowledge, it has evolved through millennia on this accretion, on tradition, on knowledge.

A: Yes.

K: It is there, and all our actions are based on that knowledge.

A: Which by definition must be repetitious.

K: Obviously it is a repetition. So what is the beginning of freedom in relation to knowledge? May I put it this way to make myself clear? I have experienced something yesterday that has left a mark. That is knowledge and with that knowledge I meet the next experience. So the next experience is translated in terms of the old and therefore that experience is never new.

A: So in a way, if I understand you correctly, you are saying that the experience that I had yesterday, that I recall . . .

K: The recollection.

A: ... upon my meeting something new that appears to have some relationship to it, I approach on the basis of holding my previous knowledge up as a mirror in which to determine the nature of this new thing ...

K: Quite.

A: ... and this could be a very distorting mirror!

K: Generally it is. You see that's what I mean. Where is freedom in relation to knowledge? Or is freedom something other than the continuity of knowledge?

A: It must be something other.

K: Which means, if one goes into it very, very deeply, the ending of knowledge.

A: Yes.

K: And what does that mean, what does it mean to end knowledge, when I have lived entirely on knowledge?

A: It means ending that immediately.

K: Ah, wait, wait. See what is involved in it. I met you yesterday and there is the image of you in my mind and that image meets you next day.

A: Yes.

K: The image meets you.

A: The image meets me.

K: And there are a dozen images or a hundred images. So the image is the knowledge, the image is the tradition, the image is the past. Now can there be freedom from that?

A: If this transformation that you speak of is to come to pass, there must be.

K: Of course. Therefore we can state it, but how is the mind which strives, acts, functions on image, on knowledge, on the known — how is it to end that? Take this very simple fact: you are in sorrow, or you praise me; that remains knowledge, and with that image, with that knowledge I meet you. So I never meet you. The image meets you.

A: Exactly.

K: Therefore there is no relationship between you and me.

A: Yes, because between us this image has been interposed.

K: Of course, obviously. Therefore how is that image to end, never to register — you follow sir?

A: I can't depend on someone else to handle it for me.

K: Therefore what am I to do? How is this mind which is registering, recording all the time — the function of the brain is to record all the time — how is it to be free of knowledge? When you have done some harm to me personally, collectively or whatever, you have insulted me, flattered me, how is the brain not to register that? If it registers, it is already an image, a memory — and the past then meets the present; and therefore there is no solution to it.

A: Exactly.

K: I was looking at the word 'tradition' the other day in a very good dictionary. Of course the ordinary word — tradere — is to give, hand over, to give across. But it also has another special meaning — betrayal.

A: Oh, yes, to traduce.

K: To traduce. And in discussing in India this came out, betrayal of the present. If I live in tradition I betray the present.

A: Yes, I do see that.

K: Which means knowledge betrays the present. I betray the present.

A: Which is in fact a self-betrayal.

K: Yes, that's right.

A: Yes, I do see that.

K: So how is the mind which functions on knowledge — how is the brain which is recording all the time — to end, to see the importance of recording and not let it move in any other direction? That is, sir, let me put it this way, very simply: you insult me, you hurt me, by word, gesture, by an actual act; that leaves a mark on the brain which is memory. That memory is knowledge, that knowledge is going to interfere in my meeting you next time – obviously. Now how is the brain and also the mind to record and not let it interfere with the present?

A: The person must, it seems to me, take pains to negate.

K: No, see what is implied, how am I to negate it? How is the brain whose function is to record, recording like a computer . . .

A: I didn't mean to suggest that it negates the recording. But it's the association, the translation of the recording into an emotional complex.

K: That's just the point: how is it to end this emotional response when I meet you next time, you who have hurt me? That's the problem.

A: That's the place from which we in practice must then begin.

K: Yes.

A: Exactly. There is an aspect of this that interests me very much in terms of the relation between the theoretical and the practical.

K: Sir, to me theory has no reality. Theories have no importance to a man who is actually living.

A: May I say what I mean by theory? I don't think I mean what you think I mean by it. I mean theory in the sense of the Greek word 'theorea' – spectacle, what is out there that I see. And the word is therefore very closely related to what you have been talking about in terms of knowledge. And yet it is the case that if we see something, that something is registered to us in the mind in terms of a likeness of it, otherwise we should have to become it in order to receive it, which in the material order would annihilate us. It seems to me, if I followed you correctly, that there is a profound confusion in one's relationship to that necessity for the finite being and what he makes of it. And in so far as he is making the wrong thing of it he is in desperate trouble and can only go on repeating himself, and in such a repetition increasing despair.

K: You see religion is based on tradition. Religion is vast propaganda, as it is now. In India, here, anywhere, propaganda of theories, of beliefs, of idolatry, worship, essentially based on the acceptance of a theory.

A: Yes.

K: Essentially based on an idea.

A: A statement, a postulate.

K: Ideas put out by thought.

A: Right.

K: And obviously that's not religion. So religion as it exists now is the very denial of truth.

A: Yes, I am sure I understand you.

K: And if a man like me wants to find out, to discover what the truth is he must deny the whole structure of religion as it is — which is idolatry, propaganda, fear, division: you are a Christian, I am a Hindu — all that nonsense, and be a light to himself. Not in the vain sense of that word. Light because the world is in darkness and a human being has to transform himself, has to be a light to himself. And the light is not lit by somebody else.

A: So there is a point at which he must stop repeating himself. In a sense we could use the analogy perhaps from surgery: something that has been continuous is now cut.

K: Yes.

A: And cut radically, not just fooled around with.

K: We haven't time to fool around any more — the house is on fire! At least I feel this enormously — things are coming to such a pass that each human being must do something. Not in terms of better housing, better security, more this and that, but basically regenerate himself.

A: But if the person believes that in cutting himself free from this accretion he is killing himself, then he is going to resist that idea.

K: Of course. Therefore he has to understand what his mind has created, therefore he has to understand himself.

A: So he starts observing himself.

K: Himself — which is the world.

A: Yes. Not learning five languages to be able to . . .

K: Attending courses where you learn sensitivity and all that rubbish.

A: The point that you are making, it seems to me, is made also by the great Danish thinker, Kierkegaard, who lived a very trying life in his own community because he was asking them to undertake what you are saying. He was saying: look, if I go to a seminary and try to understand what Christianity is by studying it myself then what I am doing is appropriating something, but then when do I know I have appropriated it fully? I shall never know that point, therefore I shall forever appropriate it and never do anything about it, as such, as a subject. The person must risk the deed, not the utterance, not simply thinking through what someone has thought before but actually embodying the meaning through the observation of himself in relation to that. And that has always seemed to me a very profound insight. But one of the ironies of that is, of course, that we have an endless proliferation of studies in which scholars have learned Danish in order to understand Kierkegaard, and what they are doing to a large extent – if I haven't misjudged the spirit of much that I have read – is simply to perpetuate the very thing he said should be cut. I do have this very strong feeling that profound change would take place if the teacher were not only to grasp what you have said but take the risk of acting on it. Since if it isn't acted on, we are back again where we were. We have toyed with the idea of being valiant and courageous, but then we think about what is involved before we do, and then we don't do.

K: Quite.

A: We think and don't do.

K: Therefore, sir, the word is not the thing. The description is not the described, and if you are not concerned with the description but only with the thing, 'what is', then we have to *do* something. When you are confronted with 'what is' you act, but when you are concerned with theories and speculations and beliefs you never act.

A: So there isn't any hope for this transformation, if I understood you correctly, if I just think to myself that this sounds marvellous: 'I am the world and the world is me', while I go on thinking that the description is the described, there is no hope. So we are speaking about a disease here, and we are speaking about something that has been stated as the case, and if I take what has been *stated* as the case, as the case *itself*, then I am thinking that the description is the described.

K: Of course.

A: And I never get out.

K: Sir, it is like a man who is hungry, any amount of description of the right kind of food will never satisfy him. He is hungry, he wants food. So, all this implies, doesn't it, sir, several things? First, can there be freedom from knowledge — and knowledge has its place — can there be freedom from tradition as knowledge?

A: From tradition as knowledge, yes.

K: Can there be freedom from this separative outlook — me and you, we and they, and all this divisive attitude or activity in life? Those are the problems we have to attend to.

A: That's what we must attend to as we move through our dialogues.

K: So first can the mind be free from the known, not verbally but actually?

A: Actually.

K: I can speculate about what is freedom and all the rest of it, but can I see the necessity, the importance, that there must be freedom from the known, otherwise life becomes repetitive, a continuous scratching of the surface which has no meaning.

A: Of course. In our next conversation I hope we can pursue this further.

18 February 1974

DIALOGUE II

Knowledge and Conflict in Human Relationships

DR ANDERSON: Mr Krishnamurti, in our previous conversation I was delighted that we had made the distinction, with regard to knowledge and self-transformation, between, on the one hand, my relationship with the world, in the sense that the world is me and I am the world, and on the other hand this condition in which one wrongly thinks that the description is the described. It would appear then that something must be done to bring about a change in the individual, and we could say that this is where the observer comes in. If the individual is not to make the mistake of taking the description for the described, then he must as an observer relate to the observed in a way that is totally different from the way he has been doing in his confusion. I thought that perhaps if we pursued that in this conversation, it would link up directly with what we had said earlier.

KRISHNAMURTI: What we said was that there must be a quality of freedom from the known, otherwise the known is merely the repetition of the past, of the tradition, the image, and so on. The past, surely, *is* the observer. The past is the accumulated knowledge as the 'me' and the 'you', 'they' and 'us'. The observer is put together by thought as the past. Thought is the past, thought is never free, thought is never new, because thought is the response of the past, as knowledge, as experience, as memory.

A: Yes, I follow that.

K: And the observer, when he observes, is observing with the memories, the experiences, knowledge, hurts, despairs, hope – with all that background he looks at the observed. So the observer then becomes separate from the observed. *Is* the observer different from the observed? So when we are talking of freedom from the known we are talking about freedom from the observer.

A: From the observer, yes.

K: And the observer is tradition, the past, the conditioned mind that looks at things, looks at itself, looks at the world, looks at me and so on. So the observer is always dividing. The observer is the past and therefore cannot observe wholly.

A: If the person uses the first person pronoun, 'I', while he is taking the description for the described, this is the observer he refers to when he says 'I'.

K: The 'I' is the past.

A: I see.

K: The 'I' is the whole structure of what has been, the remembrances, the memories, the hurts, the various demands, all that is put together in the word 'I', who is the observer and therefore division: the observer and the observed. The observer who thinks he is a Christian and observes a non-Christian or a Communist; this division, this attitude of mind which observes with conditioned responses, with memories and so on, that is the known.

A: I see.

K: I mean I think that is logically so.

A: It follows precisely from what you have said.

K: So we are asking, can the mind, its whole structure, be free from the known? Otherwise the repetitious actions, repetitious attitudes, repetitious ideologies, will go on, modified, changed, but it will be in the same direction.

So, what is this freedom from the known? I think that is very important to understand because any creative action — I am using the word creative in its original sense, not in the sense of creative writing, creative bakery, creative essays, creative pictures, I am not talking in that sense. Creation in the deeper sense of that word means something totally new being born. The other is not creative, it is merely repetitive, modified, changed — the past. So unless there is a freedom from the known there is no creative action at all. Freedom implies not the negation of the known but the understanding of the known and that understanding brings about an intelligence which is the very essence of freedom.

A: I'd like to make sure that I've understood your use of this word creative. It seems to me very important. People who use the word creative in the sense you described, creative this, that or the other . . .

K: That is a dreadful way of using that word.

A: . . . because the issue of their activity is something merely novel.

K: Novel, that's right.

A: Not radically new but novel.

K: It's like creative writing, teaching creative writing. It's so absurd.

A: Exactly. Yes, I grasp the distinction which you have made; and I must say I fully agree with it.

K: Unless you *feel* new you cannot create anything new.

A: That's right. And the person who imagines that he is creative in this other sense that we pointed to is a person whose reference for his activity is this observer that we mentioned who is tied to the past.

K: Yes, that's right.

A: So even if something does appear that is really extraordinarily novel, merely novel but still extraordinarily novel, they are fooling themselves.

K: The novel is not the creative.

A: And today especially, it seems to me in our culture we have become hysterical about this because in order to be creative one must simply rack one's brains in order to produce something which is bizarre enough to get attention.

K: That's right, attention, success.

A: Yes, it has to be novel to the degree that I feel knocked on the head by it.

K: Eccentric and all the rest of it.

A: Exactly. But if that tension is increased, then with each succeeding generation the person is under tremendous stress not to repeat the past, which he can't help repeating.

K: Repeating, quite. That's why I say that freedom is one thing and knowledge is another. We must relate the two and see whether the mind can be free from knowledge. We won't go into that point now, which is real meditation for me. You follow, sir?

A: Yes, I do.

K: To see whether the brain can record and be free not to record, to record and operate when necessary in terms of the recording, the memory, and knowledge, and be free to observe without the observer.

A: Yes. That distinction seems to me absolutely necessary, otherwise it wouldn't be intelligible.

K: So knowledge is necessary to act in the sense of my going home from here to the place I live; I must have knowledge for this; I must have knowledge to speak English; I must have knowledge to write a letter and so on. Knowledge as function, mechanical function, is necessary. Now if I use that knowledge in my relationship with you, another human being, I am bringing about a barrier, a division between you and me, namely the observer. Am I making myself clear? That is, knowledge in relationship, in human relationship, is destructive. That is, knowledge, which is the tradition, the memory, the image, which the mind has built about you, that knowledge is separative and therefore creates conflict in our relationship. As we said earlier, where there is division there must be conflict. This divisive activity – politically, religiously, economically, socially, in every way – must inevitably bring conflict and therefore violence. That's obvious.

A: Exactly.

K: Now, when knowledge comes between human beings in a relationship there must be conflict – between husband and wife, boy and girl. Wherever there is the operation of the observer who is the past, who is knowledge, there is division and therefore conflict in relationship.

A: So the question that comes up next is the one of freedom from being subject to this repetitive round.

K: Yes, that's right. Now is that posslble? It is an immense question because human beings live in relationship. There is no life without relationship. Life means to be related.

A: Exactly.

K: People who retire into a monastery are still related; however much they might like to think they are alone, they are actually related, related to the past.

A: Yes, very much so.

K: To their saviour, to their Christ, to their Buddha, you follow, all that, they are related to the past.

A: And their rules.

K: And their rules, everything. They live in the past and therefore they are the most destructive people because they are not creative in the deeper sense of that word.

A: No, and in so far as they are in this confusion you have been talking about, they are not even producing anything novel.

K: The novel would be for a man who is talkative to enter a monastery where they don't talk.

A: Yes.

K: That's novel to him and he says that's a miracle!

A: Right.

K: So our problem is: what place has knowledge in human relationship?

A: Yes, that's the problem.

K: That's one problem. Because relationship with human beings is obviously of the highest importance. Out of that relationship we create the society in which we live, out of that relationship all our existence comes.

A: This would take us back again to the earlier statement: I am the world and the world is me. That is a statement about relationship. It's a statement about many other things too, but that is a statement about relationship. The statement that the description is not the described, is the statement of the rupture of this relationship . . .

K: That's right.

A: . . . in terms of everyday activity.

A WHOLLY DIFFERENT WAY OF LIVING

K: Sir, everyday activity is my life, our life.

A: Is everything. Yes, precisely.

K: Whether I go to the office, the factory, or drive a bus or whatever it is, it is life, living. So knowledge and freedom: they must both exist together, not freedom separate from knowledge. It's the harmony between the two, and the two operating all the time in relationship.

A: Knowledge and freedom in harmony.

K: In harmony. It's as if they can never be divorced. If I want to live with you in great harmony, which is love, which we will discuss later on, there must be this absolute sense of freedom from you, not dependency and so on – this absolute sense of freedom and an operating at the same time in the field of knowledge.

A: Exactly. So somehow this knowledge, if I may use a theological word here, if correctly related to this freedom, is continuously redeemed; it is somehow no longer operating destructively but in coordination with the freedom in which I *may* live – because we haven't got to that freedom yet, we are just positing freedom.

K: No, we haven't gone into the question of freedom, what it means.

A: Yes, but I think we have established something in this conversation which is terribly important in terms of helping people not to misunderstand what you are saying.

K: Quite.

A: I have the feeling that because they are not sufficiently attentive to what you say, people simply dismiss many statements of yours out of hand as . . .

K: . . . impossible.

A: . . . either impossible, or if they like the aesthetics of it, it still doesn't apply to them. 'It's a lovely thing out there, wouldn't it be great if somehow we could do this.' But you see you haven't said that. You haven't said what they think you have said. You've said something about knowledge with respect to pathology and you've said something about knowledge which is no longer destructive. So we're not saying that knowledge as such is the bad guy and something else is the good guy.

K: No.

A: I think it is terribly important that that is seen, and I wouldn't mind it being repeated over and over again, because I do strongly feel that it's easy to misunderstand.

K: That's a very important point because religion means gathering together all one's energy to be attentive. We'll discuss that when we come to it. So freedom means a sense of complete austerity and a sense of total negation of the observer.

A: Exactly, but austerity in itself doesn't produce it.

K: It is freedom that brings about this austerity inwardly. Freedom in action in the field of knowledge and in the field of human relationship, because human relationship is of the highest importance.

A: Yes, particularly if I am the world and the world is me.

K: Obviously. So what place has knowledge in human relationship? Knowledge in the sense of past experience, tradition, image. All that is the observer and what place has the observer in human relationship?

A: What place has knowledge and what place has the observer?

K: The observer is the knowledge.

A: Is the knowledge. But there is the possibility of seeing knowledge, not simply negatively, but in coordination, in true creative relationship.

K: I have said that.

A: Right. Exactly.

K: To make it very simple, I'm related to you – you are my brother, husband, wife or whatever it is, and what place has knowledge as the observer, which is the past, in our relationship?

A: If our relationship is creative . . .

K: It is not if we state it actually as it is. I am related to you, I am married to you, I am your wife or husband; now what is the actuality in that relationship? The actuality is that I am separate from you.

A: The actuality must be that we are not divided.

K: But we are. I may call you my husband, my wife, but I am concerned with my success, I am concerned with my money, I am concerned with my ambitions, my envy, I am full of 'me'.

A: Yes, I see that, but I want to make sure that we haven't reached a confusion here.

K: Yes, we have.

A: When I say that the actuality is that we are not separate, I do not mean that at the phenomenal level a dysfunction is not occurring. I am fully aware of that. But if we are going to say that the world is me and I am the world . . .

K: We say it theoretically, we don't feel it.

A: Precisely. But if that is the case, that the world is me and I am the world, that this is actual . . .

K: This is actual only when I have no division in myself.

A: Exactly.

K: But I have a division.

A: If I have a division then there is no relationship between one and the other.

K: Therefore I am accepting the *idea* that the world is me and I am the world. But that is just an idea.

A: But if and when it happens . . .

K: Wait, just see what takes place in my mind. I make a statement of that kind, the world is you and you are the world. The mind then translates it into an idea, into a concept and tries to live according to that concept.

A: Exactly.

K: It has abstracted from reality.

A: In a destructive sense.

K: I won't call it destructive or positive, this is what is going on. So in my relationship with you what place has knowledge, the past, the image which is the observer; what place has the observer in our relationship? Actually the observer is the factor of division.

A: Right.

K: And therefore there is conflict between you and me. This is what is going on in the world every day.

A: Then one would have to say, it seems to me, following the conversation point by point, that the place of this observer, understood as you have explained it, is the point of dysrelationship.

K: It is the point where there is actually no relationship at all! I may sleep with my wife, and so on, but actually there is no relationship because I have my own pursuits, my own ambitions and idiosyncrasies, and she has hers, so we are always separate and therefore always in battle with each other. Which means that the observer as the past is the factor of division. As long as there is the observer, there must be conflict in relationship.

A: Yes, I follow that.

K: Wait, wait, see what happens. I make a statement of that kind, someone will translate it into an idea, into a concept, and say: How am I to live that concept? The fact is he doesn't observe himself as the observer.

A: That's right, that's right. He is the observer looking out there making a distinction between himself and the . . .

K: . . . and the statement.

A: Right, making a division.

K: Has the observer any place at all in relationship? I say, the moment he comes into existence in relationship there is no relationship.

A: We are talking about something, in fact, that doesn't even exist.

K: That doesn't exist. Therefore we have to go into the question of why human beings in their relationship with other human beings are so violent, because violence is spreading throughout the world. A mother came to see me, the other day in India, from a very Brahmanical family, very cultured; her son who is six, when she asked him to do something, took up a stick and began to hit her. A thing unknown! You follow, sir?

A: Yes.

K: The idea that you should hit your mother is traditionally something incredible and this boy did it. And I said, see the fact; we went into it, she understood. So to understand violence one has to understand division.

A: The division was already there.

K: Yes.

A: Otherwise he would not have picked up the stick.

K: Division between nations, you follow, sir? The armaments race is one of the factors of violence. I call myself American and he calls himself Russian or Indian or whatever it is; this division is the factor of real violence and hatred. When the mind of a man sees that it cuts away all division in himself. He is no longer an Indian, American or Russian. He is a human being with his problems which he is trying to solve, not in terms of India or America or Russia. So we come to the point: can the mind be free in relationship, which means orderly, not chaotic but orderly?

A: It has to be, otherwise you couldn't use the word relationship.

K: No. So can the mind be free of that, free of the observer?

A: If not, there is no hope.

K: That's the whole point.

A: If not, we've had it.

K: Yes. And all the escapes and going off into other religions, doing all kinds of tricks, have no meaning. Now, this demands a great deal of perception, insight, into the fact of your life, how one lives one's life. After all, philosophy means the love of truth, love of wisdom, not the love of some abstraction.

A: No, wisdom is supremely practical.

K: Practical. Therefore here it is: can a human being live in relationship in freedom and yet operate in the field of knowledge?

A: And yet operate in the field of knowledge, yes.

K: And be absolutely orderly. Otherwise it is not freedom. Because order means virtue.

A: Yes.

K: Which doesn't exist in the world at the present time. There is no sense of virtue in anything. Virtue is a creative thing, is a living thing, is a moving thing.

A: If I am following you correctly, what you are really saying is that the ability to act in the strict sense must be creative, otherwise it's not action but simply reaction.

K: A repetition.

A: A repetition. The ability to act, or virtue, as you put it, bears with it necessarily the implication of order. It must. It seems to me there's no way out of that.

K: Yes. So can I come back? In human relationship as it exists now there is conflict, sexual violence and so on and so on, every kind of violence. Now, can man live at total peace? Otherwise he is not creative – in human relationship – because that is the basis of all life.

A: I'm very taken with the way you have pursued this. I notice that when we asked this question: 'Is it possible that?', the reference for it is always a totality; and the reference over here is a fragment, or a fragmentation, or a division. Never once have you said that the passage from the one to the other is a movement that even exists.

K: No, it can't exist.

A: I think, Mr Krishnamurti, that nothing is so difficult to grasp as this statement that you have made. There is nothing that we are taught, from childhood up, to render such a possibility a matter for taking seriously. One doesn't like to make sweeping statements about how everyone has been educated, but I'm thinking of myself, from a child upward, all the way through graduate school, accumulating a lot of this knowledge that you have been talking about. I don't remember anybody saying to me, or even pointing me to a literature that so categorically makes this distinction between one and the other as *in terms of* each other, not *accessible to* each other through passage.

K: No, quite.

A: Now, I'm correct in understanding you this way, aren't I?

K: Quite right, the fragment cannot become the whole.

A: The fragment cannot become the whole.

K: But the fragment is always trying to become the whole.

A: Exactly. Now of course, in the years of very serious and devoted contemplation and exploration of this which quite clearly you have undertaken with great passion, I suppose it must have occurred to you that the first sight of this, while one is in the condition of the observer, must be very frightening – the thought that there is no passage.

K: But you see I never looked at it that way.

A: Please tell me how you looked at it.

K: From childhood I never thought I was a Hindu.

A: I see.

K: I never thought, when I was educated in England, that I was European. I was never caught in that trap. I don't know how it happened, I was never caught in that trap.

A: Well, when you were quite little and your playmates said to you, you are a Hindu, what did you say?

K: I probably put on Hinduism and all the trappings of Brahmin tradition but it never penetrated deeply.

A: As we say in the vernacular, it never got to you.

K: It never got to me, that's right.

A: I see. That's very remarkable, that's extraordinary. The vast majority of people in the world seem to have been 'got to' in this respect.

K: That's why I think, you see, that propaganda has become the means of change: but propaganda is not truth, repetition is not truth.

A: It's a form of violence too.

K: That's just it. So a mind that simply observes doesn't react to what it observes according to its conditioning. Which means there is no observer at any time, therefore no division. It happened to me, I don't know how it happened, but it happened. And in observing all this I've seen that in every kind of human relationship, there is this division and therefore violence. And to me the very essence of non-relationship is the factor of 'me' and 'you'.

This brings us to the point, sir, doesn't it, where one asks whether the human mind which has evolved in separation, fragmentation...

A: That is what evolution is, yes.

K: ... can such a mind transform, undergo regeneration which is not produced by influence, by propaganda, by threat and punishment, because if it changes because it is going to get a reward then ...

A: It hasn't changed.

K: ... it hasn't changed. So that is one of the fundamental things one has to ask, and answer it in action, not in words. The human mind has evolved in contradiction, in duality – the 'me' and the 'not me', this traditional cleavage, division, fragmentation. Now can that mind observe this fact, observe without the observer, for only then is there a regeneration. As long as there is an observer observing this, then there is conflict. I don't know if I make myself clear.

A: Yes, you do.

K: Sir, the difficulty is most people won't even listen.

A: I know that.

K: If they do listen they listen with their conclusions. If I am a Communist I will listen to you up to a point. After that I won't listen to you; and if I am slightly demented I will listen to you and translate what I hear according to my dementia.

A: Exactly.

K: So one has to be extraordinarily serious to listen. Serious in the sense of putting aside my peculiar prejudices and idiosyncrasies and listening to what you are saying, because the listening is the miracle. Not what shall I do with what you have said.

A: Not what shall I listen to ...

K: ... but the act of listening. You are good enough to listen to me because you want to find out. But the vast majority say, what are you talking about, I want to go on enjoying myself, so go and talk to somebody else. So to create an atmosphere, to create an ambience, a feeling that life is dreadfully serious, one says: my friend, do listen; it's your life, don't waste it, do listen. To bring about a human being who will listen is of the greatest importance, because we don't want to listen. It's too disturbing.

A: I understand. I have tried sometimes in class to make this very point. Sometimes I suggest that we should watch an animal, especially a wild animal, because if it's not listening it's likely to be dead.

K: Dead, yes, sir.

A: There is this extraordinary attention it has and every instant of its life is a crisis.

K: Absolutely. In America what is happening now, as I observe it, I may be mistaken, people are not serious. They are playing with new things, something entertaining, going from one thing to the other. And they think this is searching, asking, but they get trapped in each thing and at the end of it they have nothing but ashes. So it is becoming more and more difficult for human beings to be serious, to listen, to see what they are, not what they should be. In this conversation you are listening because you are interested, you want to find out. But the vast majority of people say, for God's sake, leave me alone; I have my little house, my wife, my car, my yacht, or whatever it is; for God's sake don't change anything as long as I live.

A: You know, going back to what I do know something about, I've often remarked to myself in attending conferences where papers are read that nobody is listening: it's one long monologue and after a while you get the feeling that it is really a shocking waste of time. And even when sitting down having coffee the discussion between classes usually runs on the basis of babble; we are just talking about things in which we are not genuinely interested in order to fill up space. This, however, is far more serious a matter than simply a description of what's going on.

K: It's a matter, I feel, of life and death.

A: Exactly.

K: If the house is burning I've got to do something. I am not going to discuss who burned the house – what colour his hair was, whether it was black or white or purple; I want to put that fire out.

A: Or if such and such had not happened the house would not be burning.

K: And I feel it is so urgent because I see it in India, in Europe and America. Everywhere I go I see this sense of slackness, sense of despair, sense of hopeless activity that is going on.

So to come back to what we are saying, relationship is of the highest importance. When in that relationship there is conflict, we produce a society which will further that conflict, through education, through national sovereignties, through all the rest of it. So a serious man, serious in the sense of one who is really concerned, committed, must give his total attention to this question of relationship, freedom and knowledge.

A: If I've heard you correctly, and I don't mean by that the words that have passed between us, but if I have truly heard you, I've heard something very terrifying, that this disorder we have in part described, has a built-in necessity in it. As long as it persists it can never change.

K: Obviously.

A: Any modification of it is . . .

K: . . . further disorder.

A: . . . is more of the same.

K: More of the same.

A: I have the feeling, and I hope I have understood you correctly, that there is a relationship between the starkness of this necessity and the fact that there cannot be a gradual progress. But nevertheless there is some demonic progress that takes place within this disorder that is not so much a progress as a proliferation of the same. Necessarily so. Is that what you have been saying?

K: Yes. You know I was told the other day that the word 'progress' meant, entering into an enemy's country fully armed.

A: Really! Entering into an enemy's country fully armed!

K: Sir, this is what is happening.

A: I know. Next time I would like very much to resume at this very point: namely this necessity and the necessity that produced that statement.

18 February 1974

DIALOGUE III

What Is Communication with Others?

Dr Anderson: Mr Krishnamurti, in our conversations we have been exploring the general question of the transformation of man, a transformation, which as you say, is not dependent on knowledge or time. And we arrived at a very crucial issue with regard to relationship and communication. I remember one point in our conversation that was extremely instructive for me, when you reminded us that the important thing is to begin at the right starting point. So if it is agreeable to you, it would be helpful if we could begin today with the question of communication and relationship, go into that question and begin to unravel it.

Krishnamurti: I wonder, sir, what that word 'communication' really means. To communicate implies not only verbally but a sharing, not accepting something that you or I say, but sharing together, thinking together, creating together, all that is involved in that word 'communication'. And in that word is also implied the art of listening. The art of listening demands a quality of attention in which there is real listening, a real sense of having an insight as we go along, each second, not at the end, but at the beginning.

A: So that we are . . .

K: . . . walking together on the same road all the time.

A: So there is a concurrent activity. Not one of us making a statement, the other thinking about it and then saying, 'Well, I agree, I don't agree, I accept, I don't accept, and these are the reasons I don't accept, and these are the reasons I do', but we are walking together.

K: On the same road, with the same attention, with the same intensity, at the same time, otherwise there is no communication.

A: Exactly.

K: Communication implies that we are walking together, we are thinking together, we are observing together, sharing together at the same level, at the same time, with the same intensity.

A: Would you say that this activity underlies the speaking together, or does one come to that activity after one has started to speak together?

K: Sir, we are asking: what is the art of listening. The art of listening implies, doesn't it, that there is not only verbal understanding between you and me — the fact that we are both speaking English and know the meaning of each word — but also at the same time we are sharing the problem, sharing the issue together. If you and I are both serious, we are sharing the thing. So in communication there is not only verbal communication but there is non-verbal communication, which comes into being or happens when one has the art of really listening to somebody, in which there is no acceptance, denial, comparison, judgment, just the act of listening.

A: I wonder whether I am on the right track here, if I suggest that there is a very deep relation here between communication and what we call 'communion'.

K: Communion, yes.

A: So that if we are in communion, our chance of communicating...

K: ...becomes simpler. Now to be in communion with each other both of us must be serious about the same problem at the same time with the same passion. Otherwise there is no communication.

A: Exactly.

K: If you are not interested in what is being said, well, you will think of something else and communication stops. So there is verbal communication and non-verbal communication. They are both operating at the same time.

A: One does not precede the other or follow upon the other. They move together.

K: Which means that each of us, being serious, gives our complete attention to the issue. Sir, the man who is really serious lives: the man who is flippant or merely wanting to be entertained does not live.

A: The general notion of being serious about something usually suggests either undergoing some pain, or I'm serious about something in order to get something else. These two things are, as a rule, what people imagine about seriousness. As a matter of fact, we often hear the expression, 'don't look so serious'. It's as though we fear something about being serious.

K: Sir, look! As we said yesterday, the world is in a mess and it's my responsibility living in this world as a human being who has created this mess, it's my responsibility to be serious about the resolution of this problem. I am serious. It doesn't mean I am long-faced, I am miserable, unhappy, or I want something out of it. This is a problem that has got to be solved. It's like if one has a cancer, one is serious about it, you don't play around with it.

A: Action in relation to this seriousness then is instantaneous.

K: Obviously!

A: This raises – not an additional question, I don't mean to go beyond where we haven't begun – but time means for the serious person something very different from what it would seem to mean for the unserious person. One would not then have the feeling of something being dragged out or, as we say, of time that has to be 'put in'.

K: Put in, quite.

A: So in this concurrent communication in which communion is always present, time as such would not in any way oppress.

K: Quite right. But you see, sir, I am trying to see what it means to be serious. The intent, the urge, the feeling of total responsibility and of action, the 'doing', not 'I will do'. All that is implied in the word seriousness. At least I'd put all those things into that word.

A: Could we look for a moment at one of them that you put into it? Responsibility, able to be responsive.

K: Yes, to respond adequately to any challenge. The challenge now is that the world is in a mess, confusion, sorrow, violence and all that. As a human being who has created this thing, I must respond adequately. The adequacy depends on my seriousness, in the sense I have given, on my observation of the chaos and responding, not according to my prejudices, my inclination, tendencies, pleasures or fears, but responding to the problem, not according to my translation of the problem.

A: Yes, I am just thinking as you are speaking about how difficult it is to communicate this to someone who thinks that the way to respond adequately to this chaos is to have a plan for it which one superimposes on it. And that's exactly what we assume, and if the plan doesn't work out, we blame ourselves . . .

K: . . . or change the plan. But we *don't* respond to the challenge. We respond according to our conclusion about the problem.

A: Exactly.

K: Therefore, this means really, if we can explore it a little more, that the observer is the observed.

A: Therefore the change, if it comes, is total not partial. One is no longer outside what he is operating upon.

K: That's right.

A: And what he is operating upon is not outside himself.

K: Of course. As we said yesterday – it's very interesting if we go into it rather deeply – the world is me and I am the world. That is not something intellectual or emotional, but a fact. Now, when I approach the problem, the chaos, the misery, the suffering, the violence, all that, I approach it with my conclusions, with my fears, with my despairs. I don't *look* at the problem.

A: Would you think it possible to put it this way, that one doesn't make room for the problem?

K: Yes, put it that way. Sir, let's look at this. As a human being one has created this misery which is called the society in which we live, a completely immoral society. As a human being one has created that. But that human being looking at it separates himself and says, 'I must do something about it.' The 'it' is 'me'.

A: Some people respond to that this way. They say, 'Well look, assume that I am truly serious, I am truly responsible, that I make this act and there comes about between me and the world this confluent and total relationship, yet all the things that are going on out there that are atrocious, let's say, 2,500 miles away from where I am, don't stop. Therefore, how can I say that the world is me and

I am the world?' This objection comes up again and again. I am interested to know what your reply to that would be.

K: Sir, look. We are human beings irrespective of our labels as English, French, German, all the rest of it. A human being living in America or in India has the problems of relationship, of suffering, of jealousy, envy, greed, ambition, imitation, conformity. Those are all our problems, common to all of us.

A: Yes.

K: And when I say the world is me and I am the world, I see that as a reality, not as a concept. Now, if my responsibility to the challenge is to be adequate it must be not in terms of what I think, but of what the problem *is*.

A: Yes, I follow you here. I was thinking while you were saying that, of a possible answer to the question that I posed, and I put the question simply because I know some people who may well read this, who would ask it and who would want to participate in our conversation. I wondered whether you might have said that as soon as one puts the question in that way, one has already divorced oneself from the issue?

K: That's right.

A: That from the practical point of view that question is an interposition that simply does not have a place in the activity you are talking about.

K: Yes, that's right.

A: Now this is very interesting, because it means that the person must suspend his disbelief.

K: Or his belief.

A: Or his belief . . .

K: . . . and observe the thing.

A: . . . and observe the thing.

K: Which is not possible if the observer is different from the observed.

A: Now, would you explore the practical aspect of this with me for a moment? It would seem that people at this point will say, 'Well, yes, but I can't stop it, I think I have an intuition of what you mean, but the minute that I open myself, or begin to open myself, all these things seem to rush in on me. What I had hoped doesn't seem to take place.' If I understand you correctly, they are really not doing what they claim that they are trying to do.

K: That's right. Sir, can we put the question differently? What is a human being to do confronted with this problem of suffering, of chaos, of all that is going on around us? What is he to do? He approaches it generally with a conclusion – what he should *do about* it.

A: And this conclusion is interposed between him ...

K: Yes, the conclusion is the factor of separation.

A: Right.

K: Now, can he observe the fact of this confusion without any conclusions, without any planning, without any predetermined way of getting out of this chaos? Because his predetermined conclusions, ideas and so on are all derived from the past, and the past is trying to resolve the problem and therefore he is translating it and acting according to his previous conclusions, whereas the fact demands that you look at it; the fact demands that you observe it, that you listen to it. The fact itself will have the answer, you don't have to bring the answer to it. I wonder if I am making myself clear?

A: Yes, I'm listening very, very hard. Clearly, if there is to be a change here, it has to be a change that is altogether radical. Now I must start. What do I do?

K: There are two things involved, aren't there. First, I must learn from the problem, which means I must have a mind that has a quality of humility. One does not come to it and say, 'I know all about it.' What he knows is merely explanations, rational or irrational. He comes to the problem with rational or irrational solutions. Therefore he is not learning from the problem. The problem will reveal an infinite lot of things, if I'm capable of looking at it and learning about it. And for that I must have a sense of humility and say, 'I don't know. This is a tremendous problem. Let me look at it, let me learn about it.' Not I come to it with my conclusions; which means I have stopped learning about the problem.

A: Are you suggesting that this act is a waiting on the problem to reveal itself?

K: To reveal itself. That's right! Therefore, I must be capable of looking at it. I cannot look at it if I've come to it with ideas, with ideations, mentations or every kind of conclusion. I must come to it, and say, 'Look, what is it?' I must learn from *it*, not learn according to some professor, psychologist or philosopher.

A: Some people would question that one has the capacity for this.

K: I think everybody has it. Sir, we are so vain.

A: But that there is a capacity doesn't mean that there is the doing of what must be done.

K: Look, the learning is the doing.

A: Exactly, yes. I wanted to make that clear because, if I have been following you, we comfort ourselves with the curious notion that we possess a possibility and because we possess the possibility we think that someday it will perhaps actualize itself.

K: Quite right.

A: But if I'm correct, the possibility cannot actualize itself, and in practice that never occurs, but somehow it is believed, isn't it?

K: I'm afraid it is. Sir, it is really quite simple. There is this misery, confusion, immense sorrow in the world, violence, all that. Human beings have created it, human beings have built a structure of society which sustains this chaos. That's a fact. Now, I come to it, a human being comes to it, trying to resolve it according to his plan, according to his prejudices, his idiosyncrasies or knowledge, which means he has already understood the problem whereas the problem is always new. So I must come to it afresh.

A: One of the things that has concerned me for many years as one whose daily work involves the study of scriptures, is the recurrent statement that one comes upon, sometimes in a very dramatic form. For instance, take the prophetic ministry of Jesus where he says that they are hearing but they are not listening, they are observing but they are not seeing.

K: And doing.

A: But then it seems he does not say, 'in order to attain to that, do this.' No. The closest he comes to it is, through the analogy with the child, is to speak of having faith like a little child. What is meant by faith here is not something that would perhaps be appropriate to go into, but the analogy with the child suggests that the child is doing something that is lost somewhere along the way in some respect. I'm sure he didn't mean that there is a perfect continuity between the adult and the child. But why is it that over the centuries men have said this over and over again, namely you are not listening, you are not seeing, and then they don't point to an operation, they point to an analogy. Some of them don't even point to an analogy, they just hold up a flower.

K: Sir, we live on words. Most people live on words. They don't go beyond the word. And what we talking about is not only the word, the meaning of the word, the communication that exists in using words, but the non-verbal communication, which is having an insight. That is what we are talking about all the time so far.

A: Yes.

K: That is, the mind can only have an insight if it is capable of listening. And you *do* listen when the crisis is right on your doorstep.

A: Now, I think I'm at a point here that is solid. Is it that we don't allow ourselves access to the crisis that is there continuously? It isn't a crisis that is episodic.

K: No, the crisis is always there.

A: Well, we are doing something to shut ourselves off from it, aren't we?

K: Or we don't know how to meet it. Either we avoid it, or we don't know how to meet it, or we are indifferent; we have become so callous. All these things, all three are involved in not facing the crisis. Because one is frightened, one says, 'Oh lord! I don't know how to deal with it.' So one goes off to an analyst or a priest or one picks up a book to see how it can be translated. One becomes irresponsible.

A: Sometimes people will register the disappointment that things haven't worked out. So why try something new?

K: Yes, of course.

A: And this would be a buffer.

K: Yes, that's what I mean. Avoidance. There are so many ways to avoid – clever, cunning, superficial and very subtle. All that is involved in avoiding an issue. So what we are trying to say, isn't it, is that the observer is the past, as we said yesterday. The observer is trying to translate and act according to the past when the crisis arises. The crisis is always new. Otherwise it's not a crisis. A challenge must be new, is new, is always new. But he translates it according to the past. Now, can he look at that challenge, that crisis, without the response of the past?

A: May I read a sentence out of your book? I think this may have a very direct relationship to what we are talking about. It's a sentence that arrested me when I read it. 'Through negation that thing which alone is the positive comes into being.' Through negation something is done apparently.

K: Absolutely.

A: Right. So we are not leaving it at the point where we are saying, words are simply of no consequence, therefore, I will do something non-verbal, or I will say something because I never communicate with the non-verbal. That has nothing to do with it. Something must be done. There is an act.

K: Absolutely. Life is action.

A: I should say for our readers that this is from the "Awakening of Intelligence", and it's on page 196 in the chapter on Freedom. 'Through negation' – I take it that's a word for this act – 'that thing which alone is the positive' – the word 'alone' came over to me with the force of something unique.

K: Yes sir.

A: Something that is not continuous with anything else. That thing which alone is the positive comes into being. There is no temporal hiatus here, so we are back to where we began in our earlier conversations about not being dependent on knowledge and time. Could we look at this negation together for a moment? I have the feeling that unless negation is an abiding activity, then communion and communication and the relationship that we are talking about can never be reached. Is that correct?

K: Quite. May I put it this way? I must negate, I mean negate not intellectually or verbally, but actually negate the society in which I live. The implication of immorality which exists in society, on which society is built, I must negate that immorality totally. That means that I live morally. In negating that the positive is the moral. I negate totally the idea of success. Not only in the mundane world, not only in the sense of achievement in a world of money, position, authority, which I negate completely, I also negate success in the so-called spiritual world.

A: Quite, the temptation.

K: Both are the same. Only I call that spiritual and I call that physical, moral, mundane. So in negating success, achievement, there comes an energy. Through negation there is a tremendous energy to act totally differently which is not in the field of success, imitation, conformity and all that. So through negation, I mean actual negation not just ideal negation, through actual negation of that which is immoral, morality comes into being.

A: Which is altogether different from trying to be moral.

K: Of course, trying to be moral is immoral.

A: Yes. May I try to go into this a step further? I intuit here a twofold aspect of negation. I'd like very much to see whether this is what you also feel. My desire for success in itself is a withholding myself from the problem that we talked about, and that itself is a form of negation. I have negated access to myself. I've negated, in other words, I have done violence to what it is that wishes to reveal itself. So I am then going to negate my negation as the observer.

K: You are quite right. When we use the word 'negation', as it is generally understood, it means an act of violence. And we are using the word negate not in the sense of violence, but the understanding of what success implies. The 'me', who is separate from you, wanting or desiring success which will put me in a position of authority, power, prestige. So in negating success, I am negating my desire to be powerful, which I do only when I have understood the whole process involved in achieving success. Achieving success involves ruthlessness, lack of love, an immense lack of consideration for others, a sense of conformity, imitation, acceptance of the social structure, all that is involved and therefore the understanding of all that when I negate success. It is not an act of violence. On the contrary, it is an act of tremendous attention.

A: I've negated something in my person.

K: I've negated my self.

A: Right. I've negated my self.

K: The 'me' which is separate from 'you'.

A: Exactly.

K: And therefore I've negated violence, which comes about when there is separation.

A: Would you use the term self-denial here, not in the conventional sense, but could one use that word in your context?

K: I'm afraid it wouldn't be clear. Self-denial means sacrifice, pain, lack of understanding. Why use another term when you have understood this?

A: Well, to communicate with someone.

K: But change the word so that we both understand the meaning of self-denial. I mean all religions have based their action on self-denial, sacrifice, denial of desire, refraining from looking at a woman, the denial of riches, taking a vow of poverty. You know all of them: the vow of poverty, of celibacy and so on. All these are a kind of punishment, a distorting of a clear perception. If I see something clearly, the action is immediate. So, to negate implies diligence. Diligence means giving complete attention to the fact of success. By giving my whole attention to, in this case, success, in that attention, the whole map of success is revealed.

A: With all its horrors.

K: With everything it involves; and it is only then the seeing is the doing. Then it is finished: and the mind can never revert to success and therefore become bitter and all the things that follow.

A: What you are saying, is that once this happens, there is no reversion.

K: It is finished.

A: It's not something that one has to keep up.

K: Of course not.

A: Well, fine. I'm delighted we've established that.

K: Now take an actual instance. In 1928 I happened to be the head of a tremendous organization, a religious organization, and I saw around me various religious organizations, sects, Catholic, Protestant, all trying to find truth. So I said, 'No organization can lead man to truth.' So I dissolved it, the property, an enormous business. I can never go back to it. When you see something as poison you won't take it again. It isn't that you say, 'By Jove, I've made a mistake. I should go back and ...' It is, sir, like seeing danger. When you see danger you never go near it again.

A: I hope you won't mind if I talk about words here again. But you know so many of the things that you say cast new light on common terms. For instance, we say in English, practice makes perfect. Now obviously this can't be the case if we mean by practice that we are repeating something. But if you mean by practice the Greek praxis, which is concerned directly with act, not repetition, with act, then to say it makes perfect, doesn't refer to time at all. It's that upon the instant the act is performed, perfection is.

K: Yes. But can we now go back, or go forward to the question of freedom and responsibility in relationship? That's where we left off yesterday. First of all, can we go into this question of what it is to be responsible? Because I think that is what we are missing in this world, in what is happening now. We don't feel responsible. We don't feel we are responsible because for us the people in authority, politically and religiously, are responsible. We are not. That is the general feeling all over the world.

A: Because those people over there have been delegated to do a job by me.

K: Yes. And scientists, politicians, the educationalists, the religious people, they are responsible, but I know nothing about it, I just follow. That's the general attitude right through the world.

A: One feels one gets off scot-free that way because it's the other one's fault.

K: Yes. So I make myself irresponsible. By delegating responsibility to you I become irresponsible. Whereas now we are saying, nobody is responsible except you, because you are the world and the world is you. You have created this mess, you alone can bring about clarity, and therefore you are totally, utterly, completely responsible. And nobody else. Now that means you have to be a light to yourself, not take the light of a professor, or an analyst, or a psychologist, or the light of Jesus, or the light of the Buddha. You have to be a light to yourself in a world that is becoming utterly dark. That means you have to be responsible. Now, what does that word mean? It means really to respond totally, adequately to every challenge. You cannot possibly respond adequately if you are rooted in the past, because the challenge is new, otherwise it is not a challenge, a crisis is new, otherwise it is not a crisis. If I respond to a crisis in terms of a preconceived plan, which the Communists do, or the Catholics, or the Protestants and so on, then they are not responding totally and adequately to the challenge.

A: This takes me back to something I find very germane in the dramatic confrontation between the soldier and the Lord Krishna in the Gita. Arjuna, the army general, says to Krishna, 'Tell me definitely what to do and I will do it.' Now Krishna does not turn around and say to him in the next verse, 'I am not going to tell you what to do.' But at that point he simply doesn't tell him what to do, and one of the great Sanskrit scholars has argued that that's an irresponsible reaction on the part of the teacher. But if I am understanding you correctly, he couldn't have done otherwise?

K: When the general puts the question, he is putting the question out of irresponsibility.

A: Of course, a refusal to be responsible. Exactly! A refusal to be responsible.

K: That's why, sir, responsibility means total commitment to the challenge, responding adequately, completely to a crisis. The word responsibility means that – to respond. I cannot respond completely if I am frightened, or I cannot respond completely if I am seeking pleasure, I cannot respond totally if my action is routine, repetitive, traditional, conditioned. So, to respond adequately to a challenge means that the 'me', which is the past, must end.

A: And at this point Arjuna just wants it continued right down the line.

K: That's what everybody wants. Politically, look at what is happening in this country, and elsewhere. We don't feel responsible. We don't feel responsible for the way we bring our children up.

A: In our next conversation I'd really like to continue this in terms of the phrase we sometimes use 'being responsible for my action'. But that does not seem to be saying what you are saying at all. As a matter of fact, it seems to be quite wide of the mark.

K: Quite right.

19 February 1974

DIALOGUE IV

What Is a Responsible Human Being?

DR ANDERSON: Just as we ended our last conversation the question arose of the distinction between the notion that I must be responsible for my action and my being responsible. Perhaps we could start at that point now.

KRISHNAMURTI: Sir, there is a very definite distinction between responsible for and being responsible. Being responsible for implies direction, a directed will. But the feeling of responsibility implies responsibility for everything, not just in one particular direction. Responsible for education, responsible for politics, responsible for the way I live, responsible for my behaviour. It's a total feeling of complete responsibility, which is the ground in which action takes place.

A: I think this takes us back to this business of crisis we were talking about. If the crisis is continuous it's misleading to say, I'm responsible for my action, because I've put the thing out there again and it becomes an occasion for my confusing what is at hand that requires to be done and the concept of this notion of my action. I *am* my action.

K: Yes, that's just it.

A: I am it.

K: That means, the feeling of responsibility expresses itself politically, religiously, educationally, in business, in the whole of life, responsibility for the total behaviour. Not in a particular direction. I think there is great deal of difference when one says I am responsible for my action. That means you are responsible for your action according to the idea that you have preconceived about action.

A: Exactly. People sometimes will say that the child is free because it's not responsible. But I think sometimes when we say this we have this nostalgia for the past as though our freedom would be freedom from constraint, whereas if one is his action genuinely, absolutely . . .

K: There isn't any restraint.

A: . . . there isn't any restraint at all.

K: Look, if one has this total feeling of responsibility, then what is your responsibility with regard to your children? It means education. Are you educating them to bring about a mind that conforms to the pattern which society has established? Which means you accept the immorality of the society that is. If you feel totally responsible you are responsible from the moment it is born until the moment it dies. The right kind of education, not education to make the child conform, the worship of success, and the division of nationalities which brings about war. You follow, you are responsible for all that, not just in a particular direction. Even if you are responsible in a particular direction, and can say: 'I'm responsible for my action,' what is your action based on? How can you be responsible, when you, your action is the result of a formula that has been handed down to you?

A: Yes, I follow what you mean.

K: The Communists, for example, say the state is responsible. Worship the state, the state is the god and you are responsible to the state. Which means they have conceived what the state should be, formulated it ideationally and according to that you act. That's not responsible action, that's irresponsible action. Whereas action means the doing now. The active present of the verb to do, which is to do now. The acting now must be free from the past. Otherwise you are just repeating, carrying on traditionally. That's irresponsible.

A: I'm reminded of something in the I Ching that I think reflects the principle you are pointing to. If I am quoting correctly from one of the standard translations, it goes like this, 'The superior man', by which it means the free man, not one hierarchically ranked, 'does not let his thoughts go beyond his situation'. Which would mean that he simply would be present as he is, not being responsible to something out there that is going to tell him how to be responsible or what he should do, but upon the instant that he is, he is always...

K: Responsible.

A: Yes, he simply does not let his thoughts go beyond his situation. That goes back to that word 'negation'. Because if he won't let his thoughts go beyond his situation he has negated the possibility for their doing so, hasn't he?

K: Quite.

A: Yes, I see that. The reason that I'm referring to these other quotations is because if what you are saying is true and if what they say is true, then there must be something in common here, and I realize that your emphasis is practical, eminently practical, upon the act. But it does seem to me to be of great value if one could converse, commune with the great literatures which have so many statements complaining about the fact that they are not understood. I see that as a great gain.

K: Suppose there are no books in the world.

A: The problem is the same.

K: The problem is the same.

A: Of course, of course.

K: There is no leader, no teacher, nobody to tell you do this, do that, don't do this, don't do that. You are there. You feel totally, completely responsible.

A: Right.

K: Then you have to have an astonishingly, active, clear brain, not befuddled, not puzzled, not bewildered. You must have a mind that thinks clearly. And you cannot think clearly if you are rooted in the past. You are merely continuing, modified perhaps, through the present to the future, that's all. So from that arises the question, what is responsibility in human relationship?

A: Yes, now we are back to relationship.

K: Yes, because relationship is the basic foundation of life: that is, to be related, to be in contact with.

A: *We* are at present related. This is what is.

K: What is human relationship? If I feel totally responsible, how does that responsibility express itself in relationship to my children, to my family, to my neighbour: whether my neighbour is next door or ten thousand miles away, he is still my neighbour. So what is my responsibility? What is the responsibility of a man who feels completely involved in this feeling of being a light to himself and totally responsible? I think this is a question, sir, that has to be investigated.

A: You know I think that only a person who is responsible, as you have defined the word, can make what we call a clean decision.

K: Sir, I would like to ask this. Is there decision at all? Decision implies choice. Choice implies a mind that's confused between this and that. But a mind that sees clearly has no choice. It doesn't decide, it acts.

A: Doesn't this take us back to this word 'negation' again?

K: Yes, of course.

A: Perhaps a clean decision could be interpreted in terms of what takes place at this point of negation, from which flows a different action.

K: But I don't like to use that word 'decision' because it implies deciding between this and that.

A: You don't want to use it because of its implications of conflict.

K: Yes, we think we are free because we can choose. Is a mind free that is capable of choice? Or is it a mind that is not free that chooses? Because choice implies between this and that. Obviously. Which means the mind doesn't see clearly and therefore there is choice. Choice exists when there is confusion. For a mind that sees clearly, there is no choice, it is doing. I think this is where we have got into rather a lot of trouble when we say we are free to choose, that choice implies freedom. I say, on the contrary: choice implies a mind that is confused and therefore not free.

A: What occurs to me now is the difference between regarding freedom as a property or quality of action rather than as a state. We have the notion that freedom is a state, which is quite different from the sense you are pointing to.

K: Let's come back to this, sir. What is the responsibility of a human being in relationship? Because relationship is life, relationship is the foundation of existence. Relationship is absolutely necessary, otherwise you cannot exist. Relationship means cooperation. Everything is involved in that one word. Relationship means love, generosity, all that is implied in it. Now what is a human responsibility in relationship?

A: If we were genuinely and completely sharing then responsibility would be fully present.

K: Yes, but how does it express itself in relationship? Not only between you and me now, but between man and woman, with my neighbour, relationship to everything, to Nature. What's my relationship to Nature? Would I go and kill baby seals?

A: No.

K: Would I go and destroy human beings calling them enemies? Would I destroy Nature, all the things which man is doing now? He is destroying the earth, the air, the sea, everything because he feels totally irresponsible.

A: He sees what is out there as something to operate on.

K: So I ask how does this responsibility show itself in my life? Suppose I am married, what is my responsibility? Am I related to my wife?

A: The record doesn't seem very good.

K: Not only the record, the actuality. Am I related to my wife? Or am I related to my wife according to the image I make about her? And I am responsible for that image, do you follow, sir?

A: Yes, because my input has been continuous with respect to that image.

K: So I have no relationship with my wife if I have an image about her. Or if I have an image about myself when I want to be successful and all the rest of that business.

A: Since we were talking about now, being now, there is a point of contact, I take it, between what you are saying and the phrase that you used in one of our earlier conversations, the betrayal of the present.

K: Absolutely. You see that is the whole point, sir. If I am related to you, I have no image about you, or you have no image about me, then we have a relationship. We have no relationship if I have an image about myself or about you. Our images have a relationship, but in actuality we have no relationship. I might sleep with my wife but it is not a relationship. It is a physical contact, sensory excitement, nothing else. My responsibility is not to have an image.

I must stick to this because this is really quite important. Because go where you will there is no relationship between human beings, and that is the tragedy, and from that arises all our conflicts, violence, the whole business. So when there is this responsibility, the feeling of this responsibility, it translates itself in relationship. It doesn't matter with whom. There is a freedom from the known which is the image. And in that freedom, goodness flowers.

A: Goodness flowers.

K: And that is beauty. Beauty is not an abstract thing, but goes with goodness. Goodness in behaviour, goodness in conduct, goodness in action.

A: Sometimes while we have been talking I have started a sentence with 'if', and I have looked into your eyes and immediately I knew I had said the wrong thing. We are always 'iffing' it up.

K: 'Iffing' it up! I know, sir. We are always dealing with abstractions rather than with reality.

A: Immediately we 'if', a construction is out there which we endlessly talk about.

K: That's right.

A: And we get cleverer and cleverer about it and it has nothing to do with anything.

K: So how does this responsibility translate itself in human behaviour? You follow, sir?

A: There would be an end to violence.

K: Absolutely.

A: It wouldn't taper off.

K: You see what we have done, sir? We are violent human beings, sexually, morally, in every way we are violent human beings, and not being able to resolve it we have created an ideal of not being violent, which means there is the fact – violence – an abstraction from the fact which is non-fact, and we try to live the non-fact.

A: Yes, and immediately that produces conflict because it cannot be done.

K: Conflict, misery, confusion all that. Why does the mind do it? The mind does it because it doesn't know what to do with the fact of violence. Therefore in abstracting the idea of not being violent, it postpones action. I am trying not to be violent and in the meantime I am jolly well violent.

A: Yes.

K: And this is an escape from the fact. All abstractions are escape from the fact. So the mind does it because it is incapable of dealing with the fact or it doesn't want to deal with the fact or it is lazy and says, I will try and do it another day. All this is involved when it withdraws from the fact. Now in the same way the fact is our relationship is non-existent. I may say to my wife, I love you, etc., etc., but it's non-existent, because I have an image about her and she has an image about me. So we have lived on abstractions.

A: It occurs to me that the word 'fact' itself, which there have been no end of disquisitions about . . .

K: Oh yes, of course. The fact, 'what is', let's call it, 'what is'. You see, sir, this reveals a tremendous lot. When you feel responsible, feel responsible for the education of your children, not only yours, all children. Are you educating them to conform to society, are you educating them to merely acquire a job? Are you educating them to the continuity of what has been? Are you educating them to live in abstractions, as we are doing now? So what is your responsibility as a father, mother, it doesn't matter who you are, for the education of a human being? That's one problem. What is your responsibility, if you feel responsible, for human growth, human culture, human goodness? What's your responsibility to the Earth? It is a tremendous thing to feel responsible. And also, you see, with responsibility goes love, care, attention.

A: Yes, earlier I was going to ask you about care in relation to responsibility. Something that would flow immediately.

K: Naturally. You see that involves a great deal too because the mother depends on the child, and the child depends on the mother,

A WHOLLY DIFFERENT WAY OF LIVING 61

or the father, or whoever it is. So that dependence is cultivated: not only between the father and the mother but dependence on a teacher, dependence on somebody to tell you what to do, dependence on your guru.

A: Yes, I follow.

K: Gradually the child, the man, is incapable of standing alone and therefore he says I must depend on my wife for my comfort, for my sex, for this, that, and the other thing, I am lost without her. And I am lost without my guru, without my teacher. It becomes so ridiculous. When the feeling of responsibility exists all this disappears. You are responsible for your behaviour, for the way you bring up your children, for the way you treat a dog, a neighbour, Nature, everything is in your hands. Therefore you have to become astonishingly careful about what you do. Careful, not, 'I must not do this and I must do that'. Care, that means affection, that means consideration, diligence. All that goes with responsibility, which present-day society totally denies. That's what the various gurus that are imported into the West are doing, creating such mischief making unfortunate, thoughtless people, who want excitement, join them, to do all kinds of ridiculous nonsensical things.

So, we come back: freedom implies responsibility. And therefore freedom, responsibility means care, diligence, not negligence. Not doing what you want to do, which is what is happening in America. Do what you want to do, which is not freedom but permissiveness which breeds irresponsibility. I met the other day in New Delhi, a girl who had become a Tibetan Buddhist. You follow, sir. Born in America, being a Christian, brought up in all that. Throws all that aside and becomes a Tibetan Buddhist, which is the same thing in different words. It's so ridiculous. And I've known her some years, I said, 'Where is your child?' She said, 'I've left him with other liberated Tibetans'. I said, 'At six! you are the mother'. She said, 'Yes, he is in very good hands'. I came back next year and I asked, 'Where is your child?' 'Oh, he has become a Tibetan monk.' He was seven. He was seven years old and had become a Tibetan monk. You understand, sir? The irresponsibility of it. The mother feels, 'They know better than I do, I am a Tibetan Buddhist and the lamas will help me to become . . .'

A: It puts a rather sinister cast on the Biblical statement: train up a child in the way he should go and when he is old he will not depart from it. There is a sinister note there, isn't there.

K: Absolutely. So this is going on in the world all the time. And a man who is really serious negates it because he understands the implications of all that. So he *has* to deny it. It isn't a question of will or choice, he says, 'That's too silly, too absurd'. So freedom means responsibility and infinite care.

A: The phrase that you just used, 'infinite care' would be totally impossible for what we mean by a finite being, unless the finite being did not betray the present.

K: Sir, the word 'present', the now, is rather difficult. What is the 'now'? What is the act of now, the present? To understand the present I must understand the past – not history, I don't mean that – understand myself as the past. I am the past.

A: In terms of what we said earlier about knowledge.

K: Yes. I am that. Therefore I must understand the past, which is 'me'. The 'me' is the known, the 'me' is not the unknown. I can imagine it is the unknown, but the fact is, the 'what is' is the known. That is 'me'. I must understand myself. If I don't, the now is merely a continuation in modified form of the past. Therefore it is not the now, not the present. Therefore the 'me' is the tradition, the knowledge, with all the complicated manoeuvres, cunning, all that, the despairs, the anxieties, the desire for success, fear, pleasure, all that is 'me'.

A: Since we are still involved in a discussion about relationships here, might we return for a moment to education and relationship. I want to be sure I have understood you here. Let us say that one were fortunate enough to have a school where what you are pointing to was going on.

K: We are doing it, we have got seven schools.

A: It would seem that if the teacher is totally present to the child the child will feel this. The child won't have to be instructed in what this means. Is that right?

K: Yes, but one has to find out what is the relationship of the teacher to the student. Is he merely an informer, giving information to the child? Any machine can do that. What is his relationship?

Does he put himself on a pedestal, up there and his student down there? Or is the relationship between the teacher and the student one in which there is learning on the part of the teacher as well as the student? Not 'I have learned and I am going to teach you.' In that there is a division between the teacher and the student. But when there is learning on the part of the teacher as well as on the part of the student there is no division. Both are learning.

A: Yes.

K: And therefore that relationship brings about a companionship.

A: A sharing.

K: A sharing, taking a journey together. And therefore an infinite care on both sides; which means: how is the teacher to teach mathematics, or whatever it is, to the student and yet teach it in such a way that you awaken the intelligence in the child, not simply about mathematics? And how do you bring this act of teaching in which there is order – because mathematic means order, the highest form of order is mathematics – how will you convey to the student in teaching mathematics that there should be order in his life? Not order according to a blueprint. That's not order.

A: No.

K: This is teaching which is an act of learning all the time. It's a living thing, not something I have learned and I am going to impart to you.

A: This reminds me of an essay I read many years ago by Simone Weil in which she said that everyone who teaches a subject is responsible for teaching the student the relation between what they are studying and the students making a pure act of attention.

K: Of course.

A: And that if this doesn't take place the whole thing is meaningless.

K: So, sir: what is the relationship of the teacher to the student in education? Is he training him merely to conform, is he training him to cultivate mere memory, like a machine? Is he training him or is he helping him to learn about life – not just about sex – life, the whole immensity and complexity of living. We are not doing this.

A: No, we refer students to subject matters. They take this, they take that, they take the other and there are prerequisites for taking these other things; and this builds a notion of education which has absolutely no relationship to what you have just said about life.

K: None at all.

A: And yet in the catalogues of colleges and universities across the country there is on the first page or so a rather pious remark about the relation between their going to school and the values of civilization; and that turns out to be learning a series of ideas. They used also to talk about character. Perhaps not any more.

K: So, sir, when you feel responsible there is a flowering of real affection, a flowering of care for a child, and you don't train him, or condition him to go and kill another for the sake of your country. You follow? All that is involved in responsibility. So we come to a point where, since the human being is now so conditioned to be irresponsible, what are the serious people going to do with the irresponsible people? You understand? Education, politics, religion, everything is making human beings irresponsible. I am not exaggerating: this is so.

A: No, you are not exaggerating.

K: Now I as a human being see this. I say what am I to do? You follow, sir? What is my responsibility in face of the irresponsible?

A: Well, as we say in English, if it's to start anywhere, it must start at home. It would have to start with me.

K: That's the whole point. Start with 'me'.

A: Right.

K: Then the point arises, that you can't *do* anything about the irresponsible. But something strange takes place. Which is, the irresponsible consciousness is one thing, and the responsible consciousness is another. Now when the human being is totally responsible that responsibility enters unconsciously into the irresponsible mind. I don't know if I'm making this clear.

A: Yes, go ahead.

K: Suppose I'm irresponsible, and you are responsible. You can't do anything consciously with me, and the more you actively operate on me, the more I resist. I react violently to you. I build a wall against you, I hurt you. I do all kinds of things. So you see you cannot do anything consciously, actively, let's put it that way.

A: Designedly.

K: Designedly, planned, which is what people are all trying to do. But if you can talk to me, to my unconscious, because the unconscious is much more active, much more alert, much more, it sees the danger much quicker than the conscious. So it is much more sensitive. So if you can talk to me, to the unconscious, that operates; so you don't actively, designedly attack the irresponsible. People have tried it; and they have made a mess of it.

A: Oh yes, it just compounds, complicates the thing further.

K: Whereas if you talk to me and your whole inward intention is to show how irresponsible I am, what responsibility means, you care for me.

A: Yes.

K: You care for me, because I am irresponsible. You follow?

A: Exactly.

K: You care for me, and therefore you are watching not to hurt me, you follow? In that way you penetrate very, very deeply into my unconscious. And that operates unknowingly when suddenly I say, 'By Jove, how irresponsible I am'. That operates. I have seen this, sir, in operation because I've talked for 50 years, unfortunately or fortunately, to large audiences with tremendous resistance to anything new. If I say, don't read sacred books, which I say all the time, because you are just conforming, obeying, you are not living, you are living according to some book that you have read, immediately there is resistance: 'Who are you to tell us?'

A: Not to do something.

K: Not to do this or to do that. So I say, all right. I go on pointing out I'm not trying to change them. I'm not doing propaganda because I don't believe in propaganda. So I say, look, look what you do when you are irresponsible. You are destroying your children, you send them to war, to be killed, to kill and be maimed. Is that love, is that affection, is that care? Why do you do it? And I go into it. They get bewildered, and they don't know what to do. So it begins to slowly seep in.

A: Well, at first it's such a shock. It sounds positively subversive to some people.

K: Oh, absolutely, sir. So we come to something now, which is, in my relationship to another, when there is total responsibility in which freedom and care go together, the mind has no image in relationship at all. Because the image is the division. Where there is care there is no image.

A: This would lead us into what perhaps we could pursue later, namely love.

K: Ah, that's a tremendous thing.

A: Yes, I think this would come about naturally. I've been listening to what you have been saying and it has occurred to me that if one is responsible and care is continuous with that, one would not fear. Not 'would not', 'could not', fear.

K: You see that means one must understand fear and also the pursuit of pleasure. Those two go together, they are not two separate things.

A: What I have learned here in our discussion is that what we should be concerned about understanding is not what are called values.

K: Oh no.

A: It is not a question of understanding love, but of understanding all those things in which we are trapped which militate against any possibility of love whatsoever. This is what's so hard to hear, to be told that there just is no possibility. This produces immense terror. Do you think that next time when we converse together we could discuss fear?

K: Yes, but before we go into fear there is something we should discuss very carefully: what is order in freedom?

A: Yes, fine.

19 February 1974

DIALOGUE V

Order Comes from the Understanding of Our Disorder

DR ANDERSON: Mr Krishnamurti, when we spoke last time we had reached the point where we were about to discuss order, and I thought perhaps we could begin with that today.

KRISHNAMURTI: We had been talking about freedom, responsibility and relationship, and before we went any further we thought we'd talk over together this question of order. What is order in freedom? As one observes all over the world, there is such extraordinary disorder both outwardly and inwardly. One wonders *why* there is such disorder. You go to India and you see the streets bursting with people; and you see also so many sects, so many gurus, so many teachers, so many contradictory lies, such misery. And you come to Europe: there is a little more order but you see, when you penetrate this superficial order, that there is equal disorder. And you come to this country and – you know what it is llke, better than I do – there is complete disorder. You may drive very carefully, but go behind the façade of so-called order and you see chaos, not only in personal relationships but sexually, morally, with so much corruption. All governments are corrupt, some more, some less. But how has this whole phenomenon of disorder come about? Is it the fault of the religions that have said: do this and don't do that? And now people are revolting against all that?

Is it that governments are so corrupt that nobody has any trust in governments? Is it that there is such corruption in business, nobody wants to look at it even, any intelligent man, any man who is really serious. And when you look at family life there is such disorder. So taking the phenomenon as a whole, why is there such disorder? What has brought it about?

A: Doesn't it appear that there is a sort of necessary, almost built-in progression, in the way we have mentioned earlier, and once order so conceived is superimposed upon an existing situation, not only does it not effect what is hoped for but it creates a new situation which we think requires a new approach: and the new approach is still the superimposition.

K: Like the Communists have tried to do in Russia and China. They have imposed order, what they call order, on a disordered mind: and therefore there is revolt. So looking at all this, it's very interesting, looking at this phenomenon of disorder, what then is order? Is order something imposed, as in the army on the soldier, a discipline which is a conformity, suppression, imitation? Is order conformity?

A: Not in the sense that it's artificially imposed, no.

K: In any sense. If I conform to order I am creating disorder.

A: Yes, I understand what you mean. In our use of the word 'conform' we sometimes mean by it a natural relation between the nature of a thing, and the activities that are proper to it or belong to it. But that use of the word is not the usual one that we are concerned with here.

K: So is order conformity? Is order imitation? Is order acceptance, obedience? Or is it because we have conformed, because we have obeyed, because we have accepted, that we have created disorder? Because discipline, in the ordinary, accepted sense of that word, is to conform.

A: Yes, we say in English, don't we, to someone who is undisciplined, straighten up.

K: Straighten up, yes.

A: The images that we use to refer to that correction are always rigid.

K: Yes. So that authority, whether the Communist authority of the few or the authority of the priest or the authority of someone who says, 'I know and you don't know,' that is one of the factors that has produced disorder. And another factor of this disorder is our lack of real culture. We are very sophisticated, very so-called civilized, in the sense that we are clean, we have bathrooms, we have better food and all that, but inwardly we are not cultured. We are not healthy, whole human beings.

A: The inner fragmentation spills out into our what we do outwardly.

K: So unless we understand disorder, the nature and structure of disorder, we can never find out what is order. Out of the understanding of disorder comes order. Not first seek order, and then impose that order on disorder.

A: Yes. I'm thinking as you are speaking of the phenomenon in the world of study and the world of teaching and learning as we understand them conventionally. I've noticed in our conversations that you always suggest that we study some dysfunction. We are never invited really to do that: we are told that the thing to study is the principle involved. The argument for that, of course, is that one refers to health in order to understand disease.

K: Quite.

A: But then the reference to health, when that is said, is received purely conceptually.

K: Quite right.

A: So what we are studying now is a concept.

K: Is a concept rather than the actuality, than the 'what is'.

A: And we slip away from the true task. There is a difficulty in grasping the suggestion that we study disorder simply because disorder by its own condition is without an ordering principle. Therefore it sounds when it comes out as though I am being asked to study something that is unstudiable. But on the contrary . . .

K: On the contrary. There must be an understanding of disorder, why it has come about. One of the factors, sir, I think, is basically that thought is matter, and thought by its very nature is fragmentary. Thought divides, the 'me' and the 'not me', we and they, my country and your country, my ideas and your ideas, my religion and your religion and so on. The very movement of thought is divisive, because thought is the response of memory, the response of experience, which is the past. And we need to really go into this question very, very deeply, the movement of thought and the movement of disorder . . .

A: 'Movement' seems to me to be a key word, in listening to you.

To study the movement of disorder would seem to me to take it a step deeper than the phrase, to study disorder.

K: The movement.

A: Yes, I think that removes the objection that the study of disorder is to undertake an impossible pursuit. That objection loses its force precisely at the point when one says, it's not disorder as a concept we are dealing with here, it's the movement of it, it's its own career, it's its passage, it's the whole corruption of the act as such.

K: Oh that's absolutely right.

A: But you know hardly ever is that taken seriously . . .

K: I know, sir. You see we deal with concepts, not with 'what is', actually what is. Rather than the discussion of formulas, concepts and ideas, 'what is' is disorder; and that disorder is spreading all over the world, it's a movement, it's a living disorder. It isn't a disorder that is dead. It is a living thing, moving, corrupting, destroying.

A: Yes, exactly. But it takes, as you have pointed out so often, an extreme concentration of attention to follow movement and something rebels in us against following movement which perhaps lies in disaffection because we intuit that the transition is unintelligible.

K: Of course.

A: And we don't want that. We can't stand the thought that there is something that is unintelligible, and so we just will not give that active attention.

K: It's like sitting on the bank of a river and watching the waters go by. You can't alter the water, you can't change the substance or the movement of the water. In the same way this movement of disorder is part of us and is flowing outside of us. So one has to look at it.

A: And there is no confusion in so doing.

K: Obviously not. First of all, sir, let's go into it very, very carefully. What is the factor of disorder? Disorder means contradiction, right?

A: Yes, and conflict.

K: Contradiction. This opposed to that. Or the duality of this opposed to that.

A: The contention between two things to be mutually exclusive.

K: What brings about this duality and the conflict? Is there a duality at all?

A: Certainly not in act, there is not a duality. That simply couldn't be. But the duality, of course, is present in terms of distinction, but not in terms of division.

K: Division, that's right. After all there is man, woman, black and white and so on, but is there an opposite to violence? You've understood?

A: Yes, I'm listening very intently.

K: Or only violence? But we have created the opposite. Thought has created the opposite as non-violence and then the conflict between the two. The non-violence is an abstraction from the 'what is': and thought has done that.

A: Yesterday I had a difficult time in class over this. I made the remark that vice is not the opposite of virtue. Virtue is not the opposite of vice, and somehow I just couldn't communicate that because the students insisted on dealing with the problem purely in terms of a conceptual structure.

K: You see sir, I don't know if we want to go into this now, but the necessity of measurement goes back to the ancient Greeks. And the whole of Western civilization is based on measurement, which is thought.

A: This is certainly true in continuous practice. And the irony of it is that an historian looking at the works of the great Greek thinkers would turn around and say at this point, well now just wait a minute, there are some things about Aristotle and Plato that would suggest that there's a much more organic grasp of things than simply approaching them with a slide-rule, but that doesn't meet the point you are making.

K: Sir, you can see what is happening in the world, in the Western world: technology, commercialism and consumerism is the highest activity that is going on now.

A: Exactly.

K: Which is based on measurement.

A: Yes.

K: Which is thought. Now look at it a minute, hold that a minute and you will see something rather odd taking place. The East, especially India, India exploded over the East in a different sense, they said measurement is illusion. To find the immeasurable, the measurement must come to an end. I'm putting this very crudely and quickly.

A: No, it seems to me that you are putting it very aptly with respect to this concern we have with act.

K: It's very interesting because I've watched it. In the West, technology, commercialism and consumerism, God, saviour, church, all that's outside. It is a plaything. And you just play with it on Saturday and Sunday but the rest of the week ...

A: Yes.

K: And you go to India and you find this. The word 'ma' is to measure, in Sanskrit, and they said, reality is immeasurable. Go into it, see the beauty of it.

A: Yes, I follow.

K: A mind that is measuring, or a mind that is caught in measurement, can never find truth. I'm putting it that way – they don't put it that way. So they said, to find the real, the immense, measurement must end. But then they said: thought must be controlled.

So, in order to find the immeasurable you must control thought. And who is the controller of thought? Another fragment of thought. I don't know if you follow.

A: Oh, I follow you perfectly.

K: So, they use measurement to go beyond measurement; and therefore they could never go beyond it. They were caught in an illusion of some other kind, but it is still the product of thought. I don't know if I'm conveying this?

A: Yes. There is the incredible irony of their having right in front of them in the Brihadaranyaka Upanishad this profound statement: 'This is full; that is full. The full flows out from fullness!' And then the next line, 'On taking away the full from fullness, fullness itself remains'. Now they are reading that, but if they approach it in the way you have described, they would see that they haven't attended to what's being said, because it's the total rejection of that statement that would be involved in thought control.

K: Yes, of course. You see that's what I've been trying to get at. Thought has divided the world physically: America, India, Russia, China, you follow, divided the world. Thought has fragmented the activities of man, the businessman, the artist, the politician, the beggar, you follow?

A: Yes.

K: Thought has fragmented man. Thought has created a society based on this fragmentation, and thought has created the gods, the saviours, the Christs, the Krishnas, the Buddhas – and those are all measurable, in a sense. You must become like the Christ, or you must be good. All sanctioned by a culture which is based on measurement.

A: Once you start with forecasts, as we have classically, then we are going to necessarily move to five, six, seven, 400, 4000, an indefinite division. And all in the interest, it is claimed, of clarity.

K: So, unless we understand the movement of thought, we cannot possibly understand disorder. It is thought that has produced disorder. It sounds contradictory, but it is so – thought is fragmentary, thought is time, and as long as we are functioning within that field there must be disorder. Which means, each fragment is working for itself, in opposition to other fragments. I, a Christian, am in opposition to the Hindu, though I talk about love and goodness and all the rest of it.

A: I love him so much I want to see him saved, so I will go out and bring him into the fold.

K: Saved. Come over to my camp!

A: Yes.

K: Probably the basic cause of disorder is the fragmentation of thought. I was told the other day, that in Eskimo culture, thought means the outside.

A: That's very interesting.

K: When they use the word outside, they use the word thought.

A: And we think it's inside.

K: So thought is always outside. You can say, I am inwardly thinking. Thought has divided the outer and the inner. So to understand this whole contradiction, measurement, time, the division, the fragmentation, the chaos, and the disorder, one must really go into this question of what is thought, what is thinking. Can the mind, which has been so conditioned in fragments, in fragmentation, can that mind observe this whole movement of disorder, not fragmentarily?

A: No, the movement itself.

K: The movement itself.

A: Movement itself, yes. But that's what's so terrifying – to look at that movement. It's interesting that you've asked this question in a way that keeps homing in because measure is – put in a very concise, elliptical way – possibility, which is infinitely divisible. It only comes to an end with an act. And as long as I remain divided from act, I regard myself as a very deep thinker. I'm sitting back exploring alternatives which are completely imaginary, illusory.

K: That brings up the point that measurement means comparison. Our society and civilization are based on comparison. From childhood to school, college and university, it is comparative.

A: That's right.

K: Comparison between intelligence and dullness, between the tall and the short, the black, white and purple and all the rest of it – comparison in success. And look also at our religions. The priest, the bishop, you follow, the hierarchical outlook, ultimately Pope or the archbishop. The whole structure is based on comparison, which is measurement, which is essentially thought.

A: Yes. The Protestants complain about the Catholic hierarchy, and yet their scripture, their Bible is what some Catholics call their Paper Pope.

K: Of course.

A: With the very rejection of something, something takes its place which becomes even more divisive.

K: So is it possible to look without measurement, that is without comparison? Is it possible to live a life – living, acting, the whole of life, laughter, tears, without a shadow of comparison coming into it? Sir, I'm not boasting, I'm just stating a fact, I have never compared myself with anybody.

A: That's a most remarkable thing.

K: I never thought about it even – somebody much cleverer than me, somebody much more brilliant, so intelligent, somebody greater, spiritual – it didn't occur. So I ask myself, are measurement, comparison, imitation not the major factors of disorder?

A: I've had a very long thought about what you said a few conversations ago, about when you were a boy and never accepted the distinctions that were made in a dividing way . . .

K: Oh, of course.

A: . . . and within the social order. In my own growing up, I did accept this distinction in terms of division, but I didn't do it with Nature. But that set up conflict in me, because I couldn't understand how it could be that I'm natural as a being in the world but I'm not somehow related to things the way things are, in what we call Nature. Then it occurred to me that in thinking that way I was already dividing myself off from Nature, and I'd never get out of that problem.

K: No.

A: And the thing came to me some years ago with a tremendous flash, when I was in Bangkok in a temple garden. In the early morning I was taking a walk and my eye was drawn to a globule of dew resting on a lotus leaf. It was a perfect sphere. And I thought: where's the base? How can it be stable? Why doesn't it roll off? By the time I got to the end of my 'whys' I was worn out, so I took a deep breath and said to myself, now shut up and just keep quiet and look. And I saw that everything maintained its own nature in this marvellous harmony without any confusion at all. And I was just still.

K: Quite.

A: Just still. I think that's something of what you mean about the fact. That was a fact.

K: Just remain with the fact, look at the fact.

A: That marvellous globule on the leaf *is* the fact.

K: That is correct. Sir, from this arises, can one educate a student to live a life of non-comparison – thinking in terms of a bigger car, a smaller car, you follow? You are clever, I am not clever. What happens if I don't compare at all? Will I become dull?

A: On the contrary.

K: I know I'm dull only through comparison. If I don't compare, I don't know what I am. *Then I begin from there.*

A: Yes. The world becomes infinitely accessible.

K: Oh, then the whole thing becomes extraordinarily different. There is no competition, there is no anxiety, there is no conflict with each other.

A: This is why you use the word 'total' often, isn't it? In order to express that there's nothing drawn out from one condition to the other. There is no link there, there is no bridge there: totally disordered; totally order.

K: Absolutely.

A: Yes, and you use the word 'absolute' often.

K: Sir, after all, mathematics is order. For the highest form of mathematical investigation you must have a mind that is totally orderly.

A: The other marvellous thing about maths is that whereas it's the study of quantity, you don't make passage from one integer to another by two getting larger. Two stops at two. Two and a half is no longer two.

K: Yes.

A: But as far as I know a child when he is taught mathematics is never introduced to that.

K: You see, sir, our teaching is so absurd. Is it possible to observe the movement of disorder with a mind which is itself already in a state of disorder? So disorder isn't out there but in here. Now can the mind observe that disorder without introducing the factor of an observer who is orderly?

A: Who will superimpose.

K: Yes. Therefore observe, perceive disorder without the perceiver. I don't know if I am making sense at all.

A: Yes, you are.

K: That is, to understand disorder we think an orderly mind is necessary.

A: As against a disorderly mind.

K: But the mind itself has created this disorder, which is thought and all the rest of it. So can the mind not look at disorder out there, but at the maker of disorder which is in here?

A: Which is itself the mind in disorder.

K: The mind itself is disordered.

A: Yes, but as soon as that is stated conceptually...

K: No, no, concepts are finished.

A: Yes, but we are using words.

K: We are using words to communicate.

A: Exactly. But my point is: what are we going to say when we hear the statement that it is the disordered mind that keeps proliferating disorder, but it is that disordered mind that must see.

K: I'm going to show you, you will see in a minute what takes place. Disorder is not outside me, disorder is inside me. That's a fact. Because the mind is disorderly all its activities must be disorderly. And these disorderly activities are proliferating or are moving in the world. Now can this mind observe itself without introducing the factor of an orderly mind, which is the opposite? Can it observe without the observer who is the opposite?

A: That's the question.

K: Now watch it, sir, if you are really interested in it. You will see. The observer is the observed. The observer who says, 'I am orderly, and I must put order in disorder.' That is generally what takes place. But the observer is the factor of disorder. Because the observer is the past, is the factor of division. Where there is division there is not only conflict but disorder. You can see this, sir, it is actually happening in the world. All these problems of energy, of war, peace and so on, can be solved absolutely when there are not separate governments, sovereign armies, and when we say: 'look, let's solve this problem all together, for God's sake. We are human beings. This Earth is meant for us to live on – not as Arabs and Israelis, and Americans and Russians – it is our Earth.' But we will never do this because our minds are so conditioned to live in disorder, to live in conflict.

A: And a religious vocation is conceived as the task of cleaning up the disorder with my idea of order.

K: Your idea of order is the fact that has produced disorder.

A: Exactly.

K: So a question now arises, sir, which is very interesting: can the mind observe itself without the observer? Because the observer is the observed. The observer who says, 'I will bring order in disorder,' that observer is itself a fragment of disorder; therefore it can never bring about order. So can the mind be aware of itself as a movement of disorder, not trying to correct it, not trying to justify it, not trying to shape it, but just observing? As I said previously, observing, sitting on the banks of a river and watching the waters go by. You see, then you see much more. But if you are swimming in the middle of it you will see nothing.

A: I've never forgotten that it was when I stopped questioning, when I stood before that droplet of dew on the leaf, that everything changed totally; and what you say is true; once something like that happens there is no regression from it.

K: Sir, it is not once, it is . . .

A: . . . forever.

K: It's not just an incident that took place. My life is not an incident, it is a movement; and in that movement I observe this movement of disorder. And therefore the mind itself is disorderly and how can that disorderly, chaotic, contradictory, absurd little mind bring about order? It can't. Therefore a new factor is necessary. And the new factor is to observe, to perceive, to see without the perceiver.

A: To perceive without the perceiver, to perceive without the perceiver.

K: Because the perceiver is the perceived.

A: Yes.

K: If you once grasp that then you see everything without the perceiver. You don't bring in your personality, your ego, your selfishness. You say disorder is the factor which is in me, not out there. The politicians are trying to bring about order when they are themselves so corrupt. You follow, sir? How can they bring about order?

A: It's impossible.

K: That's what's happening in the world. The politicians are ruling the world, from Moscow, from New Delhi, from Washington, wherever it is, it's the same pattern being repeated. Living a chaotic, corrupt life, you try to bring order in the world. It's childish. So that's why transformation of the mind is not of your mind or my mind, it's of the mind, the human mind.

A: Not even the mind trying to order itself.

K: How can it, it is like a blind man trying to bring about colour! And he says: 'That's grey.' It has no meaning. So can the mind observe this disorder in itself without the observer who has created disorder? Sir, this brings up a very simple thing. To look at a tree, at a woman, at a mountain, at a bird, or a sheet of water with the light on it, the beauty of it, to look without the see-er. The moment the see-er comes in, the observer comes in, he divides. Division is all right as long as it's descriptive. But when you are living, that division is destructive.

A: Yes, what was running through my mind was this continuous propaganda we hear about techniques that are available for stilling the mind: but that requires a stiller to do the stilling; and so that possibility is absolutely, I'm using your words, absolutely and totally out.

K: But that's what the gurus are doing. The imported gurus and the native gurus are doing this. They are really destroying people. But we'll talk about that later. What we are now concerned with is the fact that measurement, which is the whole movement of commercialism, consumerism, technology, is now the pattern of the world. Begun in the West, made more and more perfect in the West, and that is spreading all over the world. Go to the smallest town in India or anywhere, the same pattern is being repeated. And in the villages they are so miserable, unhappy, with one meal a day. But it is still within that pattern. And governments are trying to solve these problems separately, France by itself, Russia by itself and so on. It's a human problem, therefore it has to be approached not with a Washington mind or a London mind or a Moscow mind, but with a mind that is human and says: 'Look, this is our problem and for God's sake let's get together and solve it.' Which means care, which means accepting responsibility for every human being.

So we come back to this: as we said, order comes only with the understanding of disorder. In that there is no superimposition, in that there is no conflict, in that there is no suppression. When you suppress you react; you know all that business. So order is a totally different kind of movement. And that order is real virtue. Because without virtue there is no order. There's gangsterism.

A: Yes.

K: Politically or any other way, religiously. With virtue, virtue being conduct, there is flowering in goodness every day. This is not a theory, sir, it actually takes place, when you live that way.

A: The hexagram in the I Ching called conduct is also translated 'treading'.

K: Treading.

A: Treading, meaning a movement.

K: Of course.

A: A movement. And that's a vastly different understanding of the usual notion of conduct. But I understand from what you have said that your use of the word 'conduct' as virtue, as order, is precisely oriented to act, movement.

K: Yes sir. You see, a man who acts out of disorder is creating more disorder. Look at the life of the politician, ambitious, greedy, seeking power, position.

A: Running for election.

K: And he is the man who is going to create order in the world. The tragedy of it and we accept it! You follow?

A: Yes, we believe it's inevitable.

K: And therefore we are irresponsible.

A: Because he did it and I didn't. Yes.

K: Because we accept disorder in our life. I don't accept disorder in my life, I want to live an orderly life, which means I must understand disorder, and where there is order the brain functions much better.

A: There is a miracle here. As soon as I grasp the movement of disorder...

K: As soon as the mind grasps it.

A: Yes, yes. Then, there is order. That's truly miraculous. Perhaps it's the one and only miracle.

K: There are others but...

A: I mean in the deepest sense of the word, all of them would have to be related to that or we wouldn't have any of them, it's the real heart, the real core.

K: That's why, sir, in relationship, communication, responsibility, freedom and this freedom from disorder, there is a great sense of beauty. A life that is beautiful, a life that is really flowering in goodness. Unless we bring about such human beings the world will go to pot.

A: Yes.

K: This is what is happening. And I feel it's my responsibility: I've a passion for this, it's my responsibility to see that when I talk to you, you understand it, you live it, you function, move in that way.

A: I come back to attention, the enormous emphasis that you've made on staying totally attentive to this. I think I begin to understand something of what happens when a person begins to think that they are taking seriously what you are saying. I didn't say: begins to take it seriously, they *think* they are beginning to. As a matter of fact, they begin to watch themselves being drawn to it. Of course nothing has started yet. But something very strange happens in the mind with this notion that I am being drawn to it. I start to get afraid, I become terribly fearful of something. Next time could we discuss fear?

20 February 1974

DIALOGUE VI

The Nature and Total Eradication of Fear

DR ANDERSON: In our last talk together we had reached the point where the question of fear arose, so perhaps we could now explore that further.

KRISHNAMURTI: Yes, I think so. I wonder how we can approach this problem, because it is a common problem throughout the world. Everyone, or almost everyone, is frightened of something. It may be the fear of death, of loneliness, of not being loved, of not becoming famous or successful and also the fear of not having physical security and of not having psychological security. There are so many, multiple forms of fear. Now to go into this problem really very deeply, can the mind, which includes the brain, really be fundamentally free of fear? Because fear, as I have observed, is a dreadful thing.

A: Oh yes.

K: It darkens the world, it destroys everything. And I don't think we can discuss fear, which is one of the principles in life, without also going into the pursuit of pleasure. They are two sides of the same coin.

A: Fear and pleasure.

K: So to take fear first, there are both conscious and unconscious fears. Fears that are observable, that can be remedied and fears that are deep-rooted, deep in the recesses of one's mind.

A: At the unconscious level.

K: At the deeper levels. Now, we must be concerned with both, not only the obvious external fears, but also the deep-seated, undiscovered fears, the fears that have been handed down, the traditional fears.

A: Being told what to fear.

K: And also fears that the mind itself has produced, has cultivated.

A: In one's personal life.

K: And also in relation to others; fears of physical insecurity, losing a job, losing a position, losing something, and all the positive fears, not having something, and so on. So, if we are going to talk about this question, how should we, you and I, approach this? First take the outer, the obvious physical fears, and then from there move to the inner, and so cover the whole field, not just a particular instance of fear of an old lady, an old man, or a young man, but take the whole problem of fear.

A: Good.

K: Not just take one leaf or one branch of fear but the whole movement of fear.

A: We are back to that word 'movement' again.

K: Now, outwardly, physically it is obvious that we must have security, physical security. That is, food, clothes, and shelter are absolutely necessary. Not only for the Americans but for the whole of humanity.

A: Of course.

K: It's no good saying, 'We are secure and to hell with the rest of the world.' The world is you and you are the world. You can't isolate yourself and say, 'I am going to be secure and not bother about the others.'

A: Secure myself against them.

K: That gives rise to division, conflict, war. But physical security is necessary for the brain. The brain can only function — as I have observed in myself, in others, not that I am an expert on the brain or neurology and all that, but I have observed it — the brain can function only in complete security. Then it functions efficiently, healthily, not neurotically, and its actions won't be lopsided. The brain needs security, as a child needs security. That security is denied when we separate ourselves — as the Americans, the Russians, the Indians, the Chinese. National division has destroyed that security, because of wars.

A: Because that is a physical barrier.

K: A physical fact. And yet we don't see that. Sovereign governments, with their armies, their navies and all the rest of it, are destroying security.

A: In the name of providing it!

K: So, you see what we are trying to get at is how stupid the mind is. It wants security, and it must have security, and yet it is doing everything to destroy that security.

A: Oh yes, I see that.

K: So that's one factor. And the factor of security is one's job; either in a factory, in a business, or as a priest. So occupation becomes very important.

A: Indeed it does.

K: So, see what is involved. If I lose my job I am frightened, and that job depends on the environment, on production, business, the factory, all that commercialism, consumerism, and therefore competition with other countries. So we need physical security and we are doing everything to destroy it. If all of us said, 'Look let's all get together, not with plans, not with my plan, your plan, the communist plan or the capitalist plan, let's as human beings sit down together and solve this problem,' they could do it. Science has the means of feeding people. But they won't because they are conditioned to function so as to destroy the security which they are seeking. So that's one of the major factors in physical security. Then there is the fear of physical pain. Physical pain in the sense one has had pain, let's say last week; the mind is afraid that it will happen again. So there is that kind of fear.

A: It's very interesting with respect to physical pain that what is remembered is not the neurological reaction but the emotion that accompanied it.

K: Yes, that's it. So there is that fear. Then there is the fear of outward opinion, what people say, public opinion.

A: Reputation.

K: Reputation. You see, sir, all this is born out of disorder, which we have already discussed.

So can the mind bring about security, physical security, which means food, clothes and shelter for everybody. Not as a communist, as a capitalist, as a socialist or as a Maoist, but meeting together as human beings to resolve this problem. It can be done. But nobody wants to do it, because they don't feel responsible for it. I don't know if you have been to India; if you have gone from town to town, village to village as I have done, you see the appalling poverty, the degradation of poverty, the sense of hopelessness.

A: Yes, I have been to India and it was the first time in my life that I sensed poverty, not simply as privation, but it seemed to have a positive character about it. It was so stark.

K: I know, sir. Personally we have been through all that. So, physical survival is only possible when human beings get together. Not as communists, socialists or whatever, but as human beings who say, 'Look this is our problem, for God's sake let's solve it.' But they won't because they are already burdened with problems, with planning, how to solve that. You have your plan, I have my plan, he has his plan, so planning becomes the most important thing, plans become more important than the starvation. And we fight each other: and common sense, affection, care, love can change all this. Sir, I won't go into that.

Then there is the fear of public opinion. What my neighbour will say.

A: My image, the national image.

K: And I depend on my neighbour. If I am a Catholic living in Italy, I have to depend on my neighbour because I could lose my job if I were a Protestant there. So I accept it, I will go and salute the pope or whatever, it has no meaning. So I am afraid of public opinion. See what a human mind has reduced itself to. I don't say: 'To blazes with public opinion, they are conditioned, frightened as much as I am.' So there is that fear. And there is the physical fear of death, which is an immense fear. That fear one has to tackle differently when we come later on to talk about death.

A: Yes.

K: So there is the outward form of fear: fear of darkness, fear of public opinion, fear of losing a job, fear of not being able to survive. Sir, I have lived with people who have one meal a day. I have walked in India behind a woman with a girl, and the girl said,

'Mother, I'm hungry.' And the mother says, 'You have already eaten for the day.' So there is all that, those physical fears, pain and the fear of recurring pain, and so on. And the other fears are much more complicated, fears of dependency; inwardly, I depend on my wife, I depend on my guru, I depend on the priest, I depend on the — so many dependents! And I am afraid to lose them, to be left alone.

A: To be rejected.

K: To be rejected. If that woman turns away from me I'm lost. I get angry, brutal, violent, jealous, because I have depended on her. So dependency is one of the factors of fear. And inwardly I am afraid. I am afraid of loneliness. The other day I heard a woman on television say, 'The only fear I have in life is my loneliness.' And being afraid of loneliness I do all kinds of neurotic activities. Being lonely I attach myself to you or to a belief, or to a saviour, or to a guru. And I protect the guru, the saviour, the belief and that soon becomes neurotic.

A: Yes. I fill up the hole . . .

K: . . . with this rubbish. There is that fear. And then there is the fear of not being able to arrive, to succeed in this world of disorder, and to succeed in the so-called spiritual world. That's what they are all doing now.

A: Spiritual achievement.

K: Achievement, which they call enlightenment.

A: Expanding consciousness. I know what you mean.

K: Then there is the fear of not being, which translates itself into 'identification with'. I must identify myself.

A: In order to be.

K: To be. To identify myself with my country, and I say to myself, that's too stupid. Then I say, I must identify myself with God, whom I have invented: God has not made man in his image, man has made God in his image. You follow?

A: Oh, I follow you.

K: So, not being, not achieving, not arriving, brings about a tremendous sense of uncertainty, a tremendous sense of not being able to fulfil, not being able to 'be with', and the cry then is, 'I must be myself.'

A: Do my own thing.

K: Your own thing. Which is rubbish. So there are all these fears, both logical fears, irrational fears, neurotic fears, and fears about survival, physical survival. So how do you deal with all these fears and many more fears which we will go into presently – how do you deal with them all? One by one?

A: Well, you would just be in the mournful round of fragmentation if you do that.

K: And also there are the hidden fears, which are much more active.

A: The continual bubbling up from below.

K: Bubbling up, when I'm not conscious, they take over. So how am I to deal first with the obvious fears which we have described? Shall I deal with them one by one, to get security? You follow? Or take loneliness and tackle that, come to grips with it, go beyond it and so on? Or is there a way of dealing with fear, not with its branches but with the root of it? Because if I take each leaf, each branch, it will take all my lifetime. And if I begin to analyse my fears, that very analysis becomes paralysis.

A: Yes, and then I even fear that I might not have analysed correctly.

K: Correctly. And I am caught over and over again. So how shall I deal with this problem, as a whole, not just parts, fragments of it?

A: In our conversations we've been pointing to movement. The movement of fear is one.

K: Yes, a tremendous one.

A: And it is a unified field of destruction.

K: It is the common factor of everything. Whether a man or woman lives in Moscow or India, or wherever, there is this common thing, fear, and how shall we deal with it? Can the mind be free of fear, really, not verbally or ideologically, be absolutely free of fear? And it *is* possible to be completely free of fear and I'm not saying this as a theory, I know it, I've gone into it.

Now how shall I deal with fear? So I ask myself, what is fear? Not the objects of fear or the expressions of fear.

A: Nor the instant reaction to danger.

K: What is fear?

A: It's an idea in my mind in part.

K: What is fear, sir?

A: If we had said it's an abiding . . .

K: No. Behind the words, behind the descriptions, the explanations, the way out and the way in, and all the rest of it, what is fear? How does it come about?

A: If I have followed you through our conversations until now, I'd say that it is another expression of the observer's disordered relation to the observed.

K: What does that mean? Look, the problem is this – I will make the problem clearer. Man has tried to lop off or prune one fear after the other, through analysis, through escape, through identifying himself with something which he calls courage. Or by saying, well I don't care, I rationalize my fears and remain in an intellectual state of rationalizing, of verbal explanation. But the thing is boiling. So what shall I do? What is fear? I have to find this out, not you telling me, I have to find it out for myself as I find myself that I am hungry – nobody has to tell me I am hungry so I have to find this out.

A: In my earlier reply, when you asked me what is fear, I did the usual academic thing: 'If I have followed you up until now then it seems clear that' and so on. Whereas let's forget about the following, let's zero in on it right now and then I must say I can't tell anybody else what fear is with respect to what it is I am going to discover in me as such. All my continual descriptions about it are simply a deflection from my *immediate* issue which is *here*.

K: Yes, so I'm not escaping, I'm not rationalizing. I am not analysing, because analysis is real paralysis. When you are confronted with a problem like this merely to analyse it, with the fear of not being able to analyse perfectly and therefore going to a professional, who also needs an analysis, means that one is caught.

So I will not analyse because I see the absurdity of it. You follow, sir?

A: Yes I do.

K: I won't run.

A: No backing off or flight.

K: No explanations, no rationalizations, no analysis. I am faced with this thing. Then there are the unconscious fears which I don't know about. They express themselves occasionally when I am alert, when I see fear surfacing in me.

A: When I am alert.

K: When I am alert and watching. Or when I'm looking at something, fear comes up uninvited. Now, it is important for the mind to be completely free of fear. It's essential, as food is essential. It's essential for the mind to be free of fear. So I see outwardly what we have discussed. Now I say, what are the hidden fears, can I consciously invite them to come to the surface? You follow?

A: Yes I do.

K: Or is it that the conscious cannot touch that. The conscious can only deal with the things it knows: but it cannot observe the things it doesn't know.

A: Or have access to.

K: So, what am I to do? Are dreams the answer? Dreams are merely the continuation, in a different form, of what has happened during the day. We won't go into that for the moment. So how is all that to be awakened and exposed? The racial fears, the fears that society has taught me, the fears that the family has imposed, the neighbours, all those crawling, ugly, brutal things that are hidden, how are they all to come up naturally and be exposed so that the mind sees them completely? You understand?

A: Yes, I do. I was just thinking about what we are doing in relation to what you are saying. Here we are in a university where hardly any listening goes on at all, if any. Why? Well, if we were to relate to each other in terms of my sitting back here saying to myself, every time you made a statement, well what do I have to say back, even if my reaction were benign and I'd say to myself as a professor, now that's a very interesting concept, perhaps we could clear that up a little – we should never have begun to be together, never started, and yet we might have given ourselves the idea that we were trying very hard to be sincere.

K: I know, I know.

A: But fear is at the base of that too, because the professor is thinking to himself...

K: ... of his position, ...

A: He's got his reputation at stake here. He'd better not keep quiet too long, because someone might get the idea that either he doesn't understand a thing that is going on or he doesn't have anything to contribute to what's going on. All of which has nothing to do with anything.

K: Absolutely. Please sir, look, sir, what I have found: the conscious mind, conscious thought cannot invite and expose the hidden fears. It cannot analyse it, because analysis, as we said, is inaction, and if there is no escape, I shan't run off to a church, or Jesus or Buddha, or somebody, or identify myself with some other thing. I have pushed all those aside because I've understood their futility. So I am left with this. This is *my* baby. So what shall I do? Some action has to take place. I can't just say, 'Well I've pushed all that aside, I'll just sit here.' Now just see what happens: because I've pushed all those things aside through observation, not through resistance, not through violence, because I have negated all those, escape, analysis, running off to something and the rest of all that, I have energy, the mind now has energy.

A: Yes, it floods up.

K: Because I have pushed away all the things that dissipate energy. Therefore I am now this thing, I am confronted with that, confronted with fear. Now, what can I do? Listen to this, sir, what can I do? I can't do anything, because it is I who have created the fear.

A: Yes.

K: Right, so I cannot do a thing about fear.

A: Precisely.

K: But there is the energy which has been gathered, which has come into being when all dissipation of it has ended. There is energy. Now, what happens? This is not some hocus-pocus, some kind of mystical experience. There is actual fear and I have tremendous energy which has come about because there is no longer any dissipation of energy. So what takes place? So I ask, what has created fear? What has brought it about? Because I have the energy, you follow, to put that question and find the answer to that question, I've got energy now. So, what has brought it about? You, my neighbour, my country, my culture?

A: My self.

K: What has brought it about?

A: I've done it.

K: Who is I?

A: I don't mean 'I' as the fragmented observer off from me. I am thinking what you said earlier about the mind as disordered, which requires to empty itself of the disorder.

K: I'm asking, what has brought this fear into my consciousness? What has brought this fear? And I won't leave it till I find it. You understand, sir? Because I've got the energy to do it. I don't depend on any book, on any philosopher, on anybody.

A: Would it be that once the energy begins to flood that the question itself disappears?

K: And I'll begin to find the answer.

A: Yes.

K: I don't put the question, but I find the answer.

A: Right, right.

K: Now, what is the answer?

A: The answer couldn't be academic, a description of something.

K: What is the answer to this fact of fear which has been sustained, which has been nourished, which has carried on from generation to generation? Can the mind observe this fear, the movement of it . . .

A: The movement of it.

K: . . . not just a piece of fear.

A: Or a succession of fears . . .

K: But the movement of this.

A: The movement of fear itself.

K: Yes, observe it without the thought that has created the observer. Can there be observation of this fact, which I've called fear because the mind has recognized it, because it has had fear before? So through recognition and association it says, this is fear.

So can the mind observe without the observer, who is the thinker, observe the fact of fear only? Because the observer, which is thought, the observer as thought has produced it. I am afraid of my neighbour, what he may say, because I want to be respectable. That is the product of thought. Thought has divided the world into America, Russia, India, China and all the rest of it, and that destroys security. That is the result of thought. I am lonely and therefore I act neurotically, which is also the factor of thought operating. So I see very clearly that thought is responsible for that. Right, sir?

A: Yes.

K: So, what will happen with thought? Thought is responsible for fear. It has nourished it, encouraged it, it has done everything to sustain it. I am afraid of the pain that I had yesterday happening again tomorrow – which is the movement of thought. And thought can only function within the field of knowledge – that's its ground – and fear is something new each time. Fear isn't old. It is made old when I recognize it.

A: Yes.

K: But when the process of recognition, which is the association of words and so on, occurs, can the mind observe that without the interference of thought? If it does fear is not.

A: Right. The thing that struck me while I was sitting here was that the moment that occurs, the thought and the fear immediately disappear.

K: So fear can be put away completely. If I was living in Russia and they threatened to put me in prison I would probably be afraid. That is natural self-preservation. It's a natural fear like a bus coming towards you causing you to step aside, or when you run away from a dangerous animal, that's a natural self-protective reaction. But that's not fear. It's a response of intelligence operating and saying, for God's sake move away from the oncoming bus. But the other factors are factors of thought.

A: Exactly.

K: So can thought understand itself and know its place and not project itself? Not control thought, which is an abomination. If you control thought, who is the controller? Another fragment of thought. That is a vicious circle, a game you are playing with yourself. So can the mind observe without a movement of thought? It will only do that when you have understood the whole movement of fear. Understood, not analysed, but looked at it. It is a living thing, therefore you have to look at it. Only a dead thing can be dissected and analysed, kicked around. But a living thing you have to watch.

A: In our last conversation, we came to a point where we raised the question of someone saying to himself, I *think* I understand what I have heard, now I am going to try that.

K: You don't say, sir, when you see a dangerous animal, I will *think* about it! You move, you act. Because there is tremendous destruction waiting there. There is a self-protective reaction which is intelligence saying: get out. Here we are not using intelligence. Intelligence operates only when we have looked at all these fears, the movements, the inwardness, the ugliness, the subtlety, the whole movement of them. Then out of that comes intelligence and says, I have understood it.

A: That's beautiful, very beautiful. We were going to say something about pleasure.

K: Ah, that must also be dealt with. So, sir, look, we said there are the physical fears and the psychological fears, both are interrelated, we can't say, that's one thing and this is another. They are all interrelated; and the interrelationship and the understanding of that brings this intelligence which will operate physically. It will say, let's then work together, co-operate together to feed man. You follow, sir? Let's not be national, religious, sectarian. What is important is to feed man, to clothe him, to make him live happily. But you see unfortunately we are so disorderly in the ways we live that we have no time for anything else. Our disorder is consuming us.

A: It's interesting that one of the misuses of tradition would be that we are actually taught what to fear. In our language we have an expression, cautionary tales, an accumulation of warnings about things that are simply imaginary, fantasia, phantasmagoria, which children get from their earliest years, almost with the bottle. And when we get into adolescence we reflect on these things and if things go wrong we feel that perhaps it's because we haven't sufficiently grasped what we have been told. And then some young people will say at that point, 'I'm going to junk the whole thing.' But then immediately the question of loneliness arises.

K: Sir, this is life, you can't reject one part and accept the other part.

A: Exactly.

K: Life means all this: freedom, order, disorder, communication, relationship, responsibility — all this is living. If you don't understand and say, 'I don't want to have anything to do with this,' then you are not living: you are dying.

A: Yes, of course. What we have been saying about this movement, as a unified field, is taken by thought and, you might say, put in the refrigerator, and that's the reality to the person.

K: Quite, sir.

A: And when we want to look at it, it's one of the ice cubes we break out.

K: That's right, sir. What place has knowledge in the regeneration of man? Look, our knowledge is: you must be separate; you are an American, I am a Hindu, that's our knowledge. Our knowledge is: you must rely on your neighbour because he knows, he is respectable, society is respectability, society is moral, so you accept that. So knowledge has brought about all these factors. And you are suddenly asking me what place has that, what place has tradition, what place has the accumulated knowledge of millennia? The accumulated knowledge of science, mathematics, and so on, that is essential. But what place has knowledge which I have gathered through experience, through generation after generation of human endeavour, what place has it in the transformation of fear? None whatsoever.

A: None. Because of what we saw before that upon the instant that this is grasped, the thought that was operating as a fragment and the fear vanish; and it isn't that something succeeds it.

K: No, nothing takes its place.

A: Nothing takes its place.

K: It doesn't mean there is emptiness.

A: Oh, no. But you see it's when you start thinking about that as a thought, you get scared.

K: That's why it's very important to find out or to understand the function of knowledge and where knowledge becomes ignorance. We mix the two together. Knowledge is essential, to speak English, to drive, for a dozen other things, knowledge is essential. But that knowledge becomes ignorance when we are trying to understand actually 'what is'; the 'what is' is this fear, this disorder, this irresponsibility. To understand that you don't have to have knowledge. All you have to do is to look, look outside you and look inside you. And then you see clearly that knowledge is absolutely unnecessary, it has no value in the transformation or the regeneration of man. Because freedom is not born of knowledge; freedom is when all the burdens are not. You don't have to search for freedom. It comes when the other is not.

A: It isn't something in place of the horror that was there before.

K: Of course not.

A: Yes, I follow you. Maybe next time we could talk about pleasure, the opposite side of the coin.

20 February 1974

DIALOGUE VII

Understanding, Not Controlling, Desire

DR ANDERSON: Mr Krishnamurti, the last time we were speaking you remarked that fear and pleasure are opposite sides of the same coin. I was thinking that perhaps we could move from fear on to a discussion of pleasure. But perhaps there is something more about fear that we need still to explore.

KRISHNAMURTI: Sir, I think for most of us, fear has created such misery; so many activities, ideologies and gods, are born of fear that we never seem to be completely free from fear. And 'freedom from' and 'freedom' are two different things, aren't they?

A: Yes.

K: Freedom from fear and the feeling of being completely free.

A: Would you say that the notion even of 'freedom for' also suggests conflict?

K: Yes. 'Freedom for' and 'freedom from' involve contradiction and conflict and battle, violence, struggle. When one understands that rather deeply one can see the meaning of what it means to be free. Not 'from' or 'for', but intrinsically, deeply, by itself. Probably it's a non-verbal, non-ideational happening, a feeling that all the burdens have fallen away from you. Not that you are struggling to throw them away. The burdens don't exist, conflicts don't exist. As we were saying the other day, relationship then is in total freedom.

So these two principles of pleasure and fear seem to be deeply rooted in us. And I don't think we can understand pleasure without understanding fear. You can't separate them, really: but in order to investigate one has to separate them.

A: Yes, without fear do you think we should ever have thought of pleasure?

K: We would never have thought of pleasure. It's like punishment and reward. If there was no punishment at all nobody would talk about reward.

A: Yes, I see.

K: And when we are talking about pleasure I think we ought to be clear that we are not condemning pleasure, we are not trying to become puritanical or permissive. We are trying to investigate or examine, to explore the whole structure and nature of pleasure, as we did fear. And to do that properly and deeply the attitude of condemnation or acceptance of pleasure must be set aside. Naturally so. I mean, if I want to investigate something I must be free from my inclinations and prejudices.

A: 'Looking forward to' is, I see, beginning to emerge from what you are saying.

K: Yes.

A: We say we look forward to pleasure, we even ask a person, what is your pleasure. We get nervous, thinking that perhaps we won't meet it. Now I take it that what you are saying here suggests the anticipation of gratification.

K: That's right. Gratification, satisfaction and a sense of fulfilment. We will go into all that when we talk about pleasure. But I think we must be clear from the beginning that we are not condemning it. The priests throughout the world *have* condemned it.

A: Yes, the notion of freedom is associated with many religious approaches to this. One is free from desire.

K: Yes. One has to bear in mind that we are not justifying it, sustaining it or condemning it, but observing it. To really go into this question of pleasure I think one has first to look into desire. The more commercial the usage of things, the more desire grows. You can see it through commercialism and consumerism. Through propaganda desire is sustained, is nourished, is – what is the word I am looking for – is inflamed.

A: Inflamed, yes.

K: You see this happening all over the world now. In India, for example, not that I know India much better than I do America because I've not lived there very long, but I go there every year, this desire and this instant fulfilment is beginning to take place. Before in the Brahmanical order, there was a certain restraint, a certain traditional discipline which said, don't be concerned with the world and things, they are not important. What is important is the discovery of truth, of Brahman, of reality and so on. But now all that's gone: now desire is being inflamed; buy more; don't be satisfied with two pairs of trousers but have a dozen. This feeling of excitement in possession is stimulated through commercialism, consumerism and propaganda.

A: There's a lot of terror, isn't there, associated with commercialism on the part of those who are the purveyors, because the pleasure fades and this requires a stronger stimulus next time.

K: That's what the couturiers are doing; every year there is a new fashion. There is this stimulation of desire. It is really quite frightening in a sense how people are using, are stimulating desire to acquire money, possessions, the whole circle of a life that is utterly sophisticated, a life in which there is instant fulfilment of one's desire, and the feeling that if you don't fulfil, if you don't act, there is frustration. So all that's involved in it.

A: Would you say then that the approach to this is based on frustration; frustration itself is regarded as the proper incentive?

K: Yes.

A: And since frustration itself is a nullity we are trying to suggest that nullity is in itself interested in being filled. Whereas in fact by its nature it couldn't be.

K: As with children – don't frustrate them – let them do what they like. Sir, I think that before we enter into the complicated field of pleasure, we ought to go into the question of desire. Desire seems to be a very active and demanding instinct, a demanding activity that is going on in us all the time. Sir, what is desire?

A: I wonder if I could ask you to relate it to appetite as against what one would call natural hunger. Sometimes I feel there is a confusion here. Someone will get the idea in class, talking about appetite and desire, that if we look at Nature, the lion desires to kill the antelope to satisfy his appetite. Whereas it has seemed to me that the correct reply is: no that's not the case, the lion wants to incorporate the antelope into his own substance; he's not chasing his appetite.

K: I think that appetite and desire are both related.

A: Yes.

K: Appetite, physical appetite and psychological appetite, which is much more complex. Sexual appetite, and intellectual appetite, a sense of curiosity. I think that both desire and appetite are stimulated by commercialism and by consumerism, which is the form of civilization that is actively operating in the world at the present time – both in Russia and everywhere else, this consumerism has to be fulfilled.

A: Right, we talk about planned obsolescence.

K: Quite. So what is appetite and what is desire? I have an appetite because I am hungry, a natural appetite. I see a car and I have read a great deal about it and I would like to possess it, drive it, feel the power of it, going fast, the excitement of all that. That is another form of appetite.

A: Yes.

K: Then there is the intellectual appetite of discussing with a clever intelligent, observant man or woman in order to argue, to stimulate each other in discussion.

A: Yes.

K: And comparing each other's knowledge, a kind of subtle fight.

A: Scoring points.

K: That's right; and that is very stimulating. And then there is sexual appetite, the sexual appetite of constantly thinking about sex, chewing the cud. All that, both psychological and physical appetites, the normal and the abnormal. The feeling of fulfilment and frustration. All that's involved in appetite. And I'm not sure that religions, organized religions and beliefs, do not stimulate a peculiar appetite for rituals.

A: I think they do. It seems to me that despite pious protestations there is a theatrical display that occurs.

K: Go to a Roman Catholic mass and you see the beauty of it, the beauty of the colours, the beauty of the setting, the whole structure is marvellously theatrical and beautiful.

A: And for the moment it appears that we have Heaven on Earth: but then we have to go out again.

K: Of course. And it's all stimulated through tradition, through the usage of words, chants, certain associations of words, symbols, images, flowers, incense, all that is very, very stimulating.

A: Yes.

K: And if one is used to that one misses it.

A: Oh yes. I was thinking as you were saying how extraordinarily beautiful, at least to my ear, Sanskrit is as a language, and the chanting of the Gita, and the swaying back and forth, and then one sits down to study what the words say, and one says, now look, what on earth is going on when we are doing that as against what the word itself could disclose. But of course, it is self-seduction, one can't blame the language for being beautiful. And all this is encouraged; and I take it that what you are suggesting that we look at here is that there's a tremendous vested interest in keeping this up.

K: Of course. It is kept up commercially. And if it was not sustained by the priests then the whole thing would collapse. So this is a battle to hold the human being in his appetites – which is really very frightening when you look at it. Frightening in the sense – rather disgusting in one way – of exploiting people and being intrinsically destructive of the human mind.

A: Yes, I've had this problem in teaching my classes. Sometimes, it has seemed that maybe the first stanza of a poem that I know by heart would be appropriate. And so I'll begin to recite it and when I get to the end the expectation has arisen, the ears are there, the bodies are leaning forward and I have to stop and say: well, we can't go on, because you are not listening to *what* I am saying, you are listening to *how* it is being said. And if I read it terribly you wouldn't listen either. Your disgust would dominate just as your pleasure is dominating now. And the students have got after me for not reciting more poetry and to be upset over that is a perfect sign that they haven't started to do their work yet. And then we are up against the problem that they think I am being ascetical and denying the goodies!

K: Yes, of course. So there is desire and appetite, we have gone into this a little bit – but what *is* desire? I see something and immediately I must have it, a gown, a coat, a tie, the feeling of possession, the urge to acquire, the urge to experience, the urge of an act that will give me tremendous satisfaction. The satisfaction might be acquisition, acquiring a tie, or a coat, or sleeping with a woman. Now behind all that is desire. I might desire a house and another might desire a car, someone else might desire to have intellectual knowledge. Another might desire God or enlightenment. They are all the same. The objects vary but desire is the same. One I call noble, the other I call ignoble, worldly, stupid. But desire is behind all of them. So what is desire? How does it come about that this very strong desire is born, is cultured? You follow? What is desire? How does it take place in each one of us?

A: If I've understood you, you make a distinction between appetite associated with natural hunger, that sort of desire, and now we are talking about desire which is sometimes described as artificial. I don't know whether you would want to call it that.

K: Sir, the objects of desire vary, don't they.

A: Yes, the objects vary.

K: The objects of desire vary according to each individual, each tendency and idiosyncrasy or conditioning and so on. Desire for that and that and that. But I want to find out, what is desire? How does it come about? I think it's fairly clear.

A: You mean a sense of absence?

K: No, I am asking what *is* desire? How does it come about?

A: One would have to ask himself.

K: Yes, I'm asking you, how does it come about that there is this strong desire 'for' something or desire against desire itself. I think it's clear: there is visual perception, then there is sensation, then there is contact and desire comes out of it. That's the process, isn't it?

A: Oh, yes, I'm clear now what you are saying.

K: Perception, sensation, contact, desire.

A: And then if the desire is frustrated, anger. The whole thing goes down the line.

K: All the rest of it, violence and so on, follows. So religious people, monks throughout the world, have said, 'Be without desire, control desire, suppress desire. Or if you cannot, transfer it to something that's worthwhile – to God, or enlightenment or truth or whatever.'

A: But then that's just another form of desire – desire not to desire.

K: Of course.

A: So we never get out of that.

K: Yes, but you see they said: control desire. Because you need energy to serve God and if you are caught in desire you are caught in tribulation, in trouble, which will dissipate your energy. Therefore hold it, control it, suppress it. I have seen it so often in Rome, the priests are walking along with the Bible and they daren't look at anything else, they keep on reading it because they are attracted to whatever it may be, to a woman or a nice house or a nice cloak, so keep reading it, never expose yourself to tribulation, to temptation. So hold it because you need your energy to serve God. So desire comes about through perceptions, visual perception, sensation, contact, desire. That's the process of it.

A: Yes. And then there's the whole backlog of memory to reinforce it.

K: Of course, yes.

A: I was struck by what you just said. Here's this book, that's already outside me, it's really no more than what they put on horses when they are in a race.

K: Blinkers! The Bible becomes blinkers!

A: Yes, I follow that. But the thing that struck me was, never, never therefore quietly looking at it.

K: That's it sir.

A: Looking at desire itself.

K: I walked once behind a group of monks in India. And they were very serious people. There was an elderly monk, with his disciples around him, walking up a hill and I followed them. They never once looked at the beauty of the sky, the extraordinary blue of the sky and the mountains, the light on the grass and the trees and the birds and the water – they never once looked around. They had bent their heads down and they were repeating something in Sanskrit, and were going along totally unaware of Nature, totally unaware of the passers-by. Because their whole life had been spent in controlling desire and concentrating on what they thought was the way to reality. So desire there acted as a repressive, limiting process.

A: Of course.

K: Because they are frightened. If I look up there might be a woman, I might be tempted. So we see what desire is and we see what appetite is; they are similar.

A: Yes. Would you say appetite was a specific focus of desire?

K: Yes, put it that way if you like. But they both go together, they are two different words for the same thing. Now the problem arises, need there be control of desire at all? You follow, sir?

A: Yes, I'm asking myself, because in our conversations I've learned that every time you ask a question, if I construe it in terms of a syllogistical relation to things that have been stated as premises before, I am certainly not going to come to the one answer that is needful.

K: Sir, you see, discipline is a form of suppression and control of desire – religious, sectarian, non-sectarian, it's all based on that, control. Control your appetite, control your desires, control your thought; and this control gradually squeezes out the flow of free energy.

A: Yes, and yet, amazingly, the Upanishads in particular have been interpreted in terms of tapas as encouraging this control.

K: I know, I know. In India it is something fantastic; the monks who have come to see me, they are called sannyasis, are incredible. A monk came to see me some years ago, quite a young man, who had left his house and home at the age of fifteen to find God. And he had renounced everything and put on the robe. And as he grew older, at eighteen, nineteen, twenty, sexual appetite was burning. He had taken a vow of celibacy, as sannyasis and monks do. And he explained how day after day in his dreams, in his walking, in his going to a house and begging, this thing was raging like a fire. Do you know what he did to control it?

He had himself operated. Sir, his urge for God was so strong – you follow, sir – the idea not the reality.

A: Not the reality.

K: So he came to see me, after hearing several talks which I had given in that place. He came to see me in tears. He said, what have I done? What have I done to myself? I cannot put this right, grow a new organ, it is finished. That's the extreme case. But all control moves in that direction.

A: The person who is sometimes called the first Christian theologian, Origen, castrated himself out of, as I understand it, misunderstanding the words of Jesus, 'If your hand offends you, cut it off'.

K: Sir, authority to me is criminal in this way. It doesn't matter who says it.

A: And like the monk you just described, Origen came later to repent of this and to see that it was totally irrelevant. Was this monk also saying to you in his tears that he was absolutely no better off in any way?

K: On the contrary, sir, he said, I've committed a sin, I've committed an evil act. He realized what he had done: that such an act led to nothing.

A: Nothing.

K: I've met so many cases, not such extreme forms of control and denial, but others. They have tortured themselves for an idea, for a symbol, for a concept. And we have sat and discussed with them, and they begin to see what they have done to themselves. I met a man who was high up in the bureaucracy and one morning he woke up and he said, I'm passing judgment in court over others, and I seem to say to them, 'I know truth, you don't so you are punished.' So one morning he woke up and said to himself: 'This is all wrong; I must find out what truth is.' So he resigned, left and went away for twenty-five years to find out what truth is. Sir, these people are dreadfully serious, you understand.

A: Oh yes.

K: They are not like cheap repeaters of some mantra and such rubbish. So somebody brought him to the talks I was giving. He came to see me the next day. He said: 'You are perfectly right; I have been meditating on truth for twenty-five years and it has been self-hypnosis, as you pointed out. I've been caught in my own verbal, intellectual formulas and structure and I haven't been able to get out of it.' You understand, sir? And to admit that he was wrong needed courage, needed perception.

A: Exactly.

K: Not courage, perception. So, now seeing all this, the permissiveness, the reaction to the Victorian way of life, the world with all its absurdities, trivialities and banality, the response to that is to renounce it, to say, well I won't touch it. But desire is burning all the same, all the glands are working. You can't cut out your glands. So therefore they say, control, don't be attracted to a woman, don't look at the sky, because the sky is so marvellously beautiful and beauty may then become the beauty of a woman, the beauty of a house, the beauty of a chair in which you can sit comfortably. So don't look, control it. You follow, sir?

A: I do.

K: There is permissiveness, the reaction of restraint and control, and so there is the pursuit of an idea as God, and for that you control desire. Another man I met had left his house at the age of twenty. He was really quite an extraordinary chap. He was seventy-five when he came to see me, he had left home at the age of twenty, renounced everything and went from teacher to teacher to teacher. He went to – I won't mention names because that wouldn't be right – and he came to me, talked to me. He said, I went to all these people asking if they could help me find God. I've spent from the age of twenty till I'm seventy-five, wandering all over India. I'm a very serious man and not one of them has told me the truth. I've been to the most famous, to the most socially active, the people who talk endlessly about God. After all these years I return to my house and find nothing. And you come along, he said, and you never talk about God. You never talk about the path to God. You talk about perception. The seeing 'what is' and going beyond it. The beyond is the real, not the 'what is'. He was seventy-five.

A: Fifty-five years on the road.

K: They don't do that in Europe, years on the road. He was literally on the road, begging from village to village. When he told me I was so moved, almost in tears – to spend a whole lifetime, as they do in the business world...

A: Yes.

K: ... fifty years of going day after day to the office and dying at the end of it. It is the same thing, fulfilling desire, money, money, money, more things, things, things; and the other way, none of that but another substitute for that.

A: Yes, just another form.

K: So looking at all this, sir, one sees it is dreadful what human beings have done to themselves and to others, seeing all that one inevitably asks the question, how to live with desire? You can't help it: desire is there. The moment I see something, a beautiful flower, the admiration, the love of it, the smell of it, the beauty of the petals, the quality of the flower and so on, the enjoyment of it, one asks, is it possible to live without any control whatsoever?

A: The very question is terrifying in the context of these disorders that you are speaking about. I am seeing this in the perspective that one is in, when someone out of frustration comes to you, like the man did after fifty-five years on the road. And as soon as you put that question, if the answer is going to be something that completely negates this whole investment of fifty-five years on the road, it seems that most persons are going to freeze right there.

K: And it is a cruel thing too, sir. He has spent fifty-five years at it, and suddenly realizes what he has done. The cruelty of deception.

A: Oh, yes.

K: Self-deception, the deception of tradition, of all the teachers who have said, control, control, control. And he comes to you and you say to him, what place has control?

A: I think I am beginning to get a very keen sense of why you say go into it. If he doesn't get past that initial shock, then he is not going to go into it.

K: So we talked and we discussed for hours, we went into it. Gradually he saw. So, sir, unless we understand the nature and the

A WHOLLY DIFFERENT WAY OF LIVING

structure of appetite and desire, which are more or less the same, we cannot understand, very deeply, pleasure.

A: Yes, I see why you have established this foundation before we look at the opposite side of the coin.

K: Because pleasure and fear are the two principles that are active in all human beings. And that is reward and punishment. Don't bring up a child through punishment but reward him; you know. The psychologists are advocating something like this.

A: Oh yes, they are encouraged by the experiments on Pavlov's dogs.

K: Dogs or geese. Do this and don't do that. So unless we understand fear, understand in the sense of investigate, see the truth of it and whether the mind is capable of going beyond it, to be totally free of fear, as we discussed the other day; and also understand the nature of pleasure. Because pleasure is an extraordinary thing; to see a beautiful thing and enjoy it — what is wrong with that?

A: Nothing.

K: But see what is involved in it.

A: Right. The mind plays a trick here. I say to myself, I can't find anything wrong with it, therefore nothing is wrong with it; I don't really believe that necessarily. And I was thinking a little while ago when you were speaking about attempts through power to negate desire.

K: Negating desire is a search for power.

A: Would you say that one searches for power in order to secure a pleasure that has not yet been realized?

K: Yes, yes.

A: I see. It's a terrible thing.

K: But it is a reality. It's going on.

A: Oh, yes. But we are taught that from children.

K: That's just it, sir. So, pick up any magazine, there are the advertisements, the half-naked ladies, and so on. So pleasure is a very active principle in man, as fear is.

A: Oh yes.

K: And again society, which is immoral, has said, control. One side, the religious side says, control and commercialism says, don't control, enjoy, buy, sell. You follow? And the human mind, says this is all right. My own instinct is to have pleasure so I'll go after it. But Saturday, Sunday or Monday, or whatever day it is, I'll give to God. You follow, sir?

A: Yes.

K: And this game goes on, forever it has been going on. So what is pleasure? Why should pleasure be controlled? I'm not saying it's right or wrong, please let's be very clear from the beginning that we are not condemning pleasure, we are not saying you must give rein to it, let it run or that it must be suppressed or justified. We are trying to understand why pleasure has become of such extraordinary importance in life. Pleasure of enlightenment, pleasure of sex, pleasure of possession, pleasure of knowledge, pleasure of power.

A: And Heaven which is regarded as the ultimate pleasure...

K: The ultimate, of course.

A: ... is usually spoken of theologically as the future state.

K: Yes.

A: This is to me very interesting; even at the level of gospel songs we hear, 'When the roll is called up yonder I'll be there'. When it's called up yonder, which means at the end of the line. And then there's the terror that I won't be good enough when...

K: When.

A: Yes, so I'm tightening up my belt to pay my heavenly insurance policy on Saturday and Sunday, the two days of the weekend that you mentioned. But what if I got caught from Monday through Friday?

K: So pleasure, enjoyment and joy. There are these three things and happiness. You see joy is happiness, ecstasy, the delight, the sense of tremendous enjoyment. And what is the relationship of pleasure to enjoyment and to joy and happiness?

A: Yes, we have been moving a long way from fear; but I don't mean moving away by turning our back on it.

K: No, we have gone into it, we see the movement from that to this, it's not 'away from' pleasure. There is a delight in seeing something very beautiful, delight. If you are at all sensitive, if you are at all observant, if there is a feeling of relationship to Nature which very few people have unfortunately, they may stimulate it, but the actual relationship to Nature is when you see something really marvellously beautiful like a mountain with all its shadows and valleys and you know it's something, a tremendous delight. Now see what happens: at that moment there is nothing but that. That is, the beauty of the mountain, lake or the single tree on a hill, that beauty has knocked everything out of me.

A: Oh yes.

K: And at that moment there is no division between me and that, there is sense of great purity and enjoyment.

A: Exactly.

K: Now see what takes place.

A: I see we've reached a point where we are going to take a new step. It's amazing how this thing has moved so inevitably but not unjoyfully. In our next conversation I would love to pursue this.

21 February 1974

DIALOGUE VIII

Does Pleasure Bring Happiness?

DR ANDERSON: As one who was trying in listening to you to learn something of this inwardness, I was delighted in our last conversation, to follow the passage that we made from fear, moving on through other points, until we came to pleasure. As we left off we were still talking of pleasure and I hope we can now continue from there.

KRISHNAMURTI: Yes, sir, we were talking, weren't we, of pleasure, enjoyment, delight, joy and happiness, and what relationship pleasure has with enjoyment and with joy and happiness? Is pleasure happiness? Is pleasure joy? Is pleasure enjoyment? Or is pleasure something entirely different from these two?

A: In English we think we make a distinction between pleasure and joy without necessarily knowing what we mean. In our use of the words we will discriminate sometimes, and think it odd to use the word 'pleasure' rather than 'joy' when we think that 'joy' is appropriate. The relationship between the word 'please' and 'pleasure' interests me very much. We will say to someone, please sit down. And usually that will be thought of as . . .

K: . . . have the pleasure to sit down.

A: Yes, it's an invitation not a request.

K: Not a request.

A: Right. So within the word 'pleasure', there's the intimation of joy, an intimation that is not strictly reduced to the word.

K: I would like to question whether pleasure has any relationship with joy.

A: Not in itself, you mean.

K: Or even beyond the word. Is there a continuity from pleasure to joy? Is there a connecting link? What is pleasure? I take pleasure in eating, I take pleasure in walking, I take pleasure in accumulating money, I take pleasure in – a dozen things – sex, hurting people, sadistic instincts, violence. These are all forms of pleasure. I take pleasure in and pursue that pleasure. One wants to hurt people; and that gives great pleasure. One wants to have power; it doesn't matter whether it's over the cook or over one's wife, or a thousand people, it is the same. The pleasure in something which is sustained, nourished, kept going. And this pleasure, when it is thwarted becomes violence, anger, jealousy, fury, wanting to break things, all kinds of neurotic activities and so on. So what is pleasure and what is it that keeps it going? What is the pursuit of it, the constant direction of it?

A: I think something in our first conversation touched on this when we talked about the built-in necessity that one observes in a progress that is never consummated. It's just nothing but a termination and then a new start: but no consummation at all, no totality, no fulfilment – feeling full is what I mean by that.

K: Yes, I understand, sir. But what is it that's called pleasure? I see something which I like and I want it: pleasure in possession. Take that simple thing which the child, the grown-up man, and the priest all have: this feeling of pleasure in possession. A toy or a house or possessing knowledge or possessing the idea of God, or the pleasure the dictators have, the totalitarian brutalities. To make it very, very simple: what is pleasure? Look, sir, what happens: there is a single tree standing on the hill, a green meadow and deer. You see that and say, how marvellous. Not verbally, as when you say, how marvellous, in order to communicate with somebody. But when you are by yourself and see that it is really astonishingly beautiful. The whole movement of the Earth, the flowers, the deer, the meadows, the water and the single tree, the shadows. You see that. And it's breath-taking. And you turn away and go away. Then thought says: how extraordinary that was.

A: Compared with what is now.

K: How extraordinary, I must have it again, I must get that same feeling which I had then, for two seconds or five minutes. So see what has taken place – there was the immediate response to that beauty, non-verbal, non-emotional, non-sentimental, non-romantic, then thought comes along and says: how extraordinary, what a delight that was. And then there is the memory of it and the demand, the desire for its repetition.

A: At concerts this is what happens when we call for an encore.

K: Of course.

A: And with encores there's a creeping embarrassment. Because the first reappearance is a sign of adulation, praise and everybody is happy. But then, of course, there's the problem of how many more encores can be had, maybe the last encore is a signal that now we are fed up, we don't want any more.

K: Quite, quite. So thought gives nourishment, sustains and gives a direction to pleasure. There was no pleasure at the moment of perception of that tree, the hill, the shadows, the deer, the water, the meadow. The whole thing was really non-verbal, non-romantic, and so on, it was perception. It had nothing to do with me or you, it was there. Then thought comes along and forms the memory of it, the continuing of that memory tomorrow and the demand for and pursuit of that. And when I come back to it tomorrow it is not the same. I feel a little bit shocked. I say, I was inspired, I must find a means of getting inspired again; therefore I take a drink, have sex, this or that. You follow?

A: Do you think that in the history of culture, the establishment of festivals would be related to what you say?

K: Of course.

A: In English we have the saying: to live it up; the rest of the time we are living it down.

K: Down, yes, Mardi Gras, the whole business of it. So there it is. I see that. See what takes place, sir. Pleasure is sustained by thought – sexual pleasure, the image, the thinking over it, all that and the repetition of it. And the pleasure of it and so you go on, keep on, routine. Now, what is the relationship of pleasure to the delight of the moment, not even delight, it is something inexpressible. So is there any relationship between pleasure and enjoyment? Enjoyment becomes pleasure when thought says: I have enjoyed that, I must have more of it.

A: Which is actually a falling out of joy.

K: Yes, that's it. So pleasure has no relationship to ecstasy, to delight, to enjoyment or to joy and happiness. Because pleasure is the movement of thought in a direction. It doesn't matter what direction but in a direction. The others have no direction. Enjoyment, you enjoy. Joy is something you cannot invite any more than you can invite happiness. It happens and you do not know that you are happy at that moment. It is only the next moment that you say, how happy, how marvellous that was. So see what takes place, can the mind, the brain register the beauty of that hill, the tree, the water, the meadows and end it? Not say, I want it again.

A: Yes. What you just said now would take us back to that word 'negation' that we spoke of before, because there has to be a moment when we are about to fall out, and what you are saying is that the moment the 'about-to-fall-out' appears something must be done.

K: You will see it in a minute, sir, you will see what an extraordinary thing takes place. I see pleasure, enjoyment and happiness, see that pleasure is not related to the other two. So thought gives direction and sustains pleasure. Right? Now the mind asks: can there be non-interference of thought in enjoyment? I enjoy. Why should thought come into it at all?

A: There's no reason at all.

K: But it does.

A: It does, it does.

K: Therefore the question arises: how is the mind, the brain to stop thought entering into that enjoyment? You follow?

A: Yes.

K: Not to interfere. Therefore the ancients and the religious people said: 'Control thought.' You follow? 'Don't let it creep in. Control it.'

A: The minute it raises its ugly head, whack it off! It's like a hydra.

K: Like a hydra, it keeps on growing. Now, is it possible to enjoy, to take a delight in that lovely scene, and not let thought creep in? Is this possible? I'll show you it is possible, completely possible, if you are attentive at that moment, *completely* attentive. You follow, sir?

A: Which has nothing to do with screwing oneself up with muscular effort.

K: Right, just be wholly there. When you see the sunset see it completely. When you see a beautiful line of a car, see it. And don't let the thought begin. That means at that moment be supremely and completely attentive, with your mind, with your body, with your nerves, with your eyes, ears, everything attentive. Then thought doesn't come into it at all.

So pleasure is related to thought and thought in itself brings about fragmentation, into pleasure and not pleasure. Therefore I haven't pleasure, I must pursue pleasure.

A: It makes a judgment.

K: A judgment. And then the feeling of frustration, anger, violence, all that comes into it. There is the denial of pleasure, which is what the religious people have done; they are very violent people; they have said 'no pleasure'.

A: The irony of this is overwhelming. In classical philosophy St Thomas Aquinas never tired of saying in his examination of thought that one must distinguish in order to unite. His motive was very different from what seems to have been read. Because we have managed to distinguish, but we never see the thing whole and get to the uniting.

K: That's the whole point, sir. So unless the mind really understands the nature of thinking, really very, very deeply, mere control means nothing. Personally I have never controlled a thing. This may sound rather absurd: but it is a fact.

A: Marvellous.

K: Never. But I've watched it. The watching is its own discipline and its own action. Discipline in the sense not of conformity, not of suppression, not of adjusting yourself to a pattern but the sense of correctness, the sense of excellence. When you see something, why should you control? Why should you control when you see a bottle of poison on the shelf? You don't control, you say, that's poison, you don't drink, you don't touch it. It's only when I don't read the label properly, when I see it and think it is cordial that I take it. But if I read the label, if I know what it is I won't touch it. There's no control.

A: Of course not, it's self-evident. This reminds me of that wonderful story in the Gospel about Peter who in a storm sees his Lord walking on the water and is invited to do so too; and he actually makes it for a few steps and then the Gospel says he loses faith. It seems to me that one could see that in terms of what you have been saying, at the point where thought took over he started going down. The reason that I am referring to that is because I sense in what you are saying that there is a support that's not fragmented from something else but an abiding 'something' which must be sustaining the person.

K: I wouldn't put it that way, sir. That opens a door to the idea that in you there is God.

A: Yes, I see the trap.

K: In you there is the higher self, in you there is the Atman, the permanent.

A: Maybe we shouldn't say anything about that.

K: No, but we can say this though: to see appetite, desire, to see the implications, the structure of pleasure, and that there is no relation to enjoyment and to joy, to see all that, *see* it, not verbally but actually, through observation, attention, care, the utmost care, that brings an extraordinary quality of intelligence. After all intelligence is sensitivity. To be utterly sensitive in seeing – if you call that intelligence, the higher self or whatever has no meaning. You follow?

A: It's as though you are saying that at that instant it's released.

K: Yes, that intelligence comes *in* observation. And that intelligence is operating all the time if you are seeing. I have seen all my life people who have controlled, people who have denied, people who have negated, and who have sacrificed, suppressed furiously, disciplined themselves, tortured themselves. And I say, for what? For God? For truth? A mind that is tortured, crooked, brutalized, can such a mind see truth? Certainly not. You need a completely healthy mind, a mind that is whole, a mind that is holy in itself. Unless the mind is sacred, you cannot see what is sacred. So I say, sorry, I won't touch any of that; it has no meaning. So I don't know how it has happened but I never for a second control myself, I don't know what it means.

A: And yet amazingly you know what it is in others.

K: Oh obviously, you can see it.

A: So this is something that you are able to see without having . . .

K: . . . gone through it.

A: Without having gone through it. Now this to me is profoundly mysterious. I don't mean in the sense of mystification.

K: No, no.

A: But I mean it's miraculous.

K: No, not necessarily, sir. Must I get drunk in order to find out what it is to be sober?

A: Oh no.

K: I see a man who is drunk and I say, for God's sake, see the whole movement of drunkenness, what lies behind it, what he goes through, see it, and it is finished.

A: But it seems to me in my listening to you that you are doing more than just observing that someone over there has fallen on his face and therefore . . .

K: No, no.

A: There's something that is very deep here.

K: Of course.

A: At least to me. Control in the deepest sense is an activity, not a product, and something that you haven't experienced that we would normally call intangible is nevertheless acutely present to you.

K: Yes.

A: And I take it you've said that intelligence reveals that. If intelligence is allowed to reveal it.

K: I think, sir, not 'allowed.' That's a danger, to say 'allow' intelligence to operate. Which means you have intelligence, then you allow it.

A: Yes, I see the trap of that construction. I see what you mean, because now we've got an observer who's got a new gimmick.

K: So you see that is why discipline has a different meaning. When you understand pleasure, when you understand its relationship to enjoyment and to the beauty of happiness, the beauty of joy and so on, then you understand the utter necessity of a different kind of discipline that comes naturally. After all, the word discipline in itself means to learn. To learn, not to conform, not to say: I must discipline myself to be like that or not to be like that. To learn means I must be capable of hearing, of seeing, which means a capacity which is not cultivable. You *can* cultivate a capacity, but that is not the same as the act of listening.

A: Yes, I follow very clearly.

K: The capacity to learn demands a certain discipline. I must concentrate, I must give my time to it, I must set aside my efforts in a certain direction and all that. That is, developing a certain capacity needs time.

A: Yes.

K: But perception has nothing to do with time. You see and act, as you do when you see a danger. You act instantly because you are so conditioned to danger.

A: Exactly.

K: That conditioning is not intelligence, you are just conditioned. You see a snake and you recoil, you run away. You see a dangerous animal and you run. That's all self-protective, conditioned responses. That's very simple. But perception and action is not conditioned.

A: You know, in the history of the English language we have turned that word 'fear' upside down in terms of its derivation because, if I remember correctly, fear comes from an Anglo-Saxon word that means danger.

K: Danger, of course.

A: And now we've psychologized that word so that fear means rather my emotional response to that danger.

K: Of course.

A: And not what I want to be doing.

K: Yes, not aware of the danger of fear.

A: Yes.

K: As they are now ordinary human beings are conditioned by the culture and civilization they are living in. They accept nationalism – I am taking that as an example – they accept nationalism, the flag, and all the rest of it: but nationalism is one of the causes of war.

A: Oh yes, indubitably.

K: As is patriotism and all the rest of it. But we don't see the danger of nationalism because we are conditioned to nationalism as being security.

A: But we do see our fear of the enemy.

K: Of course.

A: Yes, right. And contemplating that fear of the enemy dulls our capacity to deal with the danger.

K: So fear, pleasure, and discipline. Discipline means to learn; I am learning about pleasure, the mind is learning about pleasure. Learning brings its own order.

A: Yes. That's what I've been calling a miracle.

K: It brings its own order, and that order says, don't be silly, control is out, finished. A monk once came to see me. He had a great many followers and was very well known; he is still very well known. And he said, I have taught my disciples – and he was very proud of having thousands of disciples – and it seemed rather absurd for a guru to be proud.

A: He was a success.

K: And success means Cadillacs or Rolls Royces, European and American followers, you follow, all that circus that goes on. And he was saying, 'I have arrived because I have learned to control my senses, my body, my thoughts, my desires. I've held them as the Gita says: reining in, riding a horse,' you know, holding. He went on about it for some length. I said, 'Sir, what is at the end of it? You have controlled. Where are you at the end of it?' He said, 'What are you asking, I have arrived.' 'Arrived at what?' 'I have achieved enlightenment.' Just listen to it. Follow the sequence of a human being who has a direction, which he calls truth. And to achieve that there are the traditional steps, the traditional path, the traditional approach. And he has done it. And therefore he says, 'I have got it, I have got it in my hand, I know what it is.' I said, 'All right, sir.' He began to be very excited about it because he wanted to convince me about being a big man and all that. So I sat very quietly and listened to him and he quietened down. And we were sitting by the sea, and I said to him, 'You see that sea, sir?' He said, 'Of course.' 'Can you hold that water in your hand? When you hold that water in your hand, it's no longer the sea.'

A: Right.

K: He couldn't make it out. I said, 'All right' – and the wind was blowing from the North, a slight breeze, cool – and I said, 'There is a breeze. Can you hold all that?' 'No'. 'Can you hold the Earth?' 'No.' 'So what are you holding? Words?' You know sir, he was so angry he said, 'I won't listen to you any more, you are an evil man!' And walked off.

A: I was thinking of the absurd irony of that. All the time he thought he was holding on to himself and he just let go as he got up and walked away.

K: So learning about pleasure, about fear, really frees you from the tortures of fear and the pursuit of pleasure. Then there is a sense of real enjoyment in life. Everything becomes a great joy. It isn't just a monotonous routine, going to the office, sex, and money.

A: I've always thought it a great misfortune that in the splendid rhetoric of our Declaration of Independence we have that phrase 'the pursuit of pleasure'.

K: Pursuit of pleasure.

A: Because the child, the bright child is reared on that.

K: Oh, rather, sir.

A: And when you are very young you are not about to turn around and say, everybody's daft.

K: I know, I know. So from this you see that discipline in the orthodox sense has no place in a mind that really wants to learn about truth – not philosophize about truth, not theorize about truth, as you say tie ribbons round it, but learn about it, learn about pleasure. It is really out of that learning that there comes an extraordinary sense of order, which we were talking of the other day. The order which comes with the observation in oneself of pleasure. And there is enjoyment, a marvellous sense of ending each enjoyment as you live each moment. You don't carry over the past enjoyment; that becomes pleasure; then it has no meaning. Repetition of pleasure is monotony, is boredom; and they are bored in this country and other countries; they are fed up with pleasure. But they want other pleasures in other directions, and that is why there is the proliferation of gurus in this country. Because they all want, you know, the circus kept going.

So discipline is order; and discipline means to learn about pleasure, enjoyment, joy and the beauty of joy. When you learn, it is always new.

A: What flashes across my mind here is that it seems that a profound confusion has arisen between perception and practice.

K: Oh yes.

A: I have grasped that. It's as though we had the idea that perception is perfected at the end of practice.

K: Practice is routine, is death!

A: But we do have that idea.

K: You see, sir, they always say freedom is at the end, not at the beginning. On the contrary, the beginning, the first step is the one that counts, not the last step. The understanding of this whole question of fear and pleasure, joy, can only come in freedom to observe. And in the observation is the learning and the acting. They are all at the same moment, not learn then act. The doing, the seeing are all taking place at the same time. That is whole.

A: All these marvellous participles being in the infinite mood in themselves. Yes, a little while back it occurred to me that if we paid attention to our language as well as to the flowers and the mountains and the clouds . . .

K: Oh yes.

A: . . . to the language not only in terms of individual words, but words in context so that we would refer them to what we call usage, then words would through perception, intelligence, disclose themselves completely.

K: Quite.

A: But we don't pay attention to what we say.

K: That's right, sir. I came back after lunch and somebody said: have you enjoyed your meal? And there was a man there who said: we are not pigs to enjoy.

A: I suppose he must feel very righteous in view of what he denied himself during the meal.

K: It is really a question of attention, isn't it, whether you are eating or whether you are observing pleasure. Attention, that's the thing we have to go into very, very deeply. What it means to attend. Whether we attend to anything at all or is it only a superficial listening, hearing, seeing which we call attending; or the expression of knowledge in doing. Attention, I feel, has nothing to do with knowledge or with action. In the very attending *is* action. And one has to go into this question of what is action.

A: Yes, I see a relation between what you've just said about action and what a few conversations ago we came to with the word 'movement'.

K: Yes.

A: On-goingness. And while you were talking about looking at the tree on the hill, I remembered when I was staying at an ashram in India; I got to my quarters and a monkey was sitting on the window sill with her little baby, and looked full into my face, and I looked full into hers, but she looked fuller into mine; I had the strange feeling that I was actually a human being being . . .

K: Investigated.

A: . . . investigated by this monkey, and it was a profound shock to me.

K: Sir, once I was in Benares at the place I go to usually, I was doing yoga exercises when a big monkey with a black face and long tail came and sat on the veranda. I had closed my eyes and I looked up and there was this big monkey. She looked at me and I looked at her. A big monkey, sir, they are powerful things; and she stretched out her hand, so I got up and held her hand, like that, held it.

A: Held it.

K: And it was rough but very, very supple, extraordinarily supple; and we looked at each other; and she wanted to come into the room. I said, 'Look, I am doing exercises, I have little time, come another day.' I kind of talked to her. So she looked at me and I stepped back. She stayed there for two or three minutes and gradually went away.

A: A complete act of attention between you.

K: There was no sense of fear: she wasn't afraid, I wasn't afraid. There must have been a communication, there must have been a sense of friendship, you know, without any antagonism, without any fear. And I think attention is not something to be practised, or to be cultivated: going to a school to learn how to be attentive. That's what they do in this country and in other places, they say, 'I don't know what attention is, I'm going to learn from somebody who will tell me how to get it.' Then it's not attention.

A: Speed reading, it's called.

K: Speed reading, yes.

A: A thousand words a minute.

K: Sir, that's why I feel there is a great sense of care and affection in being attentive, which means diligently watching. To 'read' exactly what is, what is there. Not interpret, not translate it, not contrive to do something with it, but to read what is there. There is an infinite lot to see. There is a tremendous lot to see in pleasure, as we have said. And to understand it. And to do that you must be watchful, attentive, diligent, careful. But we are negligent, the opposite – what's wrong with pleasure?

So that what we have done is really read this whole map.

A: Yes.

K: Beginning with responsibility, then relationship, fear and pleasure. All that. Just observing this extraordinary map of our life.

A: And the beauty of it is we've been moving within the concern for the transformation of man, which is not dependent on knowledge or time, without worrying whether we are getting off the track. It is happening naturally. That I take it is not a surprise to you.

K: And also that's why, sir, it is right to live with the company of the wise. Live with a man who is really wise. Not with people who are faking it, not in books, not attending classes where you are taught wisdom. Wisdom is something that comes with self-knowing.

A: It reminds me of a hymn in the Veda that says of the goddess of speech that she never appears except among friends.

K: Yes.

A: Actually that means that unless the care and the affection that you mentioned are continuous and concurrent with attention there can be nothing but babble.

K: Of course.

A: There can only be verbal babble.

K: Which the modern world is encouraging.

A: Yes.

K: Which again means the superficial pleasures not enjoyment. You follow? Superficial pleasures have become the curse. And to go behind that is one of the most difficult things for people to do.

A: Because it goes faster and faster.

K: That's just it, that's what is destroying the Earth, the air, everything. There is a place I go to every year in India, where there is a school with which I am concerned: the hills there are the oldest hills in the world. Nothing has been changed, there are no bulldozers, no houses; it's an old place, with these old hills. And you feel the enormity of time, the feeling of absolute non-movement – which is so far away from civilization, all this circus that is going on. And when you go there you feel this utter quietness which time has not touched. And when you leave it and come back to civilization you feel rather lost, a sense of what is all this about? Why is there so much noise about nothing? That's why it is so odd and rather inviting, a great delight, to see everything as it is, including myself. To see what I am, not through the eyes of a professor, a psychologist, a guru, a book, just to see what I am and to read what I am. Because all history is in me. You follow?

A: Of course. There is something immensely beautiful in that. Do you think that in our next conversation we could talk about the relation of beauty to what you have said?

21 February 1974

DIALOGUE IX

Sorrow, Passion, and Beauty

DR ANDERSON: Mr Krishnamurti, in our last conversation we had moved from discussing fear, and its relation to the transformation of the individual which is not dependent on knowledge or time, on to pleasure, and just as we reached the end of that conversation the question of beauty arose.

KRISHNAMURTI: One often wonders why museums are so full of pictures and statues. Is it because man has lost touch with Nature and therefore has to go to museums to look at other people's famous paintings? And some of them are really marvellously beautiful. Why do museums exist at all? I'm just asking. I'm not saying they should or should not. I've been to many of them all over the world, been shown around by experts, and I've always felt as though I was looking at things that were, for me, so artificial, other people's expression of what they considered beauty to be. And I wondered what beauty is. Because when you read a poem of Keats, a poem that a man writes with his heart and with very deep feeling, he wants to convey to you something of what he feels, what he considers to be the most exquisite essence of beauty.

I have also looked at a great many cathedrals, as you must have, throughout Europe and again there is this expression of man's feelings, devotion and reverence in masonry, in marvellous buildings. And looking at all this, I'm always surprised when people talk or write about beauty, whether it is something created by man or something that you see in Nature or rather has nothing to do with stone or paint or words but is something that is deeply inward. And so often in discussing with so-called professionals, it appears to me that it is always somewhere 'out there', modern painting, modern music, pop music and so on, it's always somehow so dreadfully artificial. I may be wrong.

But what is beauty? Must it be expressed? That's one question.

Does it need the word, stone, colour, paint? Or it is something that cannot possibly be expressed in words, in a building, in a statue? So let us go into this question of what is beauty. I think to go into it very deeply one must know or understand what suffering is; because without passion you can't have beauty – passion in the sense, not of lust but the passion that comes when there is immense suffering; and remaining with that suffering, not escaping from it, brings this passion. Passion means the complete abandonment of the 'me', of the self, the ego. And therefore great austerity, not austerity in the sense the religious people have given it – following the original meaning of the word which means ash, severe, dry – but rather the austerity of great beauty.

A: Yes, I'm following you.

K: A great sense of dignity, beauty that is essentially austere. And being austere, not verbally or ideologically, but really being austere means total abandonment, letting go of the 'me'. And one cannot let that take place if one hasn't deeply understood what suffering is. Because passion comes from the word 'sorrow'. The root meaning of the word is sorrow, suffering.

A: To feel.

K: To feel. You see, sir, people have escaped from suffering. I think it is very deeply related to beauty, not that this means you must suffer.

A: Not that you must suffer.

K: But we must go a little more slowly, I am jumping ahead too quickly. First of all, we assume we know what beauty is. We see a Picasso or a Rembrandt or a Michelangelo and we think how marvellous that is. We *think* we know. We have read about it in books, the experts have written about it and so on. One reads it and says, yes; we absorb it through others. But if one is really enquiring into what is beauty there must be a great sense of humility. One must begin by saying: I don't know what beauty is *actually*, I can imagine what beauty is, I've learned what beauty is, I have been taught in schools, in colleges, I've read books and gone on guided tours and all that, visited thousands of museums, but actually to find out the depth of beauty, the depth of colour, the depth of feeling, the mind must start with a great sense of humility: *I don't know*. Just as one really doesn't know what meditation is.

One *thinks* one knows. We will discuss meditation when we come to it. So one must start, if one is enquiring into beauty, with a great sense of humility, not knowing. That very not knowing is beauty.

A: Yes, I've been listening and trying to open myself to this relation that you are making between beauty and passion.

K: You see, sir, man suffers not only personally but there is the immense suffering of mankind. It is a thing that pervades the Universe. Man has suffered physically, psychologically, spiritually, in every way for centuries upon centuries. The mother cries because her son is killed, the wife cries because her husband is mutilated in a war or accident – there is tremendous suffering in the world: and it is really a tremendous thing to be aware of this suffering.

A: Yes.

K: I don't think people are aware let alone feel this immense sorrow that is in the world. They are so concerned with their own personal sorrow, they overlook the sorrow of a poor man or woman in a little village in India or China or the East, where they possibly never have a full meal, clean clothes, a comfortable bed. And there is the sorrow of thousands of people being killed in war; or in the totalitarian world, millions being executed for ideologies, through tyranny, the terror of all that. So there is all this sorrow in the world. And there is also personal sorrow. And without really understanding it very, very deeply and resolving it, passion won't come out of sorrow. And without passion, how can you see beauty? You can intellectually appreciate a painting or a poem or a statue, but you need this great sense of an inward bursting of passion, an explosion of passion. And that creates in itself the sensitivity that can see beauty. So it is, I think, rather important to understand sorrow. I think that beauty, passion, and sorrow are related.

A: I'm interested in the order of those words. In relation to the transformation we have been speaking about, I take it that there is a passage from sorrow to passion to beauty.

K: That's right, sir.

A: Yes. Please go on.

K: You see, in the Christian world, if I am not mistaken, sorrow is delegated to a person, and through that person we somehow escape from sorrow, or at least we hope to escape from sorrow. And in the

Eastern world, sorrow is rationalized through the doctrine of karma. You know the word karma means 'to do'. And they believe in karma. That what you have done in the past life you pay for in the present or have a reward in the present, and so on and so on. So there are these two categories of escapes. And there are thousands of escapes – whisky, drugs, sex, going off to attend mass and so on. Man has never stayed with the thing. He has always either sought comfort in a belief, in an action, or in identification with something greater than himself but he has never said, look, I must see what this is, I must penetrate it and not delegate it to somebody else. I must go into it, face it, look at it, I must know what it is. So when the mind doesn't escape from this sorrow, either personal or the sorrow of mankind, if you don't escape, don't rationalize, if you don't try to go beyond it, if you are not frightened of it, then you remain with it. Because any movement away from 'what is' is a dissipation of energy. It prevents you actually understanding 'what is'. The 'what is' is sorrow. And we have devised cunning means and ways to escape from it. Now if there is no escape whatsoever you remain with it. I do not know if you have ever done this. Because in everyone's life there is an incident, a happening that brings you tremendous sorrow. It might be an event, a word, an accident, a shattering sense of absolute loneliness, and so on. These things happen and with that comes the sense of utter sorrow. Now when the mind can remain with that, not move away from it, out of that comes passion. Not cultivated passion, not artificial trying to be passionate, but the movement of passion is born out of this non-withdrawal from sorrow. Out of total, complete *remaining with* sorrow.

A: I am thinking that when we speak of someone in sorrow we say that they are disconsolate.

K: Yes.

A: And immediately we think that the antidote to that is to get rid of the 'dis', not to stay with the 'dis'. While you have been speaking I've been seeing the interrelation in a polar sense between action and passion. Passion being able to undergo, able to be changed. Whereas action is doing to effect change. And this would be the movement from sorrow to passion at the precise point, if I have understood you correctly, where I become able to undergo what is there.

K: When there is no escape, when there is no desire to seek comfort away from 'what is', then out of that absolute, inescapable reality comes this flame of passion. And without that there is no beauty. You may write endless volumes about beauty, or be a marvellous painter, but without that inward quality of passion which is the outcome of a great understanding of sorrow, I don't see how beauty can exist. Also, one observes man has lost touch with Nature.

A: Oh yes.

K: Completely, especially in big towns, and even in small villages and hamlets, man is always outward-going, pursued by his own thought, and so he has more or less lost touch with Nature. Nature means nothing to him: it is just very 'nice'. Once I was standing with a few friends and my brother many years ago at the Grand Canyon, looking at that marvellous, incredible thing, the colours, the depth and the shadows; and a group of people came up and one lady said, isn't it marvellous, and the next one said, 'Let's go and have tea.' And off they trotted. You follow? That is what is happening in the world. We have lost touch completely with Nature. We don't know what it means. And also we kill. We kill for food, we kill for amusement, we kill for sport – I won't go into all that. So there is this lack of intimate relationship with Nature.

So, sir, you see we are becoming more and more artificial, more and more superficial, more and more verbal, moving in a linear direction, not vertical at all, but linear. And so naturally artificial things become more important – theatres, cinemas, you know the whole business of the modern world. And very few have the sense of beauty in themselves, beauty in conduct. You understand, sir?

A: Oh yes.

K: Beauty in behaviour, beauty in the usage of language, the voice, the manner of walking, the sense of humility. With that humility everything becomes so gentle, quiet, full of beauty. We have none of that. We go to museums, we study pictures, and we have lost the delicacy, the sensitivity, of the mind, the heart, the body, and when we have lost this sensitivity how can we know what beauty is? And when we haven't got sensitivity we go off to some place to learn to be sensitive. To a seminar or an ashram or some rotten hole where I am going to learn to be sensitive. It becomes disgusting. So as you are a professor and teacher, how can you educate – this becomes very, very important – students to have this quality? Then one has to ask, what are we educating for? What are we being educated for? Everybody is being educated. Ninety per cent of people probably in America are being educated, know how to read and write and all the rest of it, but what for?

A: And yet it's a fact, at least in my experience of teaching year after year, that with all this proliferation of so-called educational techniques, students nowadays care less for the written and the spoken word than was the case not so many years ago.

K: Sir, that's why when I have talked at various universities and elsewhere, I've always asked what are we being educated for? Just to become glorified clerks?

A: That's the way it turns out.

K: Of course it does. Glorified businessmen and God knows what else. What for? If I had a son that would be a tremendous problem for me. Fortunately, I haven't got a son, but it would be a burning question to me: what am I to do with the children that I have? Send them to all these schools, where they are taught nothing but just how to read and write a book, and how to memorize, and to forget the whole field of life? They are taught about sex and reproduction and all that kind of stuff. But what then? To me this is a tremendously important question because I am concerned with seven schools in India and one in England, and we are going to form one here in California. It is a burning question: what is it that we are doing with our children? Making them into robots or into clever, cunning clerks, great scientists who invent this or that and are otherwise ordinary, petty little human beings with shoddy minds? You follow, sir?

A: I do.

K: So can a human being educate another to grow in beauty, grow in goodness, to flower in great affection and care? Because if we don't do that we are destroying the Earth, as is now happening, polluting the air. We human beings are destroying everything we touch. So this becomes a very, very serious thing: we are talking about beauty, pleasure, fear, relationship, order and so on, all that, but none of these things are being taught in any school.

A: No. I raised that very question with my class yesterday, and they were very ready to agree that here we are doing an advanced university course, and we have never heard about this.

K: It is tragic, sir.

A: And because we haven't heard about it, the question arises whether we can really listen to something like this.

K: And whether the teacher or professor is honest enough to say: I don't know, I am going to learn about all these things. So, sir, that is why Western civilization – I am not condemning it – is mainly concerned with commercialism and consumerism, and is a society that is immoral. And when we talk about the transformation of man, not in the field of knowledge or of time, but beyond that, who is interested in this? Who really cares about it? Because the father goes off to his job to earn a livelihood, the mother does too and the child is just an incident.

A: This will probably appear an extravagant statement for me to make but I think it's getting to the point now where if, say, a teenager raises this issue at the level that you have been raising it, and is persistent about it, the question is seriously raised whether he is normal.

K: Yes, quite.

A: It makes one think of Socrates, who was very clear that he knew only one thing: that he didn't know, and he didn't say that very often, but he said it enough times to get himself killed: but at least they took him seriously enough to kill him! Today I think he would be put in some institution for study. The whole thing would have to be 'checked out'.

K: That's what has happened in Russia. They send them off to a mental hospital and destroy them. Sir, here we neglect everything for some superficial gain, for money. Money means power, position, authority, everything.

A: It goes back to the point about success that you mentioned before. It is always later, always later, on a horizontal axis.

As you were speaking about Nature, I wanted to share with you something that has a wry humour about it in terms of the history of scholarship: I thought of those marvellous Vedic hymns to Dawn.

K: Oh yes.

A: The way Dawn comes, rosy-fingered, and scholars have expressed surprise that the number of hymns to her are, by comparison, few compared with some other gods. Attention is drawn in the study not to the quality – the wonderful beauty – of the hymns: the important thing for scholars is to find out which god, in this case Indra, is mentioned most often in the Rig Veda. Now, I'm not trying to suggest that quantity should be overlooked, but if the question had been approached in the way you have been enquiring into it, more and more deeply, then I think scholarship would have taken a very different course. We should have been taught how to sit and let that hymn disclose itself, and stop measuring it.

K: That's what I was going to say. You see when discussing beauty and passion and sorrow we ought also to go into the question: what is action? Because action is related to all that.

A: Yes, of course.

K: What is action? Because life is action, living is action, speaking is action. Everything is action, sitting here is an action. Talking, a dialogue, discussing, going into things, is a series of actions, a movement in action. So what is action? Action obviously means acting now; not having acted or will act. It is the active present of the word: to act, which is acting all the time. It is movement in time and out of time – we will go into that a little bit later. Now what is action that does not bring sorrow? One has to put that question because every action, as we do it now, is either regret, contradiction, a sense of meaningless movement, repression or conformity and so on. That is action for most people, the routine, the repetition, the remembrance of things past and acting according to that remembrance. So unless one understands very deeply what action is, one will not be able to understand what sorrow is. So action, sorrow, passion and beauty. They are all together, they are not divorced, not something separate, with beauty at the end and action at the beginning. It isn't like that at all, it is all one thing. But, looking at it, what is action? As far as one knows now, action is according to a formula, according to a concept, or according to an ideology: the communist ideology, the capitalist ideology, or the socialist ideology, or the ideology of a Christian or a Hindu with his ideology. So action is approximation to an idea. I act according to my concept,

That concept is traditional, or put together by me, or put together by some expert. Lenin, Marx have formulated it, and they conform according to what they think Lenin, Marx formulated. And action is according to a pattern. You follow?

A: Yes I do. What's occurring to me is that under the tyranny of that, one is literally driven.

K: Absolutely. Driven, conditioned, brutalized. You don't care for anything except for ideas and carrying out ideas. See what is happening in China, and in Russia. And here too, the same thing operates in a modified form. So action as we know it now is conformity to a pattern, either in the future or in the past, to an idea which I carry out. A resolution or a decision which I fulfil in acting. The *past* is acting so it is not *action*. I don't know if I am making this clear?

A: Yes, we suffer a radical conviction that if we don't generate a pattern there will be no order.

K: So you follow what is happening? Order is in terms of a pattern.

A: Yes, a preconceived pattern.

K: Therefore it is disorder, against which an intelligent man fights – fights in the sense of he revolts. So that is why it is very important if we are to understand what beauty is to understand what action is. Can there be action without the idea? Idea means – we know this from the Greek – to see. The idea means to see, which means seeing and doing. Not seeing, drawing a conclusion from that and then acting according to that conclusion. Not perceiving, and from that perception drawing a belief, an idea, or formula, and acting according to that belief, idea, or formula. When we do that we are removed from perception. We are acting only according to a formula, therefore mechanically. You see how our minds have become mechanical.

A: Necessarily so.

K: You see that's why one must ask this essential question: what is action? Is it a repetition? Is it imitation? Is it an adjustment between 'what is' and 'what should be' or 'what has been'? Or is it conformity to a pattern or belief or a formula? If it is, then inevitably there must be conflict. Because between idea and action there is an interval, a time lag, and in that interval a great many things happen. A division in which other incidents take place and therefore there must inevitably be conflict. Action is therefore never complete, never total, never ending. Action means ending. You know, you used the word Vedanta the other day. I was told it means the ending of knowledge; not the continuation of knowledge, but the ending. So is there an action which is not tied to the past as time or to the future or to a formula, or a belief or an idea, but action? Action in which the seeing is the doing.

A: Yes.

K: Now, the seeing is the doing becomes an extraordinary movement in freedom. The other is not freedom; and therefore, the communists say there is no such thing as freedom, that's a bourgeois idea. Of course it is a bourgeois idea, because they live in ideas, concepts, not in action. They live according to ideas and carry those ideas out in action, which is not action, doing.

A: Oh, yes.

K: This is what we do in the West and in the East, all over the world, acting according to a formula, idea, belief, a concept, a conclusion, a decision; and never the seeing and the doing.

Sir, you see one begins to see what freedom is in action.

A: That's right.

K: The seeing and the doing is prevented by the observer who is the past, the formula, the concept, the belief. That observer comes in between perception and the doing. That observer is the factor of division, the idea and the conclusion in action. So can we act only when there is perception? We do this when we are at the edge of a precipice; the seeing of danger then is instant action.

A: If I remember correctly the word alert comes from the Italian which points to standing on the edge of a cliff.

K: You see, it's very interesting, we are conditioned to the danger of a cliff, a snake or a dangerous animal and so on; but we are also conditioned to the idea that you must act according to an idea, otherwise there is no action.

A: Yes, we are conditioned to that, terribly so.

K: So we have this conditioning to danger; and conditioning to the fact that you cannot act without a formula, without a concept, belief and so on. So these two are the factors of our conditioning. And now someone comes along and says, 'Look, that's not action; that is merely a repetition of what has been; modified, but it is not action. Action is when you see and do.'

A: And the reaction to that is, 'Oh I see, he has a new definition of action.'

K: I'm not defining. I've done this all my life, I see something and I do it. For instance, as you may know, I am not being personal, a very large spiritual organization with thousand of followers and a great deal of land, 5000 acres, castles and money and so on was formed around me as a boy. And in 1928 I said this is all wrong, I dissolved it, returned the property and so on. I saw how wrong it was. The seeing; not conclusions, comparisons, see how religions have done it. I saw and acted: and therefore there has never been any regret. Never any saying, oh, I have made a mistake because I shall have nobody to lean on. You follow?

A: Yes, I do. Could we in our next conversation relate beauty to seeing and to listening?

22 February 1974

DIALOGUE X

The Art of Listening

DR ANDERSON: Last time we spoke about beauty, and just as we came to the end of our conversation the relationship between seeing and the transformation of man was something we agreed we would take up next.

KRISHNAMURTI: Sir, what is seeing, what is listening and what is learning? I think the three are related to each other: learning, listening and seeing. What is seeing, perceiving? Do we actually see, or do we see through a screen darkly? A screen of prejudice, a screen of our idiosyncrasies, experiences, wishes, pleasures, fears, and obviously our images about that which we see and about ourselves? So we have screen after screen between us and the object of perception. Then do we ever see the thing at all? Or is it that the seeing is coloured or prevented by our knowledge, experience, by our images or the beliefs that condition the mind, the memories which the mind has cultivated so that seeing may not take place at all? And is it possible for the mind not to have these images, conclusions, beliefs, memories, prejudices, fears, and without having those screens just to look? I think this becomes very important because when there is seeing of that which I am talking about, you can't help but act. There is no question of postponement.

A: Or of succession or interval.

K: Because when action is based on a belief, a conclusion, an idea, then that action is time-binding. And such action will inevitably bring conflict, regrets and all the rest of it. So it becomes very important to find out what it is to see, to perceive, what it is to listen. Do I ever listen? When one is married, has a wife or husband, or has a girl friend or a boy friend, do I ever listen to her or him? Or do I listen through the image I have built about them? Through the screen of irritations, of annoyance, domination, you know all the dreadful things that occur in relationship? So do I ever listen directly to what you say, without translating, without transforming it, without twisting it? Do I ever listen to a bird call or a child weep or a man crying in pain? You follow, sir? Do I ever listen to anything?

A: It's as though people consider that listening requires an act of will, that they have to screw themselves up into some sort of agonized twist here. Not only to please the one who is insisting that they are not listening, but in order to get themselves to listen.

K: Quite. So does a human being, Y or X, listen at all? And what takes place when I do listen? Listen in the sense without any interference, without any interpretation, conclusion, like or dislike, all that. What happens when I actually listen? Sir, we said last time that we cannot possibly understand what beauty is if we don't understand suffering and passion. You hear that statement: what does the mind do? It draws a conclusion; it has formed an idea, a verbal idea; it hears the words, draws a conclusion, and forms an idea. A statement of that kind has become an idea. Then I say, how am I to carry out that idea? And that becomes a problem.

A: Yes, of course it does. Because the idea doesn't conform to nature and other people have other ideas and want to get theirs carried out. So we have a clash.

K: Yes. Can the mind listen to that statement without any forming of an abstraction? Just listen. I neither agree nor disagree but just actually listen completely to that statement.

A: What you are saying is that were I to listen adequately, or let's just say listen – either I am absolutely listening or I am absolutely not listening . . .

K: That's right, sir.

A: . . . I would not have to contrive an answer.

K: No, you are in it.

A: The action and the seeing are one.

K: Yes.

A: They are one act.

K: That's right. So can I listen to a statement and see the truth in the statement or the falseness in the statement, not through comparison but in the very statement that you are making. That is, I listen to the statement: beauty can never exist without passion and passion comes from the understanding of sorrow. I listen to that statement. I don't abstract an idea from it or make an idea from it. I just listen. What takes place? You may be telling the truth or you may be making a false statement. I don't know because I am not going to compare.

A: No, you are going to see.

K: I just listen. Which means I am giving my total attention — just listen to this, sir, you will see what is going to happen — I give my total attention to what you are saying. Then it doesn't matter what you say or don't say. You see this thing?

A: Of course, of course.

K: What is important is my act of listening. And that act of listening has brought about a miracle of complete freedom from all your statements — whether true, false, real — my mind is completely attentive. Attention means no border. The moment I have a border I begin to fight you — to agree, disagree — the moment attention has a frontier then concepts arise. But if I listen to you completely without a single interference of thought or ideation or mentation, just listen to you, the miracle has taken place. Which is that my total attention absolves me, my mind from the statement. Therefore my mind is extraordinarily free to act.

A: This has happened for me with our series of conversations. With each conversation, since this is being video-taped, one begins when one is given the sign and we're told when the time has elapsed; and usually, in an activity of this sort, one is thinking about the production as such.

K: Of course.

A: But one of the things that I have learned is that I've been listening very intensely and I've not had to divide my mind in this way. But one also asks oneself how can I afford not to make the distinction between paying attention to the production aspect of the programme and engaging in our discussion?

K: Quite.

A: But the more intensely the discussion is engaged . . .

K: You can do it.

A: . . . the more efficiently the whole thing proceeds.

K: Sir, don't you think that our minds are so commercial, unless I get a reward I won't do a thing. And one's mind lives in the marketplace: I give you this, you give me that. We are so used to commercialism, both spiritually and physically, that we don't do anything without a reward, without gaining something, without a purpose. It must all be exchange, not a gift, but exchange: I give you this and you give me that; I torture myself religiously and God must come to me. It's all a matter of commerce.

A: Fundamentalists have a phrase they apply to their devotional life. They say, I am claiming the promises of God. In the context of what you are saying, what couldn't that lead to in the mind!

K: I know, sir. You see when one goes very deeply into this: when action is not based on an idea, formula or belief, the seeing is the doing. Then what is seeing and listening, which we went into? The seeing is complete attention and the doing is in that attention. And the difficulty is, people will ask, how will you maintain that attention?

A: Yes, and they haven't even started.

K: No, how will you maintain it. Which means they are looking for a reward.

A: Exactly.

K: I will practise it, I will do everything to maintain that attention in order to get something in return. Attention is not a result, attention has no cause. What has a cause has an effect and the effect becomes the cause. It's a circle: but attention isn't that. Attention doesn't give you a reward. With attention, on the contrary, there is no reward or punishment because it has no frontier.

A: Yes, this calls up an earlier conversation we had when you mentioned the word virtue.

K: Yes, exactly.

A: And although it is difficult for a thinking child to believe, given the way he is brought up, he's somehow supposed to understand that virtue is its own reward.

K: Oh, that.

A: And, of course, it is impossible to see what is sound about that in the conditioned situation in which he lives.

K: Yes, then it's just an idea, sir.

A: And then later when we need to remind somebody that they are asking too much of a reward for something good that they did, we tell them, 'Have you forgotten that virtue is its own reward?' It becomes a form of punishment.

K: Then one must also ask: what is learning? Because they are all interrelated: learning, seeing, listening, and action, all of them. It is all one movement: they are not separate chapters but one chapter.

A: Distinction is no division.

K: No. So what is learning? Is learning a process of accumulation? And is learning non-accumulative? We are putting both questions together. Let's look at it. I learn – one learns a language – Italian, French, whatever it is – and accumulates words and the irregular verbs and so on, and then one is able to speak. So there is learning a language and being able to speak it, learning how to ride a bicycle, learning how to drive a car, learning how to put together a machine, electronics and so on. Those are all learning to acquire knowledge in action. And I am asking, is there any other form of learning? The first one we know about, we are familiar with the acquisition of knowledge. Now is there any other kind of learning, which is not accumulated, and which is acting?

A: Yes, this accumulation doesn't mean we have understood anything.

K: No, I learn in order to gain a reward or in order to avoid punishment, I learn a particular job or craft in order to earn a livelihood. That is absolutely necessary. Now I am asking: is there any other kind of learning? The first kind is the cultivation of memory, which is the result of experience and knowledge stored in the brain, and which operates, when asked to ride a bicycle, drive a car, and so on. Now is there any other kind of learning? Or only that? When one says, I have learned from my experience, it means

I have learned, stored up from that experience certain memories, and those memories either reward or punish. So all such forms of learning are mechanical. And education is usually to train the brain to function in routine, mechanically, because in that there is great security. Then it is safe: and so our mind becomes mechanical. My father did this, so I do it — you follow, the whole business is mechanical. Now is there a non-mechanical brain at all? A non-utilitarian learning in that sense which has neither future nor past and is therefore not time-binding. I don't know if I am making this clear.

A: Don't we sometimes say; I have learned from experience, when we wish to convey an insight that we feel can't, in a strict sense, be dated?

K: Sir, do we learn anything from experience? I read somewhere that we have had five thousand wars since written history began. Five thousand wars. Killing, killing, killing, maiming. And have we learned anything, have we learned anything from sorrow? Man has suffered, have we learned anything from the experience of the agony of uncertainty and all the rest of it? So when we say, we have learned, I question it. You follow? It seems such a terrible thing to say, I have learned from experience. We have learned nothing, except in the field of knowledge.

A: Yes, that's really very remarkable.

K: You see that's why our education, our civilization, all the things about us, have made our mind so mechanical, with repetitive reactions, repetitive demands, repetitive pursuits. The same thing being repeated year after year, for thousands of years: my country, your country, I kill you and you kill me. You follow, sir, the whole thing is mechanical. Now that means the mind can never be free. Thought is never free, thought is always old. There's no new thought.

A: Some people I imagine would object to the notion that we don't learn from the experience of wars, because wars tend to happen sequentially, from generation to generation, and one has to grow up. But that is not true because more than one war will very often happen in the same generation and so nothing has been learned.

K: What are they talking about, we have had two wars!

A: Nothing has been learned at all. It's a terrifying thing to hear someone just come out and say: nobody learns anything from experience.

K: No, the word experience also means to go through.

A: Yes.

K: But you never go through.

A: That's right.

K: You always stop in the middle or you never begin.

A: Right. It means, if I remember correctly, in terms of its radical root, it means to put a thing to the test and behave correctly while that's going on, which means you certainly have to see, you have to look.

K: Of course. Our civilization, our culture, our education have brought about a mind that is becoming more and more mechanical and therefore time-binding and so there is never a sense of freedom. Freedom then becomes an idea, you play around with it philosophically but it has no meaning. But a man who says, 'Now I want to find out, I want to really go into this and discover if there is freedom,' such a man has to understand the limits or rather the ending of knowledge and the beginning of something totally new. I don't know if I am conveying anything?

A: You are.

K: Then what is learning? If it is not mechanical what is learning? Is there learning at all, learning about what? I learn how to go to the moon, how to assemble this, that and drive and so on. In that field there is only learning. Is there a learning in any other field, psychologically, spiritually? Can the mind learn about what they call God?

A: When one learns about God one can't be doing what you are pointing to if this is something added on to the list.

K: Sir, it is so clear.

A: Yes, it is.

K: I learn a language, ride a bicycle, drive a car, put a machine together. That's essential. Now I want to learn about God. Just listen to this. God is of my making, God hasn't made me in his image, I have made him in my image. Now I am going to learn about him.

A: Yes, I am going to talk to myself.

K: Learn about the image which I have built about Christ, Buddha, whoever it is. The image *I* have built. So I am learning what? Learning about the image which I have built.

A: That's right.

K: Therefore is there any other kind of learning except mechanical learning? You understand my question?

A: Yes, I do.

K: So is there only learning the mechanical process of life? See what that means, sir. I can learn about myself. Myself is known. Known in the sense – I may not know it, but I can know by looking at myself, I can know myself. So myself is the accumulated knowledge of the past. The 'me' who says I am greedy, I am envious, I am successful, I am frightened, I have betrayed, I have regret, all that is the 'me', including the soul which I have invented as being in the 'me' – or the Brahman, the Atman, it's all 'me' still. The 'me' has created the image of God and I am going to learn about God. This has no meaning. So if there is no other learning, what takes place? You understand? The mind is used for the acquisition of knowledge of matter – we'll put it differently – of mechanical things. And when the mind is employed there, is there any other process of learning? Which means psychologically, inwardly – is there? The inward is the invention of thought as opposed to the outer. I don't know if you see this. If I have understood the outer I have understood the inner. Because the inner has created the outer. The outer in the sense of the structure of society, the religious sanctions, all that is invented or put together by thought – the Christ, the Buddha, all that. And what is there to learn? See the beauty of what is coming out.

A: Yes, it goes back to your remark about Vedanta as the end of knowledge. The interesting thing to me about the Sanskrit construction is that, unless I am mistaken, it doesn't mean the end of it as a terminus, as a term, because that would simply start a new series.

It is a consummation which is a total end in the sense that a totally new beginning is made.

K: That means, sir, the mind knows the activity of the known.

A: That's right, yes. That's the consummation of knowledge.

K: Of knowledge. Now what is the state of the mind that is free from the known and yet functions in knowledge?

A: And yet functions in it.

K: You follow?

A: Yes. It is seeing perfectly.

K: Do go into it, you will see very strange things take place. First of all, is this possible? You understand? Because the brain functions mechanically, it wants security, otherwise it can't function. If we hadn't security we wouldn't be sitting here together. Because we have security we can have a dialogue. The brain can only function in complete security. That security is found in a neurotic belief – all beliefs and all ideas are neurotic in that sense – so the brain finds it, say, in accepting nationality as the highest form of good or success as the highest virtue. It finds belief, security there. Now you are asking the brain, which has become mechanical and been trained in that way for centuries, to see the other field which is not mechanical. *Is* there another field? You follow the question?

A: Yes, I do. That's what so utterly devastating.

K: Is there – wait, wait – is there another field? Now unless the brain and the mind understand the whole movement of knowledge – it is a movement, it is not just static, there is adding, taking away, and so on – unless it understands all that it cannot possibly ask that other question.

A: Exactly.

K: And when it does ask that question, what takes place? Sir, this is real meditation, you know. So you see what this all implies. One is always listening with knowledge, seeing with knowledge.

A: Which is seeing through a glass darkly.

K: Yes. Now is there a listening out of silence? That is attention; and that is not time-binding because in that silence I don't want anything. It isn't that I am going to learn about myself, it isn't that I am going to be punished or rewarded. In that absolute silence I listen.

A: The wonder of the whole thing is that this meditation isn't something which is done in succession.

K: Sir, when we talk about meditation we will have to go very deeply into that because the term has lost its meaning. These shoddy little men coming from India or elsewhere have destroyed it.

A: I heard the other day about someone who was learning transcendental meditation and had to do it at 3 o'clock in the afternoon.

K: Paying so many dollars to learn that. It's so sacrilegious.

A: So 3 o'clock in the afternoon was Judgment Day. If you didn't do it according to your schedule then the world had obviously come to an end.

K: So you see, sir, that is what takes place. We began this morning with beauty, then passion, then suffering, then action. Action based on idea is inaction. It sounds monstrous, but there it is: and from that we said what is seeing, and what is listening. The seeing and the listening have become mechanical. We never see anything new. Even the flower which has blossomed overnight is never new. We say, that's a rose, I have been expecting it, it has come out now, it's beautiful. It's always from the known to the known, a movement in time, and therefore time-binding, and therefore never free. Yet we are talking about freedom, philosophy, going to lectures on freedom and so on and so on. And the communists call it a bourgeois thing, which it *is* in the sense that when you limit it to knowledge it is foolish to talk about freedom. But there is a freedom when you understand the whole movement of knowledge. So can you observe out of silence, and observe and act in the field of knowledge so that both together are in harmony?

A: Seeing then is not scheduled. Yes, of course. I suppose you could say that the classical definition of freedom in terms of the career of knowledge would be that it is a property or quality of action. In the context of what we have been saying, what a horror that one could read that statement and not let it disclose itself to you.

K: Quite.

A: If it disclosed itself to you, you would be up against it, you'd have to be serious. If you were a philosophy student and you read that and it began to operate in you, you'd say, I've got to get this settled before I go on. Maybe I'll never graduate, that's not important.

K: It's not important, quite right. And I was thinking, in the West as well as in the East you have to go to the factory or the office every day of your life. Get up at 6 o'clock, 8 o'clock, drive, walk, work, work, work for fifty years, routine, and get kicked about, insulted, worship success. Again repetition. And occasionally talk about God, if it is convenient, and so on. That is a monstrous life! And that is what we are educating our children for.

A: That's the real living death.

K: And nobody says, for God's sake let's look at all this anew! Let's wipe our eyes clear of the past and look at what we are doing, give attention, care to what we are doing.

A: Now we have this question instead: what shall we do about it? And then that becomes the next thing done that is added to the list.

K: It is a continuity of the past in a different form.

A: And the chain is endlessly linked, linked, linked, linked.

K: The cause becoming the effect and the effect becoming the cause. So it's a very serious thing when we talk about all this, because life becomes dreadfully serious. And it's only this serious person that lives, not these people who seek entertainment, religious or otherwise.

A: I had a very interesting occasion to understand what you are saying in class yesterday. I was trying to assist the students to see that the classical understanding of the four causes in operation is that they are *intemporally* related. And I said when the potter puts his hand to the clay, the hand touching the clay is not responded to by the clay after the hand has touched it. And this struck a professor who was visiting the class as maybe not so, and I could tell by the expression on his face that he was having some difficulty so I said, 'What's the matter?' 'Well,' he said, 'It seems like there is a time interval.' So I asked him to pick something up that was on the desk; and I said, 'Touch it with your finger and tell me at the moment of the touching with the finger whether the thing reacts to the finger after it is touched. Now do it.' Well, even to ask somebody to apply a practical test like that to a datum of knowledge like the four causes is to interrupt the process of education as we have known it. Because you teach a student about the four causes and he thinks about them, he never goes out and looks at things or does anything about it. And so we were picking stuff up in class, and we were doing this until finally it seemed like a revelation that what the classical teaching has said, which of course in modern society is rejected, happens to be the case. And I said, this has to be seen. This is what you mean.

K: Seeing, of course.

A: Of course. But to go back to that step there: why was that person and so many other students anguished at the point where the practical issue arose? There was a feeling, I suppose, that they were on the cliff.

K: Quite, quite.

A: So naturally alertness was required. But alertness registers that we are on a cliff, so therefore the best thing to do is to turn around and run back!

K: Sir, I think, you see, we are so caught up in words. To me the word is not the thing, the description is not the described. To us the description is all that matters because we are slaves to words.

A: And to ritual.

K: To ritual and all the rest of it. So when you say, 'Look, the thing matters more than the word,' and then they say, 'How are we to get rid of the word, how are we to communicate if we have no word?' You see how they have gone off? They are not concerned with the thing but with the word.

A: Yes.

K: And the door is not the word. So when we are caught up in words, the word 'door' becomes extraordinarily important, and not the door itself.

A: And I don't really need to come to terms with the door, I say to myself, because I have the word, I have it all.

K: Education has done this. A great part of education is the acceptance of words as an abstraction from the fact, from the 'what is'. All philosophies are based on that: theorize, theorize, theorize, endlessly, about how one should live: and the philosopher himself doesn't live.

A: Yes, I know.

K: You see this everywhere.

A: Some philosophers have seemed to me quite bizarre in this respect. I have asked my colleagues from time to time, 'If you believe that stuff why don't you do it?' And they look at me as though I am out of my mind, as though nobody would seriously ask that question.

K: Quite.

A: But if you can't ask that question, what question is worth asking?

K: Quite right.

A: I was thinking about that story you told about the monkey; when she shook hands with you, nobody had told her how to shake hands. It wasn't something that she was taught to do through a verbal communication, it was the appropriate thing at the time, without anyone measuring its appropriateness.

K: Quite.

A: As you were saying earlier, these issues relate directly to meditation. Are we ready, do you think to . . .

K: Oh, we must discuss several things yet – what is love, what is death, what is meditation, what is the whole movement of living? We've got a great deal to do.

22 February 1974

DIALOGUE XI

Being Hurt and Hurting Others

DR ANDERSON: During our conversations one thing has emerged for me very forcefully. We have been talking about having a dysfunctional relationship to thought and knowledge, but never once have you said that we should get rid of thought or that knowledge as such, in itself, has something profoundly the matter with it. So the question of right relationship between intelligence and thought arises, of what it is that maintains a creative relationship between intelligence and thought – perhaps some primordial activity which abides. And in thinking about this I wondered whether you would perhaps agree that in the history of human existence the concept of God has been generated out of a relationship to this abiding activity, and that this concept has been very badly abused. And this raises the whole question of the phenomenon of religion itself. I wondered if we might discuss that?

KRISHNAMURTI: You know, words like religion, love, or God, have lost almost all their meaning. There has been enormous abuse of these words and religion has become a vast superstition, a combination of propaganda, incredible beliefs and superstitions, the worship of images made by the hand or by the mind. So when we talk about religion I would like, if I may, to be quite clear that both of us are using the word 'religion' in the real sense of that word, not in the Christian, the Hindu, the Muslim or the Buddhist sense, or of all the stupid things that are going on here in America and elsewhere in the name of religion.

I think the word 'religion' means gathering together all one's energy, at all levels, the physical, moral and spiritual, so that it will bring about great attention. In such attention there is no frontier and then from there – move. To me that is the meaning of religion: the gathering of total energy to understand what thought cannot possibly capture. Thought is never new, never free and therefore, as we have already said, it is always conditioned and fragmentary. So religion is not a thing put together by thought or by fear or by the pursuit of satisfaction and pleasure, but something totally beyond all this, which has nothing to do with romanticism, speculative belief or sentimentality. And I think if we could keep to that meaning of the word, putting aside all the superstitious nonsense that is going on in the world in the name of religion, which has really become quite a circus, however beautiful, then I think we could start from there. If you agree to that meaning of that word.

A: Yes. I have been thinking as you have been speaking that in the biblical tradition there are statements by the prophets which seem to point to what you are saying. Such things come to mind as Isaiah's taking the part of the divine, when he says: 'My thoughts are not your thoughts, my ways are not your ways, as high as the heavens are above the Earth so are my thoughts and your thoughts, so stop thinking about me in that sense. And don't try to find a means to me that you have contrived since my ways are higher than your ways.' And while you were speaking about the act of attention, this gathering together of all the energies of the whole man, I was reminded of the very simple phrase: be still and know that I am God. Be still. It's amazing when one thinks of the history of religion, how little attention has been paid to that as compared with ritual.

K: But I think when we lost touch with Nature, with the Universe, with the clouds, lakes, birds, when we lost touch with all that, then the priests came in. Then all the superstition, fears, exploitation, all that began. The priests became the mediators between the human and the so-called divine. I was told that in the first Rig Veda there is no mention of God at all: there is only the worship of something immense, expressed in Nature and in the earth, in the clouds, in the trees, in the beauty of vision. But being very, very simple, the priests said: that is too simple.

A: Let's mix it up.

K: Let's confuse it a little bit. And so it began. I believe this is traceable from the ancient Vedas to the present time, where the priest became the interpreter, the mediator, the explainer, the exploiter, the man who said, this is right, this is wrong, you must believe this or you will go to perdition, and so on. He generated fear, not the adoration of beauty, not the adoration of life lived totally, wholly without conflict, but something outside, beyond and above, something that he considered to be God which he then made propaganda for.

So I feel we should from the beginning use the word 'religion' in the simplest way. That is, in the sense of gathering of all energy so that there is total attention, and in that quality of attention the immeasurable comes into being. Because as we said the other day, the measurable is the mechanical. Which the West has cultivated, doing marvellous things, technologically, physically, in medicine, science, biology and so on, but making the world so superficial, mechanical, mundane, materialistic. And that is spreading all over the world. And in reaction to this materialistic attitude, there are all these superstitious, nonsensical, unreasoned religions that are going on. There is the absurdity of these gurus coming from India and teaching the West how to meditate, how to hold one's breath: they say, 'I am God, worship me' – it has become so absurd, so childish, so utterly immature. All that indicates the degradation of the word 'religion' and of the human mind that can accept this kind of circus and idiocy.

A: Yes. I was thinking of a remark of Sri Aurobindo's in a study that he made of the Veda, where he traced its decline in one sentence. He said it issues as language from sages, then it falls to the priests, then it falls to the scholars or the academicians. But in that study I found no explanation as to *how* it fell to the priests.

K: I think how the priests got hold of the whole business is fairly simple. Because man is so concerned with his own petty little affairs, petty little desires and ambitions, with superficiality, he wants a little more than that: he wants something a little more romantic, a little more sentimental, something other than the daily beastly routine of living. So he looks around and the priests say, come over here, I've got the goods. I think it is very simple how the priests came into this. You see it in India, you see it in the West. You see it everywhere where man begins to be concerned with daily living, the daily earning of bread and butter, his home and all the rest of it, he demands something more than that. He says: after all this I'll die but there must be something more.

A: So fundamentally it's a matter of securing for himself some . . .

K: . . . heavenly grace.

A WHOLLY DIFFERENT WAY OF LIVING

A: ... some heavenly grace that will preserve him from falling into this mournful round of coming to be and passing away. Thinking of the past, on the one hand, anticipating the future on the other, you're saying he falls out of the now.

K: Yes, that's right.

A: I understand.

K: So if we could keep to that meaning of the word 'religion' the question then arises, can the mind be so totally attentive that the unnameable comes into being? You see, personally I have never read the Veda, Gita, Upanishads, the Bible, all the others, or any philosophy. But I questioned everything.

A: Yes.

K: Not questioned only, but observed. And one sees the absolute necessity of a mind that is completely quiet. Because it's only out of quietness that you perceive what is happening. If I am chattering I won't listen to you. If my mind is constantly rattling away, I won't pay attention to what you are saying. To pay attention means to be quiet.

A: There have been some priests, who usually ended up in a great deal of trouble, who had it seems a grasp of this. I was thinking of Meister Eckhart's remark that whoever is able to read the book of Nature doesn't need any scriptures at all.

K: That's just it.

A: Of course, he had a lot of trouble toward the end of his life and after he died the Church denounced him.

K: Of course. Organized belief in the form of a church, and all the rest of it, isn't subtle, it hasn't got the quality of real depth and real spirituality. You know what it is.

A: Yes, I do.

K: So I'm asking, what is the quality of a mind, and therefore of the heart and brain, that can perceive something beyond the measurement of thought? What is the quality of such a mind? Because that quality is the religious mind; that quality of a mind that has this feeling of being sacred in itself, and is therefore capable of seeing something immeasurably sacred.

A: The word 'devotion' seems to imply this when used in its proper sense. To use your earlier phrase, gathering all our energy towards a one-pointed attentive . . .

K: Would you say attention is one-pointed?

A: No, I didn't mean to imply focus when I said that.

K: Yes, that's what I wondered.

A: I meant rather, integrated into itself as utterly quiet and unconcerned about taking thought for what is ahead or for what is behind. Simply being there. The word 'there' isn't good either because it suggests that there is a 'where' and a 'here' and all the rest of it. It is very difficult to find, it seems to me, language to do justice to what you are saying, precisely because when we speak our utterance is in time and is progressive; it has a quality, doesn't it, more like music than graphic art. You can stand before a picture, whereas to hear music and grasp its theme you virtually have to wait until you get to the end to gather it all up. And with language you have the same difficulty.

K: Quite. So let us enquire further into the question: what is the nature and structure of a mind, and therefore the quality of a mind, that is not only sacred and holy in itself but is capable of seeing something immense? We were talking the other day about suffering, both personal and the sorrow of the world: it isn't that we must suffer, suffering is there. Every human being has a dreadful time with it; and there is the suffering of the world. It isn't that one must go through it, but as it is there one must understand it and go beyond it. And that's one of the qualities of a religious mind, in the sense in which we are using that word: it is incapable of suffering; it has gone beyond it. Which doesn't mean that it becomes callous. On the contrary it is a passionate mind.

A: One of the things that I have thought much about during our conversations is language itself. Over and over again it seems to me that our customary use of language deprives us of really seeing what the word points to in itself. Take again the word 'religion'. Scholars differ as to where that came from: some say it means to bind and others say no, it means the numinous or the splendour that cannot be exhausted by thought. It seems to me that there is another sense to bind that is not a negative one, in the sense that if one is making this act of attention, one isn't bound as with cords of rope.

K: Again, let's be clear. When we use the word 'attention' there is a difference between concentration and attention. Concentration is exclusion. I concentrate, that is, I bring all my thinking to a certain point and therefore it is excluding, building a barrier so that it can focus its whole concentration on that. Whereas attention is something entirely different from concentration. In attention there is no exclusion, no resistance, and no effort – and therefore no frontier, no limits.

A: How would you feel about the word 'receptive'?

K: Again, who is it who receives?

A: Already we have made a division.

K: Yes. I think the word 'attention' is really a very good word. Because it not only understands concentration, not only sees the duality of reception, the receiver and the received, it also sees the nature of duality and the conflict of the opposites; and attention means not only the brain giving its energy but also the mind, the heart, the nerves, the total entity, the whole human mind giving all its energy to perceive. I think that, for me at least, that is the meaning of to be attentive, to attend. Not to concentrate but to attend. That means listen, see, give your heart to it, give your mind to it, give your whole being to attend, otherwise you can't attend. If I am thinking about something else I can't attend, if I am hearing my own voice, I can't attend.

A: It's interesting that in English we use the word 'attendant' for one who waits on. I'm trying to penetrate the notion of waiting and patience in relation to this.

K: I think, sir, that again waiting means one who is waiting for something: again there is a duality. And when you wait you are expecting: again a duality. One who is waiting and is about to receive. So if we could for the moment keep to that word 'attention', then we should enquire what is the quality of a mind that is so attentive that it has understood and lives, acts in relationship and with responsibility in behaviour, has no fear psychologically in the way we talked about, and therefore understands the movement of pleasure. Then we come to the question, what is such a mind? I think it would be worthwhile at this point to discuss the nature of hurt.

A: Of hurt?

K: Why human beings are hurt. Everyone is hurt.

A: You mean both physically and psychologically?

K: Psychologically especially. Physically we can tolerate it, we can bear with a pain and say I won't let it interfere with my thinking, I won't let it corrode my psychological quality of mind, the mind can watch over that. But the psychological hurts are much more important and difficult to grapple with and understand. I think it is necessary because a mind that is hurt is not an innocent mind. The very word 'innocent' comes from innocere, not to hurt. A mind that is incapable of being hurt: there is a great beauty in that.

A: Yes, there is. We usually use the word 'innocence' to indicate a lack of something.

K: So I think in discussing religion we ought to enquire very deeply into the nature of hurt, because a mind that is not hurt is an innocent mind; and you need this quality of innocency to be totally attentive.

A: If I have been following you correctly maybe you would say that man becomes hurt when he starts thinking that he is hurt.

K: Look sir, it's much deeper than that, isn't it? From childhood the parents compare one child with another child.

A: That's when the thought arises.

K: When you compare you are hurting.

A: Yes.

K: But we do it.

A: Oh yes, of course we do it.

K: So is it possible to educate a child without comparison, without imitation? And therefore the child never gets hurt in that way. Also one is hurt because one has built an image about oneself, an image which is a form of resistance, a wall between you and me; and when you touch that wall at its tender point I get hurt. So not to compare in education, not to have an image about oneself. That's one of the most important things in life, not to have an image about oneself; if you have you are inevitably going to be hurt. Suppose one has an image that one is very good or that one should be a great success or that one has great capacities, gifts, you know the images that one builds, inevitably someone is going to come and prick it. Inevitably accidents and incidents happen that are going to break the image, and one gets hurt.

A: Doesn't this raise the question of name.

K: Oh yes. Name, form.

A: The child is given a name, the child identifies himself with the name.

K: Yes, the child can identify itself but without the image, just with the name: Brown, Mr Brown. There is nothing to it: but the moment he builds an image that Mr Brown is socially, morally different, superior or inferior or comes from a very old family, belongs to a certain higher class, the aristocracy or whatever, the moment that begins and is encouraged and sustained by thought, snobbism, you know the whole of that business, then you are inevitably going to be hurt.

A: What you are saying, I take it, is that the radical confusion here is in the imagining oneself to be his name.

K: Yes, identification with the name, with the body, with the idea that you are socially different, that your parents, your grandparents were lords or this or that. You know the whole snobbism of England, and the different kind of snobbism here in America.

A: We speak in language of preserving a name.

K: Yes, and in India it is the Brahmin, the non-Brahmin, the whole of that business. So through education, through tradition, through propaganda we have built an image about ourselves.

A: Is there a relation here in terms of religion, with the refusal in the Hebraic tradition, for instance, to pronounce the name of God?

K: The word is not the thing anyhow. So you can pronounce it or not pronounce it. If you know the word is never the thing, the description is never the described, then it doesn't matter.

A: No, one of the reasons I've always been over the years deeply drawn to the study of the roots of words is simply because for the most part they point to something very concrete.

K: Very.

A: It's either a thing or it's a gesture, more often than not it's some act.

K: Quite.

A: Some act. When I used just now the phrase, thinking about being hurt, I should have been more careful of my words and referred to mulling over the image, which would have been a much better way to put it, wouldn't it?

K: Yes. So can a child be educated never to get hurt? I have heard professors, scholars say a child must be hurt in order to live in the world. And when I asked one of them: Do you want your child to be hurt, he kept absolutely quiet: he was just talking theoretically. Now unfortunately through education, through the social structure and the nature of the society in which we live, we have been hurt, we have images about ourselves which are going to be hurt, so is it possible not to create images at all? I don't know if I am making myself clear.

A: You are.

K: That is, suppose I have an image about myself — which fortunately I haven't — if I have an image, is it possible to wipe it away, to understand it and therefore dissolve it and never to create a new image about myself? You understand? Living in a society, being educated, I have inevitably built an image. Now can that image be wiped away?

A: Wouldn't it disappear with this complete act of attention?

K: That's what I'm coming to gradually. It would totally disappear. But I must understand how this image is born. I can't just say, right, I'll wipe it out.

A: Yes.

K: Using attention as a means of wiping it out — it doesn't work that way. In understanding the image, in understanding the hurt, in understanding the education one has had, the way one has been brought up in the family, society, in understanding all that, out of that understanding comes attention; not attention first and then wipe it out. You can't attend if you're hurt. If I am hurt how can I attend? Because that hurt is going to prevent, consciously or unconsciously, this total attention.

A: The amazing thing, if I understand you correctly, is that even in the study of the dysfunctional history, provided I bring total attention to that, there's going to be an intemporal relationship between the act of attention and the healing that takes place.

K: That's right.

A: While I am attending the thing is leaving.

K: The thing is leaving, yes, that's it. So, there are two questions involved: Can the hurts be healed so that not a mark is left? And can future hurts be prevented completely, without any resistance? You follow? Those are two problems; and they can be understood and resolved only when I give attention to the understanding of my hurts. When I look at them, not translate them, not wish to wipe them away, just look at them — as we said when we went into the question of perception. Just to see my hurts. The hurts I have received, the insults, the negligence, the casual words, the gestures, all those hurts. And the language one uses, especially in this country.

A: Oh yes, yes. There seems to be a relationship between what you are saying and one of the meanings of the word 'salvation'.

K: Salvare, to save.

A: To make whole.

K: To make whole. How can you be whole, sir, if you are hurt?

A: It's impossible.

K: That is why it is tremendously important to understand this question.

A: Yes, it is. But I am thinking of a child who comes to school and has already got a freight-car filled with hurts, not a little one in a crib but a child who is already hurt and hurt because it is hurt; the thing multiplies endlessly.

K: Of course. Because of that hurt he's violent: because of that hurt he is frightened and therefore withdrawn; because of that hurt he will do neurotic things; because of that hurt he will accept anything that gives him safety — God, his idea of God is a God who will never hurt.

A: Sometimes a distinction is made between ourselves and animals with respect to this. An animal, for instance, that has been badly hurt will react toward everyone in terms of emergency and attack. But over a period of time, it might take three or four years, if the animal is loved . . .

K: Sir, you see, you said, loved. We haven't got that.

A: No.

K: Parents haven't got love for their children. They may talk about love. Because the moment they compare the younger to the older one they have hurt the child: your father was so clever, you are such a stupid boy. That is where it starts. In school where they give you marks it is a hurt, not marks, it is a deliberate hurt. And that is stored in the memory and from that there is violence, there is every kind of aggression. So a mind cannot be made whole or be whole unless this is understood very, very deeply.

A: The point I had in mind was that this animal, if loved, will, provided there is not say brain damage, in time love in return. But with the human person love cannot be coerced in that way. It isn't that one would coerce the animal to love but that the animal, because it is innocent, does in time simply respond, accept.

K: Accept, of course.

A: But then a human being is doing something we don't think the animal is doing.

K: No, the human being is being hurt and is hurting all the time.

A: Exactly. While he is mulling over his hurt he is likely to misinterpret the very act of generosity and love that is made toward him. So we are involved in something very frightful here: by the time the child comes into school, seven years old . . .

K: He is already gone, finished, tortured. There is the tragedy of it, sir, that is what I mean.

A: And you are asking the question whether there is a way to educate the child so that the child . . .

K: . . . is never hurt. That is part of education, that is part of culture. But our civilization is hurting. Sir, you see this all over the world, this constant comparison, constant imitation, constant saying: you are that, I must be like you. I must be like Krishna, like Buddha, like Jesus, you follow. That's a hurt. Religions have hurt people.

A: A child is born to a hurt parent, sent to a school where it is taught by a hurt teacher. Now you are asking: is there a way to educate this child so that the child recovers?

K: I say it is possible when the teacher, the educator realizes that he is hurt and the child is hurt, when he is aware of his hurt and he is aware also of the child's hurt, then the relationship changes. Then he will in the very act of teaching mathematics, or whatever it is, not only be freeing himself from his hurt but also helping the child to be free of his hurt. After all, that is education: to see that I, who am the teacher, am hurt, I have gone through agonies of hurt and I want to help that child not to be hurt and he has come to the school being hurt. So I say, 'All right, my friend, we both are hurt, let us see, let's help each other to wipe it out.' That is the action of love.

A: Comparing the human organism with the animal, I return to the question whether this relationship to another human being must necessarily bring about this healing.

K: Obviously, sir, if relationship exists: we have said a relationship can exist only when there is no image between you and me.

A: Let us say there is a teacher who has come to grips with this in himself very deeply, who has, as you put it, 'gone into' the question in depth and come to a point where he is no longer hurt-bound. The child or the young student or even a student his own age, because we have adult education, that he meets, is a person who is hurt-bound; will he not, because he is hurt-bound, be prone to misinterpret the activity of the one who is not hurt-bound?

K: But there is no one who is not hurt-bound, except very, very few. Look, sir, lots of things have happened to me personally, but I have never been hurt. I say this in all humility, in the real sense, I don't know what it means to be hurt. Things have happened to me, people have done every kind of thing, praised me, flattered me, kicked me around, everything. It is possible not to be hurt. And as a teacher, an educator, it is my responsibility to see that the child is never hurt, not just to teach some beastly subject: this is far more important.

A: I think I have some grasp of what you mean. I don't think I could ever say that I have never been hurt. Though I do have difficulty, and have since a child, in dwelling on it. I remember a colleague once saying with some testiness when we were discussing a situation in which there was conflict in the faculty: 'Well, the trouble with you is you can't hate.' And it was looked upon as a disorder, as an inability to focus the enemy and devote total attention to that.

K: Sanity is taken for insanity! So the question is then: can a teacher observe his hurts, become aware of them, and in his relationship with the student resolve his hurts and the student's? That's one problem. It is possible if the teacher is really, in the deep sense of the word, an educator, that is, cultivated. And from that the next question arises: is the mind capable of not being hurt, knowing it has been hurt so that no more hurts are added? Right?

A: Yes.

K: I have these two problems: one, being hurt, that is the past; and never to be hurt again. Which doesn't mean I build a wall of resistance, that I withdraw, that I go off to a monastery or become a drug addict or some silly thing like that, but there is no more hurt. Is that possible? You see the two questions? Now, what is hurt? What is the thing that is hurt? We said that physical hurt is not the same as psychological hurt.

A: Yes.

K: So we are dealing with psychological hurt. What is the thing that is hurt? The psyche? The image which I have about myself?

A: It is an investment that I have in the image.

K: Yes, it's my investment in myself.

A: Yes. I've divided myself off from myself.

K: Yes, now why should I invest in myself? What is myself? You follow?

A: Yes, I do.

K: In which I have to invest something. What is myself? All the words, the names, the qualities, the education, the bank account, the furniture, the house, the hurts, all that is 'me'.

A: In an attempt to answer the question, what is myself, I must immediately bring in all that.

K: Obviously.

A: There isn't any other way: and still I haven't got it. Then I praise myself because I must be so marvellous as somehow to slip out.

K: Quite.

A: I see what you mean. I was thinking back to a moment ago when you were saying it is possible for the teacher to have a relationship with the student so that an act of healing happens.

K: If I were in a class that's the first thing I would begin with, not with some subject. I would say, 'Look, you are hurt and I am hurt, we are both of us hurt,' and point out what hurt does, how it kills people, how it destroys people; out of that there is violence, out of that there is brutality, out of that I want to hurt people. You follow? All that comes in. I would spend ten minutes talking about that every day in different ways till both of us see it. Then as an educator I would use the right words and the student will use the right words; so we are both involved. But we don't do that. The moment we come into class we pick up a book and off we go! If I were an educator, whether with the older people or the younger people, I would establish this relationship. That's my duty, that's my job, that's my function, not just to transmit some information.

A: Yes, that's really very profound. I think one of the reasons that what you have said is so difficult for an educator reared within the whole academic . . .

K: We are so vain!

A: Exactly. We want not only to hear that it is possible for this transformation to take place, but we want it to be regarded as demonstrably proved and therefore not merely possible but predictably certain.

K: Certain, yes.

A: And then we lapse back into the whole mess.

K: Of course.

A: Next time could we take up the relationship of love to this? It would seem to me . . .

K: . . . it would all come together.

25 February 1974

DIALOGUE XII

Love, Sex and Pleasure

DR ANDERSON: In our last conversation we were talking about religion in relation to the transformation of each human being, a transformation that is not dependent on knowledge or time, and during our discussion you spoke about what you regarded religion to be in the true sense, its relation to the act of attention, and how when the whole personal history of hurt is still operating this act of attention is simply vitiated, it cannot come to pass. And towards the end of the discussion we had touched on love, so perhaps we could explore the question of love now.

KRISHNAMURTI: Sir, when you use the word 'explore', are you using it intellectually, exploring with the intellect or exploring in relation to the word and seeing in that word the mirror which will reveal ourselves?

A: I hope the latter.

K: That is, the word is the mirror in which I, as a human being, am observing. So the word 'explore' really means observing myself in the mirror of the word that you have used. The word then becomes the thing, not just a word by itself.

A: Right.

K: And therefore it is not intellectual or theoretical exploration.

A: It could be the beginning of a meditation.

K: That's what I want to make quite clear. And 'exploring' also means that the mind must be very serious, not caught up in the mere desire to achieve something, such as how to acquire the neighbour's love. You follow, sir?

A: Yes.

K: So I think when we explore that word, the meaning and significance of it, one has to be very, very serious about the matter because this word is used so loosely; it has become so corrupt – love of God, love of my wife, love of my property, love of my country, loving to read, loving to go to the cinema. And one of our difficulties is that modern education is not making us serious. We are becoming specialists – a first class doctor, a first class surgeon, a first class physicist and so on, and so on. The specialist becomes a menace in that way.

A: A learned ignoramus.

K: Education, as we were saying previously, is to encourage, to see that the human mind is serious; serious to find out what it means to live, not just how to become a specialist. So if all that is understood, what is love? Is love pleasure? Is love the expression of desire? Is love sexual appetite fulfilled? Is love the pursuit of a desired end? Identification with a family, with a woman, with a man? Is love a thing that can be cultivated, that can be made to grow when I have no love? So I think about it, do all kinds of things so that I will know how to love my neighbour?

A: We sometimes hear the admonition that one has to work at it. In terms of our conversations up to now, that would be a denial of it.

K: So, is love pleasure? Apparently it is now.

A: It seems to have been debased to that.

K: That is what we call love. Love of God. I don't know what God is and yet I am supposed to love Him. And therefore I transfer my pleasures of the world, of things, of sex, to a higher level which I call God. It is still pleasure. So what is pleasure in relation to love? What is enjoyment in relation to love? What is joy, the unconscious feeling of joy? The moment I recognize joy it is gone. And what is the relationship of joy, enjoyment and pleasure to love? Unless we understand that we shan't understand what love is.

A: Yes, I have followed you.

K: Take what is happening. Love has been identified with sex, love-making, sexual love. You follow, sir?

A: The very construction of the words, love-making, making love.

K: It's a horrible thing. It gives me a shock, 'love-making' as though that were love. You see, sir, Western civilization has put this over the whole of the Earth, through cinemas, books, pornography and through every kind of advertising, the sense of love is identified with sex: which is basically pleasure.

A: The whole glamour industry is based on that.

K: On that. The whole thing. So can the mind — again we must come back to this point — can the mind understand the nature of pleasure and its relationship to love? Can the mind that is pursuing pleasure, an ambitious mind, a competitive mind, a mind that says, I must get something out of life, I must reward myself and others, I must compete: can such a mind love? It can love sexually. But is love of sex the only thing? Why have we made sex such an enormous affair? Volumes are written on it. Unless one really goes into this very, very deeply, the other thing is not possible even to understand. We can talk endlessly about what love is and what love is not theoretically. But if we use the word love as a mirror to see what is happening inwardly, then I must inevitably ask whether it is pleasure in its multiple forms? Can a man who has got into a top position through drive, through aggression, through deception, through ruthlessness — can he know what love is? Can the priest who talks everlastingly of God, who is ambitious to become a bishop, archbishop or whatever it is — to sit next to Jesus . . .

A: To sit on the right hand of God.

K: So can such a priest who talks about it know what love means?

A: No, he thinks he can with reference to something called a higher love which is based on denial of a lower one.

K: That's just words.

A: In that conflict there can be no love.

K: So our whole social, moral structure is immoral.

A: Yes.

K: I mean, sir, this is an appalling thing. And nobody wants to change that. On the contrary, they say, yes, let's carry on, put a lot of gloss on it of different, more pleasant colours. So if a man is really concerned to come upon this thing called love he must understand the place of pleasure, whether intellectual pleasure, acquisition of knowledge as pleasure, acquisition of a position as power, you follow, and negate the whole of that. And how can a mind that has been trained, conditioned, sustained in this rotten social conditioning free itself before it talks about love? It *must* first free itself of that. Otherwise you talk of love, but it's just another word which has no meaning.

A: We do seem, in Western culture particularly, to be very sex-bound. On the one hand we are threatened with unhappiness if we don't succeed sexually. Yet on the other hand the whole history of clinical psychology focuses precisely on the pathology of sexuality, as somehow able in itself as a study to free us. The interrelationship between those two activities, the desire to succeed on the one hand and the necessity to study what's wrong with the drive on the other, brings about a paralysis.

K: Yes, so you see this thing, sex, has now become of such enormous importance right through the world. In Asia they cover it up, they don't talk about it there. If you talk about sex it is something wrong. Here you talk endlessly about it. But there you don't talk about certain things, you can talk about them in the bedroom, or perhaps not even in the bedroom. It's not done. And when I talk in India, I bring it out. They are a little bit shocked because a religious man is not supposed to deal with that kind of stuff!

A: He is supposed to be beyond that.

K: He is supposed to be, but he mustn't talk about it. Why has sex become so important? You see, love is, after all, a sense of total absence of the 'me' – my ego, my ambitions, my greed – a total negation of all that. Negation, not brutal denial or a surgical operation but the understanding of it. When the 'me' is not, the other is. Obviously. It's so simple. You know, sir, I was told that the Christian sign, the cross, is a very, very ancient symbol, previous to Christian acceptance of that symbol. It meant, wipe out the I.

A: I had never heard that.

K: Wipe out the I. You understand, sir? So when we are inquiring into this question of love we must inquire into pleasure; pleasure in all its varieties, and its relationship to love, this thing which can never be invited. The world has made sex into an immense thing and the priests right through the world have denied it. They won't look at a woman though they are burning with lust inside. They shut their eyes. And they say, only a man who is a celibate can go to God. Think of the absurdity of such a statement! So anybody who has sex is damned for ever.

A: Then you have to invent some story to explain how we fell into this.

K: Fell into it. The whole idea of the Virgin Mary.

A: Yes, the whole thing.

K: Which is a farce. So why have we made sex such a fantastic, romantic, sentimental affair? Is it because intellectually we are crippled? Because we are second-hand people? I repeat what Plato, Aristotle, Buddha, somebody has said, and therefore my mind is third rate. So it is never free: intellectually I am a slave, emotionally I become romantic, sentimental. And the only escape is sex, where I am free, if the woman and the man agree, if they are compatible and all the rest of it; it is the only door through which I can go and say, for God's sake, at least I am free here. In the office I am bullied, in the factory I just pull levers. So it is the only escape for me. The peasants in India, the poor villagers, that is the only thing they have. And religion is seen as something else: I agree we *should* be celibate, we *should* be all the rest of it but for God's sake leave us alone with our pleasures, with our sex. So that is what it looks like: that we are intellectually, morally, spiritually crippled and degenerate human beings, and sex is the only thing that gives us some release, some freedom.

In other fields I have no freedom: I have to go to the office every day. I have to go to the factory every day, I have to look at a film three times a week, or whatever it is you do, you've got to, and here at last I am a man, I am a woman. So I have made sex into an enormous affair. And if I am not sexual I have to find out why I am not. I spend years finding out. You follow, sir? Books are written. It has become nauseating, stupid. And we have also in relation to that to find out what is celibacy. Because every religion has talked about having to be celibate. Christians speak of the Virgin and the Buddhists too have the same sort of story about the Buddha: because they don't want sex to be associated with religion: and yet every priest is burning with it; so they say you must be celibate and take a vow of celibacy.

And what is celibacy? Is it in there, in your heart and your mind? Or does it refer just to the act?

A: If I have been following you correctly, it seems to me that you point to sex here as undergone in a utilitarian way. It's a means to an end and therefore . . .

K: A routine, an insistence, encouragement, you follow?

A: Yes, always a goal that lies outside the activity.

K: Quite right. Therefore conflict.

A: Therefore conflict and repetition.

K: And therefore what is celibacy? Is it the act or the mind that is chaste?

A: It must be the mind.

K: The chaste mind; which means a tremendously austere mind. Not the austerity of severity and ruthless acceptance of a principle and all the rest of it.

A: This goes back to the earlier conversation when we were talking about hurt.

K: That's right.

A: The chaste mind would never be hurt.

K: Never: and it is therefore an innocent mind; which has no picture of the woman or the man or the act; none of that imagination.

A: This is very fundamental. I know in our conversations that I keep bringing up things that I've read and studied because that has largely been the occupation of my life. And the thing that moves me so deeply in listening to you is that so many of the things that have been said and written over the centuries ought to have been understood in the way in which you've been presenting them. We even have a tradition in Christian theology that what is called the fall of Man began at the point of imagination; and yet that hasn't been properly understood, it seems to me. If it had been, we would not be in this immense conflict we are in.

K: Christians have first invented the sin and then all the rest of it.

A: It has been the cart before the horse. Yes, I do see what you are saying.

K: So, can the mind be chaste? Not can the mind take a vow of celibacy and have burning desires! And we talked the other day about desire. We are burning with desire; all our glands are full of it. So chastity means a mind that has no hurt, no image, no sense of pictures of itself, its appetites, all that. Can such a mind exist in this world? Otherwise love is not. I can talk endlessly about love of Jesus, love of this, love of that, but it becomes so shoddy.

A: Because it's love of.

K: Yes.

A: Love as an activity is not the same as love as a means.

K: Yes, sir. So is love pleasure? I can only answer it is not, when I have understood pleasure. And understood not verbally, but deeply, inwardly, seen the nature of it, the brutality of it, the divisive process of it. Because pleasure is always divisive. Enjoyment, joy are never divisive. It is only pleasure that is divisive. When you listen to an Arab about oil, it is his pride, you follow? You see it in him. And you see it in the ministers, in the politicians, this whole sense of arrogance, of power. And at the same time they talk about love.

A: But it's always love of.

K: Of course, love of my country, and my love is going to kill you.

A: Yes.

K: So, you see, we have to understand this killing too. Western civilization has made killing into a perfect art and war into a science. They have taught the whole world this. And probably the Christians are the greatest killers, after Muslims, and I believe the genuinely religious, original Buddhists were really non-killers.

A: Yes.

K: They said don't kill. But I must tell you this lovely story. I was in Ceylon several years ago and a Buddhist couple came to see me. They said. 'We are Buddhists by practice, we don't kill, but we eat meat.' I said 'What do you mean?' He said 'We change our butchers, therefore we are not responsible; and we like meat.' I said, 'Is that the problem?' He said, 'No, not at all. Our problem is, should we eat a fertilized egg because that contains life?'

A: Oh dear me.

K: So when we talk about love, we must also talk about violence and killing. We kill, we have destroyed the Earth, polluted the Earth. We have wiped away species of animals and birds, we are killing baby seals, you've seen that on television?

A: Oh, I have.

K: How a human being can do such a thing...

A: It's deeply shocking.

K: ... so a woman can wear the fur. And the killer will go home and say, 'I love my wife.' And we are trained to kill. All the generals are preparing endlessly means of killing others. That's our civilization. And can a man who is ambitious, love?

A: No.

K: No. Therefore finish with ambition. But they won't, they want both. So don't kill under any circumstances, don't kill an animal to eat. I have never eaten meat in my life, never, I don't know what it tastes like. Not that I am proud or anything, but I couldn't do it. And killing has become an industry, killing animals to feed human beings.

A: Yes, it has, right. I was thinking, as you were speaking, about chastity and it came to me that the chaste mind would have to be an undivided mind.

K: Yes sir. Not killing and loving.

A: And trying to get them together. And then taking all manner of means to palliate my obvious failure to get them together.

K: Of course.

A: The enormity of what you have brought out is truly staggering and I would like to stay with it for a moment, if you don't mind. I've been listening very intently. It's that your radical counsel to make this stop in oneself is so radical that it requires a kind of seriousness whose meaning we don't really understand. The relationship between seriousness and love has been coming into my awareness here.

K: Yes, sir, if I am serious I will never kill, and love then has become something, it is really compassion. Passion for all, compassion for all.

A: When you say one will never kill if he loves, you mean within the context of this image-making activity where one kills by design.

K: Sir, suppose my sister — I have no sister — my sister were attacked, a man comes to rape her. I will act at that moment.

A: Precisely.

K: Because I love, have compassion, that compassion creates intelligence and that intelligence will operate at that moment. If you tell me, what will you do if your sister is attacked, I will say, I don't know. I will know *then*.

A: Yes, I quite follow that. But we have made an industry of designing.

K: Designed killing.

A: At all levels, not only ourselves.

K: The other day on television there was an enormous intercontinental missile on the Red Square which would kill blindly if launched; and the Americans have it, the Indians have it, the French have it, you follow?

A: Have to have it.

K: So can the mind be free of this urge to kill? Which means can the mind be free of being hurt? When there is hurt it does all kinds of neurotic things. Is pleasure love, is desire love? But we have made pleasure and desire into love. I desire God. You follow, sir? I must learn about God. You know the whole business. God is my invention, my image, out of my thought I have made that image, and so I go around in circles. So I must know what enjoyment is. Is enjoyment pleasure? When I enjoy a good meal or a sunset or see a beautiful tree or woman or whatever, if it doesn't at that moment end it becomes pleasure. If thought carries over that enjoyment and wants it to be repeated the next day it has become pleasure, it is no longer enjoyment. I enjoy and that's the end of it.

A: William Blake has very beautifully, it seems to me, pointed to this: and, of course, he was regarded as a madman! Part of his stanza goes: 'he who kisses the joy as it flies, lives in eternity's sunrise'. It's the joy that he kisses as it flies, not the pleasure. And it's as it flies. And what you have said is, that if you won't let it fly, but hold it, then we fall out of the act of joy into the . . .

K: . . . pursuit of pleasure.

A: . . . endless, repetitive in the end mournfully boring thing.

K: And I think that is what is happening in this country and in Europe and in India too, but primarily in this country, the desire to fulfil instantly – the pleasure-seeking principle. Be entertained, with football or whatever it is, be entertained.

A: This goes back to what you pointed out in our last conversation about feeling empty, needing to be filled.

K: Yes.

A: Lonely, looking for what we call fulfilment, filling up full.

K: Quite, filling up full.

A: And yet if one undertakes to make this act of attention that you referred to in our discussion about religion *in order to* fill up the hole, then we've had it. We're not going to do that. But there has been an endless attempt to do that through control of thought.

K: Of course.

A: It would seem that if one doesn't begin in love one will not make this act of attention in a non-utilitarian way but inevitably in a utilitarian way.

K: It is not in the market-place, quite.

A: And that's why in one of the very early conversations we had you said that the beginning is the end.

K: The first step is the last step.

A: The first step is the last step. What I've been thinking about all through our conversations so far is that we are speaking about an act that is a radical end to all this nonsense that's been going on and which is terrifyingly destructive nonsense.

K: I know, sir.

A: There is the doing of something.

K: That is the seeing of all this.

A: And you have said the seeing is the doing, is the act.

K: As I see danger, I act. I see the danger of the continuity of thought in terms of pleasure, I see the danger of it, therefore end it instantly. If I don't see the danger I carry on. If I don't see the danger of nationality, I'm taking that as a very simple example, I carry on, murdering, dividing, seeking my own safety; but if I see the danger it is finished.

A: May we relate here, just for a moment, love to education?

K: Yes.

A: As a teacher I'm immensely concerned about this.

K: Sir, what we have been discussing in our dialogue this last week and now is *part* of education.

A: Of course it is.

K: Educating the mind differently.

A: I'm thinking of the student who sometimes comes to the teacher and says, 'I simply must change my way of life.' That is, once in a while you will find a student who is 'up to here', as we say. The first question they will usually ask you is, what must I do. Now, of course, that's a trap because they are looking for a means when they say that. I've come to see that now with much greater clarity than I observed for myself before. Here we are not talking about a means.

K: The means is the end.

A: I am thinking of the history of Christianity in this respect. You've got the question, what must I do to be saved. The answer is 'believe'.

K: Yes.

A: And then one is stuck with what this means and ends up believing in belief.

K: Yes, believing.

A: And that of course is abortive. The student comes and says, 'What must I do?' Now in our earlier conversation together we reached the point where the teacher and the student were talking together.

K: We are doing that now. I am not your teacher, but we are doing that now.

A: Well, no, I understand that is not your role in our conversations but I must confess that it has been working out that way because I have learned immensely. There are two things here that I want to get clear and I need your help. On the one hand to make this pure act of attention, I need only myself. Is that correct?

K: No, not quite, sir.

A: Not quite.

K: Not quite. Sir, let's put the question first. The question is: What am I to do in this world?

A: Yes.

K: What is my place in this world? First of all: the world is me, I am the world. That is an absolute fact. And what am I to do? The world is this, corrupt, immoral, killing, there is no love, there is superstition, idol worship of the mind and the hand, there is war. That is the world. What is my relationship to it? My relationship to the world only is *if I am that*. If I am not that I have no relationship to it.

A: I understand that in terms of act.

K: That's it.

A: In terms of act, not a notion that I have.

K: For me the world is corrupt, is geared to kill. And I won't kill. What is my relationship to the man who goes and kills a baby seal? I say, my God, how can you do such a thing! I want to cry about it. I do. How can you educate that man or a society which allows such a thing to happen?

A: Then perhaps I should rephrase the question and say, well, when I do whatever is done in making this pure act of attention, I am not separated from the world in which I am, and the world is not separated from me.

K: I look at the world from a different angle altogether.

A: Exactly, fine.

K: I come to it, sir, because there is something different operating in me. Compassion, love, intelligence, all that is operating in me.

A: But it seems that there are two possibilities here. On the one hand, making this pure act of attention doesn't require that I be in the physical presence of another human being, but of course I am always in relation whether I am there or not.

K: Of course.

A: Yes, I fully grasp that. But then the second possibility is that within conversation, as we are enjoying it now, something occurs, something takes place. It's not that we must be together for it to take place: and it's not that we must be alone for it to take place. Therefore what we have established is that something occurs which is quite beyond all these distinctions of inner and outer, of you're over there and I'm over here.

K: See what takes place, see what takes place. First of all we are serious, really serious. Second, the killing, the corruption, we have finished with. So we stand alone — alone — not isolated. Because when the mind is not that, it is alone. It hasn't withdrawn, it hasn't cut itself off, it hasn't built an ivory tower for itself, it isn't living in illusion. It says, that is false, that is corrupt, I won't touch it, psychologically. I won't touch inwardly, psychologically, that falseness and corruption. Therefore the mind is completely alone.

A: And it is saying this amidst all this mournful round.

K: Therefore, being alone it is pure; and purity can be cut into a million pieces and still remain pure. It is not my purity, or your purity, it is purity; like pure water remaining pure water.

So you see, sir, what has come out of this conversation is very interesting. The thing is — we are frightened of being alone. Which means we are frightened of being isolated. But every act a human being does *is* isolating himself. That is, his ambition is isolating himself. When he is nationalistic he is isolating himself, when he says 'my' family, he is isolating himself, 'I want to fulfil', he is isolating himself. When you negate all that, not violently but see the stupidity of all that, then you are alone. And that has tremendous beauty in it. And that beauty you can spread everywhere, but it still remains alone. The quality of compassion is that. But compassion isn't a word, it happens, it comes with intelligence. If my sister is attacked, this intelligence will dictate at that moment what I do. But it is not intelligent if you ask: What will you do if — such a question and an answer to that is unintelligent. I don't know if you see . . .

A: Oh yes, I am following you precisely.

K: But it is unintelligence, to say, I am going to prepare to kill all those people who are my enemies, which is what the armed forces of all sovereign governments are preparing to do. So love is something that is really chaste. Chastity is the quality of aloneness and therefore never hurt.

A: It's interesting that in this one act one neither hurts himself nor another; it's a total abstention from hurt.

K: Sir, wait a minute. I have given you all my money because I trust you. And you won't give it back to me; I say, please, give me a little of it. You won't. What shall I do? What is the act of intelligence? You follow, sir? The act of affection, act of compassion, what will it do? You follow my question? A friend of mine during the Second World War found himself in Switzerland. He had a large amount of money; and he had a great friend from childhood. He explained to that friend that he had to leave the country immediately because of the war. So he took all this money and said to his friend: 'Keep it for me; I'll come back when the war is over.' He came back after the war and asked for his money back. His friend said: 'What money?'

A: Goodness me.

K: You follow, sir? So what should he do? Not theoretically. Put yourself in that position. You entrust me with something and I say, yes, quite right, you have given me this, now you can whistle for it. What is your responsibility? Do you just walk away?

A: No. If there were a means to recover it then that would be done upon the instant. Intelligence would take over.

K: That's what I am saying. Love is not forgiveness — you follow — I forgive you and walk away. Love is intelligence; and intelligence means sensitivity, to be sensitive to the situation. And if you are sensitive to the situation, it will tell you what to do. But if you are insensitive, if you have already determined what to do, if you are hurt by what has been done, then insensitive action takes place.

A: Yes, of course. This raises very interesting questions about what we mean about conscience.

K: Yes.

A: And the word conscience, it seems to me, has invited an astonishing amount of . . .

K: . . . rubbish.

A: . . . miscomprehension of what's going on.

K: Therefore, sir, one has also to investigate what is consciousness.

A: Yes.

K: We'll do that another day: what is consciousness and what is conscience, and what is it that tells you to do or not to do?

A: Consciousness and relationship is something that, when we have a chance, I should like to explore with you. I hope that when we have the opportunity in our next conversation we could do that.

K: We have also to discuss the question of living, love, and this immense thing called death. Are they interrelated or are they separate – is living, existing, different from love?

25 February 1974

DIALOGUE XIII

A Different Way of Living

DR ANDERSON: At the end of our last conversation, we had begun to look into the relationship between living and love and death. I was hoping today that we might pursue this in relation to our continuing concern for the transformation of man.

KRISHNAMURTI: As usual, this is such a complex question, living, what it means and what it actually is; and love, which we talked about the other day in some detail and rather closely; and also this enormous problem of death; every religion has offered comforting beliefs, comforting ideas, hoping they would provide a solution to the fear, sorrow, and to everything that death involves. So I think perhaps we should begin with the question: what is living, and then go on from there to love and death.

A: Good.

K: Shouldn't we look at what we call living now, at what is actually taking place?

A: Yes.

K: What is actually going on, which we call existence, living, those two words which cover this whole field of man's endeavour to better himself – not only in the technological world but also psychologically man wants to be different, he wants to be more than what he is and so on. So when we look at man in whatever country, of whatever race or religion, it is a constant struggle from the moment you are born to the moment you die, it is a battle. Not only in relationships with other human beings, whether intimate or otherwise, but also economically, socially, morally, it is a vast battle. I think everyone agrees to that – it's obvious. The conflict, the struggle, the suffering, the pain, the frustrations, the agony, the despair, violence, brutality, killing, all that is what is actually going on. Spending forty or fifty years in an office, in a factory and occasional holidays for a month – of a wild kind because the holidays are a reaction to a monotonous life.

A: Time out.

K: You see them all over Europe, Americans for example, going from museum to museum, looking at this and that, rushing about as an escape from the monotony of their daily routine. And they go off to India; there are I believe about 15,000 oddly dressed so-called hippies in various monasteries and cities doing the most fantastic things – selling drugs, some of them, and putting on Indian clothes, dressing up as monks and all that. It is a kind of vast, romantic, sentimental escape from their daily monotonous, routine life. That is what we call living: the battle in relationship, the battle in business, in the economic environment. It is constant struggle.

A: But what you've said seems to be ingrained in living itself. We have a saying, life is a battle, we interpret it in terms of what you have said.

K: And nobody seems to say, why should it be that way? We have all accepted it. We say, yes, it is part of our existence. If we don't struggle we are destroyed, it is a part of our natural inheritance. We see how the animal struggles, so we are part animal, part ape and so we must go on struggling, struggling, struggling. We have never said, is this right? Is this the way to live? Is this the way to behave, to appreciate the beauty of living?

A: The usual question turns on how to engage the battle more effectively.

K: Effectively or successfully, with least harm, least strain, least heart failure and so on. But the ground is prepared for struggle. The monks do it, the religious people do it, the businessman, the artist, the painter, every human being, compartmentalized as he is, is in battle. And that is what we call living. And the man who looks at it intelligently might say, for God's sake, that's not the way to live, let's find out if there is a different way of living. Nobody asks that! I have talked with a great many politicians all over the world and to a great many gurus, I've talked to artists, to businessmen, to artisans, to labourers, very, very poor people, it is one constant battle – the rich, the poor, the middle class, the scientists, you follow, sir?

A: Oh yes, I'm following you.

K: And nobody says, this is wrong, this isn't living – it's bleeding!

A: I was thinking about the visionary literatures of the world of a nature that tend to be divided into three in terms of their form and content. On the one hand we have epics that deal precisely with the battle of life . . .

K: We have the Odyssey, we have the Mahabharata, so many other books all praising this.

A: . . . and then others deal with what we call the journey of life, the Odyssey would be a specific instance of that, though there are many battles in it in terms of confrontation between individuals. And then there are literary works on the notion of life as fulfilment. But we hardly ever get to the question of fulfilment itself. When these are studied they are studied in terms of literary form and the question that you've raised, which it seems to me would be a question that should be put to the student, never arises.

K: And it is an authentic question, a question that must be put.

A: I was reflecting as you were speaking that in the classroom this battle is taken for granted. It is to be related to with fortitude and so forth, but questioning of it doesn't occur.

K: No, it has occurred to some young people but they go off at a tangent.

A: Exactly.

K: Either to a commune or to become a Hindu, they go off to some ancient country and just disintegrate, do nothing, think nothing, just live.

A: Which is just a lateral movement, not a vertical one.

K: That's right. So it is a valid question and it must have a valid answer, not a theoretical one but one that says: well, I will live a different way. I will live without conflict. See what it means. I question whether you will be wiped out by society if you don't struggle. Personally I never struggled, I have never thought of battling with myself or with anybody else. So I think a question of that kind must not only be put verbally but in the expression of it one must see if it is possible for each of us to live another way, to live without a single conflict. That means without division: conflict means division; conflict means the battle of the opposites; conflict means you and me, we and they, Americans and Russians, division, division, division; fragmentation not only inwardly but outwardly. Where there is fragmentation there must be battle, one fragment assuming power and dominating the other fragments. So an intelligent man — if there is such a person — has to find out a way of living which is not going to sleep, which is not just vegetating, which is not just escaping to some fanciful, mystical vision and all that stuff, but a way of living in daily life in which conflict of any kind has come to an end. It is possible. I have watched this all around me for the last fifty years, the battle going on around me, spiritually, economically, socially, one class battling the other class, the dictatorships, the Fascists, the Communists, the Nazis, you follow, sir?

A: Yes I do.

K: All of them have their roots in this: encouraging obedience, discouraging obedience, imitating, conforming, all battle. So life has become a battle. And to me personally, to live that way is the most destructive and uncreative way of living. I won't live that way, I would rather disappear!

A: I think perhaps that some confusion has arisen here in our minds when we identify ourselves with this battle in terms of your description of it. When we begin to think about the question: 'Ought this to continue?' and we have the image of battle before us, we tend to imagine that what we are really talking about is the human equivalent of 'nature red in tooth and claw'. But if I am following you correctly this is a cardinal mistake because in our previous conversations you have very clearly indicated that we must distinguish between fear and danger; and the animals, in their own environment, act with clean and immediate dispatch in the presence of danger whereas it seems we make a mistake if we attempt to study human conflict on the basis of this analogy because the analogy, if I have understood you correctly, simply doesn't apply.

K: It doesn't, no.

A: Don't you agree that this is what we tend to do?

K: Oh rather, sir, rather. We study animals or birds in order to understand man.

A: Right.

K: Whereas you can study man, which is yourself. You don't have to go to the animal to know man. So that is, sir, really a very important question because I have, if I may talk a little about myself, watched it all. I've watched it in India: the sannyasis, the monks, the gurus, the disciples and the politicians all over the world, I happen somehow to have met all of them. Well-known writers, some painters, most of them have come to see me. And they have a sense of deep anxiety that if they don't struggle they will be nothing, they will be failures, for them that way of living is the only and the righteous way of living.

A: To drive oneself to be what is called productive.

K: And we are taught this from childhood.

A: Yes.

K: Our education *is* that. To battle, not only with yourself, but with your neighbour, and yet love your neighbour, you follow? It becomes too ridiculous. So having stated that, is there a way of living without conflict? I say there is – obviously – which is to understand the division, to understand the conflict, to see how fragmented we are, not try to integrate the fragments, which is impossible, but out of that perception the action is entirely different from integration. Seeing the fragmentation which brings about conflict, which brings about division, which brings about this constant battle, anxiety, strain, heart failure. You follow, sir? That is what is happening. To see it, to perceive it, and that very perception brings an action which is totally different from the action of conflict. Because the action of conflict has its own energy, brings its own energy, which is divisive, destructive, violent. But the energy of perception and acting is entirely different, it is the energy of creation. Anything that is creative cannot be in conflict. An artist who is in conflict with his colours is not a creative human being. He may have perfect craftsmanship, perfect technique, a gift for painting, but . . .

A: It interests me very much that you used the word 'energy' here in relation to both activities.

K: Both, yes.

A: And you haven't said that the energy at root is different.

K: No.

A: The phenomenon is different.

K: Yes.

A: It would appear that when one makes success, prosperity, victory, the object of his activity and engages this conflict, which he interprets as engaging *him*, he always tends to think that things are coming at *him*. When he does this, if I have understood you correctly, energy is released, but it is released in fragmentary patterns.

K: The way of conflict, yes.

A: Yes. Whereas the energy that's released with perception is the same energy but it is always whole.

K: Whole. Yes, sir, that's right. Therefore sane, healthy, holy.

A: Yes, I have the feeling that this release of energy which shatters out into patterns of energy as fragmentation is really what we mean by the word 'demonic'.

K: That's right.

A: That's giving it a hard name.

K: It's an excellent name, it is the most destructive thing.

A: Exactly.

K: And that's what our society, our culture is.

A: What we've done to that word, demonic! I was just thinking about Socrates, who refers to his 'daemon', meaning the energy that operates in wholeness.

K: That's right, sir.

A: And we have taken that word from the Greek clear out of the context of the Apology and turned it upside down and now it means . . .

K: . . . the devil.

A: Right. And the same thing happened with the use of the word 'asuras'. Originally in the Vedas this was not a reference to the demonic, there was no radical polarization. And yet finally we end up with gods and demons.

K: Quite.

A: Which I take it you are suggesting is nothing other than the sheerest projection of our own . . .

K: . . . fragmented . . .

A: . . . demonic behaviour which we have generated ourselves.

K: That's right.

A: This makes tremendous sense to me.

K: So the way we live now is the most impractical, insane way of living; and we want the insane way of living made more practical! That is what we are demanding all the time. We never say, let's find a way of living which is whole and therefore healthy, sane and holy. And in such a way of perceiving of living, acting is the release of total energy which is non-fragmentary, nothing to do therefore with that of the artist, the businessman, the politician, the priest or layman. Now to bring about such a mind, such a way of living, one has to observe what is actually taking place outside and inside, in us and outside; and look at it, not try to transform it, not try to bring about different adjustments, but see actually what it is. I look at a mountain, I can't change it; even with a bulldozer I can't change it: but we want to change what we see. The observer *is* the observed, you understand, sir? Therefore, there is no change in that. Whereas in perception there is no observer; there is only seeing and therefore acting.

A: This holds a mirror up to an earlier conversation we had when you referred to beauty, passion, suffering and action.

K: And action, yes.

A: I remember asking you whether in order to recover the correct relationship among them we must begin with suffering which, if perceived as it ought to be perceived, generates passion.

K: That's right.

A: One doesn't have to work it out, it happens. And upon the same instant beauty and love break out. So the passion in itself is compassion. The 'com' comes in exactly with the passion.

K: With passion, that's right.

A: Yes.

K: Now, sir, if you as a professor or teacher or parent could point this out, the impracticality of the way we are living, the destructiveness of it, the utter indifference to the Earth — we are destroying everything we touch. And point out a way of living in which there is no conflict. That, it seems to me, is the function of the highest form of education.

A: Yes, although it seems to me that this clearly requires that the teacher himself must be without conflict. This is a very different point of departure from what occurs in our general educational structure. I have noticed that my colleagues with degrees in education place tremendous emphasis on educational techniques.

K: Of course.

A: And the question of the individual teacher having undergone a transformation of the sort you have been discussing is not seen as a matter of radical concern. What is, of course, an altruistic concern is that the teacher has the interests of the students at heart and that sort of thing, which is certainly laudable in itself, but that would come after the teacher's transformation.

K: Sir, you see first I must transform myself so I can teach.

A: Precisely.

K: But you see, there is something in that which is not quite accurate. That means I have to wait till I change. Why can't I change, if I am an educator, in the very act of teaching? The boys, girls, the students live in conflict, the educator lives in conflict. Now if I was an educator with a lot of students, I would begin with that and say, I am in conflict, you are in conflict, let us see in discussing, in becoming aware of our relationship in teaching, if it is not possible for me and for you to resolve this conflict. Then there is action. But if I wait till I'm free of all conflict I can wait until doomsday.

A: I see now exactly what you are saying. What you are saying is literally this: the teacher, who is at present in conflict, simply acknowledges this, walks into the classroom . . .

K: That's right, sir.

A: ... not as somebody who is free from conflict ...

K: That's right.

A: ... but he walks into the classroom and here it is, we are facing it; and he looks at his students and lays it out.

K: That's the first thing I would discuss, not the technical subjects. Because that is *living*! And also in the very teaching of a technical subject I would say, all right, let us see how we approach it, learn from that so that both the student and the educator know their conflicts and are interested in dissolving them and are therefore tremendously concerned. That produces an extraordinary relationship: I have watched it; I go to several schools in India and in England and it takes place.

A: In this taking place love breaks out.

K: Of course, that is the very essence of it; because I care, I feel responsible.

A: May I go into this just a little bit. One of the things that has concerned me in this series of dialogues is that someone would feel that in our discussions of thought and knowledge what we have been saying is that there is some dysfunction in thought and in knowledge which relates to their own nature, the nature of thought and the nature of knowledge, which could very well give the impression that thought is a disease or that knowledge is a disease, rather than giving the impression, as I have understood from you, that thought and knowledge have their proper uses.

K: Of course.

A: Their natures are not corrupt as such.

K: Certainly not, it is the usage of them.

A: Right. Therefore it becomes of utmost importance, I think in understanding what you are saying, to be aware of the corrective that we bring to bear on the uses of thought and the uses of knowledge, while at the same time, not assuming that the principle of thought and the principle of knowledge are in their own nature corrupt.

K: Obviously not. A microphone is a microphone. There is nothing corrupt about it.

A: Exactly, but you know the thing comes home to me with tremendous force that one must begin to do this in his relationship with his students. I must tell a little story about myself here. Years ago I went to hear a lecture of yours and I listened, I thought, very carefully. And, of course, one lecture is not in itself, at least for someone like me, enough. Or to put it more honestly, *I* was not enough at the time for the lecture because it seems as I recall it now, that the principles that we have been discussing you stated at that time very clearly. I went away from that lecture with the impression that there was a very close relationship between what you were saying and Buddhism, and I was thinking about the whole thing in terms of labels, as scholars are wont to do – you know how we divide the world up into species. And in our series of conversations now I've come to see that I was profoundly mistaken. And I pinch myself to think, you know, I might have gone on thinking what I thought before, which had nothing to do with anything that you were concerned with. It is a revelation to face it that one doesn't have to have a credential to start with before one walks into the classroom. We believe that there are things that we must avoid talking about because they create dissension, disruption and put us off; and therefore let's not talk about conflict. Or if we are going to talk about it let's talk about it in terms of our being the ones who have the light over against those who don't, and we have to take the good news to them.

K: Like a guru.

A: Right, but simply to come into the classroom and say: Let's have a look without any presuppositions such as my thinking that I have this in hand and you don't, or you have it and I don't. We're going to just hold it together.

K: Right, sir, share together.

A: Share it together. After our conversation comes to an end, I will walk into the classroom and do this!

K: So, sir, the energy that is created through conflict is destructive. The energy that is created through conflict, struggle, battle, produces violence, hysteria, neurotic actions, and so on. Whereas the action of perception is total, non-fragmented, and therefore it is healthy, sane and brings about intense care and responsibility. Now that is the way to live: seeing, acting, seeing, acting, all the time. I cannot see, if there is an observer different from the observed: the observer *is* the observed.

A: This does a very marvellous thing through what we call our confrontation with death.

K: We'll come to that, yes.

A: Perhaps I'm jumping too far ahead.

K: No, sir, that's right. So you see, our whole content of consciousness is battle, a battleground, and this we call living. And in that battle how can love exist? If I am hitting you, if I am competing with you, if I am trying to go beyond you, being successful, ruthless, where does the flame of love or compassion, tenderness, gentleness, come into all that? It doesn't. And that's why our society as it is now has no sense of moral responsibility with regard to action or with regard to love. It doesn't exist.

A: I would like to go back to my own experience in the classroom. It has always seemed to me that the first stanza of the first chapter of the Gita, which begins: 'dharma-kshetre kuru-kshetre' – 'in the field of Dharma, in the Kuru field', is a statement in apposition and that the field is one. I have walked into class when we have started to do the Gita and I've tried to show both linguistically, as it seemed to me was clear from the text, and in terms of the spirit of the whole, that this was really what was being said, that it's one field, not two fields. But now that I've listened to you, I think it would have been better if I had started the other way by saying, let's have a look and see together whether it is one field. We are not going to read the book at all at this point, we are just going to start here. This is the field. The *classroom* is the field. Now, let's take a look. That would have been the better way.

K: If you have understood that the classroom is the field you have understood the whole thing.

A: Exactly. But I went in with the notion that, having grasped this, it was enough simply to expound it verbally. But it's patently not. And this is terrifying. Because even if you say in the classroom what ostensibly passes for what we call the right thing, it still will not prevail in terms of this act . . .

K: Act, yes.

A: ... that we've been talking about.

K: Quite right. Let us go, sir, from there. We've discussed life, living, in which love does not exist at all. Love can only exist when the perceiver is the perceived and acts, as we said. Then that flame, that compassion, that sense of holding the Earth in your arms, as it were, if that is understood and from that there is behaviour – because that is the foundation, if there is no behaviour in the sense of conflicting behaviour – then after establishing that in ourselves or in observing it we will proceed next to the question of death. Because the question of death is an immense thing. To me living, love and death are not separate: they are one movement. It isn't death over there which I am going to meet in twenty years or next day. It is there, it is there with love and with living: it is a continuous movement, non-divisive. This is the way I live, think, feel. That's my life. I mean this, these are not just words to me.

But before we enter into the question of death we have to go into the question: What is consciousness? Because one has to understand what consciousness is, not the explanation, not the description, not the word, but the reality of consciousness. Am I as a human ever conscious? And what is it to be conscious? What is it to be aware? Am I aware totally or am I aware just occasionally when a crisis arises, otherwise I am dormant. So that's why it becomes very important to find out what is consciousness.

A: Yes, what you have just said seems to me to indicate that we are making a distinction between consciousness as a continuing movement, utterly situated in act as against these blips, these so to speak eruptions within the 'sleepy course of nature'.

K: That's right.

A: Yes, I see that.

K: So what is consciousness? Consciousness is its content. I am putting it very simply. I prefer to talk about these things very simply, not through elaborate, linguistic descriptions and theories and suppositions and all the rest of it. Personally that has no meaning to me.

A: If it is true it will be simple.

K: Simple. Consciousness is its content: the content is consciousness. The two are not separate. That is: the thoughts, the anxieties, the identifications, the conflicts, the anxiety, the attachments, the detachments, the fears, the pleasures, the agony, the suffering, the beliefs, the neurotic actions, all that is my consciousness. Because that is the content.

A: This is a statement equivalent to saying that the world is me and I am the world.

K: That's right.

A: So there's a continuity there.

K: Yes, so the content that says: that is my furniture, that's my God, that's my belief, with all its nuances and subtleties, all that is part of my consciousness, is part of the consciousness that says: I am, I am that, I am the furniture. When I say: that's my furniture, I am identifying with it, then I am attached to it, I am that. I am that knowledge which I have acquired, which I have grown up with, which I have been successful with, which has given me great comfort, a house, a position, power. That house is me. The battle which I have been through, suffering, agony, that is me, that is my consciousness. So consciousness *is* its content, there is no division as consciousness separate from its content. I can extend or widen the consciousness, horizontally or vertically, but it is still within that field. I can extend it, saying God is immense: that's my belief. And I've extended my consciousness by imagining that it is extended. Whatever thought has created in the world and which is inside me is the content. The whole world, especially in the West, is based on thought: its activities, its explorations, its achievements, its religions and so on are fundamentally the result of thought, with its images and so on. So that is the content of consciousness. Right?

A: Right.

K: Now from that arises: what is death? Is death the ending of consciousness with its content? Or is death a continuity of that consciousness? Your consciousness is no different from mine. It may have minor variations, minor modifications, a little more expansion, a little more contraction and so on, but essentially consciousness is yours as well as mine, because I am attached to my house, so are you. I am attached to my knowledge, I am attached to my family, I am in despair, whether I live in India or in England or in America or wherever. So that consciousness is common. This is irrefutable. You follow?

So see what happens. I have never examined this content. I have never looked at it closely and I am frightened, frightened of something which I call death, the unknown. Let us call it for the moment, the unknown. So I'm frightened. There is no answer to it. Somebody comes along and says, yes my friend, there is life after death, I have proof of it. I know it exists because I have contacted my brother, my son – we will go into that presently. So I, frightened, anxious, fearful, diseased, you follow, I accept that tremendously, instantly, say: Yes there is reincarnation. I am going to be born next life; and that life is related to karma. The word karma means to act, not all the rigmarole attached to it, just to act. See what is involved. That is, if I believe in reincarnation, that is this consciousness with its content, which is the 'me', my ego, my self, my activities, my hopes, pleasures, all that is my consciousness, that consciousness is going to be born next life, which is the common consciousness of you and me, and him and her. That's going to be born next life; and they say if you behave properly now you'll be rewarded next life; that's part of the causation.

A: That's part of the content of consciousness.

K: Cause and effect.

A: Yes.

K: So behave, because otherwise you are going to be punished in your next life. If you do behave you will be rewarded in your next life. The whole of the Eastern world is based on and believes in reincarnation. So what happens? I have taken comfort in a belief which says behave now, be good now, don't hurt another now – but actually I don't carry it out!

A: The idea is that I should behave now, I should this, I should that, I should the other because of what will take place later. But then I take comfort in the thought that it's an endless process and has somehow built into it that I'll get another chance. So I can sort of stall, I can stall.

K: I can stall, I can postpone, I can misbehave.

A: Yes, because we are all destined to make it in the end.

K: Eventually. Yes.

A: Which shows that there's no grasp of what you've been talking about throughout these conversations: the immediacy and urgency of act.

K: That's right.

A: Yes, I follow.

K: The Hindus were probably the originators of this idea – cause and effect. The effect will be modified by the next cause, so there is this endless chain. And if it's endless we'll break it sometime. Therefore it doesn't matter what you do now. Such a belief gives you great comfort by assuring that you will continue, you will be with your brother, wife, husband, whoever it is. But in the meantime don't bother too much, don't take life too seriously.

A: Exactly, yes.

K: Have a good time, in fact enjoy yourself. Or do whatever you want to do, pay for it a little next life, but carry on.

A: I was speaking to a well known Hindu teacher about this and I made this very same point that you have just made, and I thought it would have some force. And I said, 'You see there's no hope of stopping repetition, if an act is not made immediately with respect to this; therefore in terms of the content of the consciousness of a whole people that basks in this notion, there can be nothing but an endless repetition and no true concern about it.'

K: What did he say?

A: All he did was to laugh as though I had somehow perceived something which most people apparently are not really bothering their heads to look at. But the extraordinary thing to me was that he showed no concern for what he discerned intellectually.

K: Sir, they are hypocrites when they believe that and do something quite contrary.

A: Yes, in the strict Biblical sense. In our next conversation could we continue with the subject of death because it seems to me . . .

K: Oh, yes, there is a great deal more involved in this. We'll go into it.

26 February 1974

DIALOGUE XIV

Death, Life and Love Are Indivisible – the Nature of Immortality

DR ANDERSON: In our last conversation we began to talk about consciousness and its relation to death in the context of living as a total movement; and towards the end we even touched on the word reincarnation. I do hope we can resume our discussion.

KRISHNAMURTI: You see one of the factors in death is that the mind is so frightened of the very word and nobody talks about it. It isn't a subject for daily conversation, it is something to be avoided, something that is inevitable, so for God's sake keep it as far away as possible!

A: We even paint corpses to make them look as if they are not dead!

K: That's the most absurd thing. Now what we are discussing, sir, is the understanding of death, its relation to living and this thing called love. One cannot possibly understand the immensity – and it is immense – of this thing called death unless there is real freedom from fear. That's why we talked sometime ago about the problem of fear. Unless the mind really frees itself from fear there is no possibility of understanding the extraordinary beauty, strength, and vitality of death.

A: That's a very remarkable way to put it: 'The vitality of death'. Normally we regard it as the total negation of life.

K: As the negation of life, that's right. So if we are inquiring into the question of death, fear must be completely non-existent in us. Then I can proceed, then I can find out what death means. We have touched a little bit on reincarnation, the belief maintained in the East which has no reality in daily life; it is like going to church every Sunday and being mischievous for the rest of the week. So if a person who is really serious, really attentive, goes into this question of death, he must understand what it means, the quality of it, not the ending of it. That's what we will go into a little this time.

The ancient Egyptians, the pharaohs of the various dynasties, prepared for death. They said, we will cross that river with all our goods, with all our chariots, with all our belongings, with all our property; and therefore their caves, their tombs were filled with all the things of their daily life, corn and so on. So living was only a means to an ending: dying. That's one way of looking at it. The other is reincarnation, which is the Indian, Asiatic outlook. And there is the whole idea of resurrection which the Christians have. Being reborn and carried by the Angel Gabriel to heaven for one's reward. Now, what is the fact? These are all theories, suppositions, beliefs, and non-facts. I mean, someone supposed to be born Jesus comes out of the grave, resurrected physically. That is just a belief. There were no cameras there! Ten people say: yes, I saw it. It is only something somebody imagined.

So there is this living and preparing for death as the ancient Egyptians did; then there is reincarnation; then there is resurrection. Now, if one isn't deeply frightened, then what is death? What is it that dies, apart from the organism? The organism may continue, if you look after it very carefully, for eighty, ninety, or a hundred years. If you have no disease, if you have no accidents, and have a way of living that is sane, healthy, perhaps you will last a hundred or a hundred and ten years. And then what? You live a hundred years, for what? For *this* kind of life – fighting, quarrelling, bickering, bitterness, anger, jealousy, futility, a meaningless existence? It is a meaningless existence as we are living now.

A: And as we have already said, this is all the content of consciousness.

K: That's right. So what is it that dies? And what is it one is frightened of? What is it one is frightened of in death? Losing the known? Losing my wife? Losing my house? Losing all the things I have acquired? Losing this content of consciousness? So my question is: can the content of consciousness be totally emptied? You follow, sir?

A. Yes I do.

K: Which is living. Dying is living, when the content is totally emptied. That means no attachment. It isn't a brutal cutting off but the understanding of attachment, of dependency, of acquisition, power, position, anxiety, all that. The emptying of that is the real death. And therefore the emptying of consciousness means that the consciousness which has created its own limitation, by its content, comes to an end. I wonder, have you got it?

A: Yes, I was following you very carefully and it occurred to me that there is a radical relation between birth and death, but that the two, when looked upon as moments in a total cycle, are not grasped at the depth that you are beginning to speak about. Am I correct?

K: That is right. So death becomes living when the content of consciousness, which makes its own frontier, its own limitation, comes to an end. And this is not a theory, not a speculative, intellectual grasping, but the actual perception of attachment – I am taking that as an example, being attached to something, to property, a man, a woman, the book I have written or the knowledge I have acquired. Attachment: and the battle to be detached; because attachment brings pain. Therefore I say to myself, I must be detached; and the battle begins. And the whole content of my consciousness is this, the battle which we described previously. Now can that content empty itself, or can it be emptied by an act of perception? Which means can this whole content be observed, including its unconscious content? You follow, sir?

A: Yes, I do.

K: I can be consciously aware of the content of my consciousness – my house, my property, my wife, my children, my job, the things I have acquired, the things I have learned. I can be consciously aware of all that. But there is also a deeper content in the very recesses of my mind which is racial, collective, acquired, the things that unconsciously I have gathered, the influences, the pressures, the strains of living in a world that is corrupt. All that has seeped in, all that has gathered in there.

A: Both personal and impersonal. This includes then what the depth psychologists are calling the collective unconscious as well as the personal consciousness.

K: The collective as well. Now can all that be exposed? Because this is very important. Because if the mind really wants to understand and grasp the full meaning of death, the vastness of it, the great quality of a mind that says: yes, that's ended, it gives a tremendous vitality, energy. So my question is: can the mind be aware totally of all the content, the hidden as well as the open, the collective, the personal, the racial, the transitory? You follow? The whole of that. Now, we usually say it is possible through analysis.

A: Yes we do.

K: I have said: analysis is paralysis. Because every analysis must be perfect, complete; and you are frightened that it might not be complete; and if you have not completed it you carry it over as a memory which will then analyse the next incident. So each analysis brings its own incompleteness: therefore it is a total paralysis.

A: In following what you are saying, I'm very taken with what we usually regard as death which has a very clear relationship to what you've said about the endless series of analytical acts.

K: Yes, sir.

A: We regard death as a terminus in terms of a line.

K: Quite, because we think laterally.

A: We think laterally. But what you're saying is, on the contrary, we must regard this vertically.

K: Yes.

A: And in the regarding of it vertically we no longer see death as simply a moment of termination. There is a total qualitative change here which is not the cessation of something that we have to regret as though we had lost something valuable.

K: Yes, I am leaving my wife and children.

A: Right.

K: And my property, my bank account! You see, sir, if one goes very deeply into this: there is this content, which is my consciousness, acquired, inherited, imposed, influenced, propaganda, attachment, detachment, anxiety, fear, pleasure, all that, and also the hidden things. I see that since analysis is really paralysis, not an intellectual supposition, but is actually not a complete act, it can never produce a complete act; after all the very word 'analysis' means to break up.

Therefore I reject that totally. I won't analyse because I see the

A WHOLLY DIFFERENT WAY OF LIVING

stupidity, the paralytic process of it. Then what am I to do? Because that's the tradition: introspection, or analysis by myself or by a professional, which is now the fad. So if the mind sees the truth of this, and therefore analysis falls away, then what is the mind to do with the content? We know what the content is; we don't have to describe it in detail. Now, what is it to do? It has to be emptied. Otherwise it is merely continuity.

A: No, it is no use analysing what is already there because that will not change it in any shape or form. That seems to be very, very clear. Perhaps you would for a moment explain why we simply refuse to see that? We do believe that an analytical enquiry is revelatory, we do believe that.

K: Sir, you can see it in a minute: analysis implies the analyser and the analysed.

A: Yes.

K: The analyser *is* the analysed.

A: Yes, we are back to the observer and the observed.

K: I am analysing my anger. Who is the analyser? Part of the fragment which is anger. So the analyser pretends to be different from the analysed. But when I see the truth that the analyser *is* the analysed then a totally different action takes place. Then there is no conflict between the analyser and the analysed. There is instant action, a perception, which is the ending and going beyond the 'what is'.

A: The reason I asked for the explanation was because of the concern raised earlier about knowledge.

K: After all, the observer is knowledge.

A: Yes, I was concerned that study, in its proper form, was not regarded in our discussions as unprofitable as such.

K: No.

A: We don't mean that.

K: We didn't even discuss that, it's so obvious.

A: Exactly, I couldn't agree more. Yes, I see what you mean now about analysis as such.

K: Analysis implies, sir, the analyser and the analysed.

A: Precisely.

K: The analyser is the analysed. And also analysis implies time, duration. I must take time to unearth, to uncover, and it will take me the rest of my life.

A: This is a confusion we have about death too in relation to time.

K: That's right, I'm coming to that. So the mind in perceiving discards analysis completely. Not because it's not profitable, not because it doesn't get me where I want to be, but I see the impossibility of emptying the consciousness of its content, if the mind approaches it through that channel: analyser, time, and the utter futility of the fact that after forty years I am still analysing!

A: And the content of my consciousness has not qualitatively changed at all; it's become intensified in its corruption.

K: That's right. But the mind must see its content, must be totally aware of it, not fragments of it. How is that to be done? You follow, sir?

A: Yes I do.

K: Because that's very important in relation to death. Because the content of my consciousness is consciousness. That consciousness is me, my ego, my saying, 'I and you', 'we and they' – whether 'they' be the communists, the catholics, the protestants or the Hindus – 'we and they'. So it is very important to find out whether it is possible to empty consciousness of its content. Which means dying to the 'me'. You follow?

A: Yes I do.

K: Because that *is* the 'me'!

A: This is where the terror starts.

K: That's where the terror starts.

A: Precisely. There's the intuition that if I die to the content of this consciousness I am wiped out.

K: Yes, so I, who have worked, who have lived a righteous life or unrighteous life, who have done so much, whether mischief or good, I have struggled to better myself, I've been so kind, so gentle, so angry, so bitter, and when you say, empty your consciousness, it means you are asking me to die to all that. So you are touching at the very root of fear.

A: Yes, exactly.

K: At the root of terror of not being. Oh yes, that's it, sir! And I want to immortalize that 'me'. I do it through writing a famous book. Or through a painting, through works, good acts, through building this or that, I immortalize myself.

A: This has very pernicious effects within the family, because we must have a son in order to ...

K: ... carry on

A: ... immortalize the name in time.

K: Therefore the family becomes a danger.

A: Exactly.

K: So look what we have done, sir: the ancient Egyptians immortalized themselves, made their life immortal by thinking of carrying on.

A: In perpetuity.

K: In perpetuity. And the robbers come and tear it all to pieces. Tutankhamen is merely a mask now, a golden mask and a mummy, and so on. So man has sought immortality through works, through every kind of way to find that which is immortal, that is, which is beyond mortality.

A: It's a very remarkable thing that the very word 'immortal' is a negative.

K: Yes, not mortal.

A: It's not saying what it is (laughs).

K: We are going to find out what it is. You follow, sir, this is a very, very serious thing. It isn't a plaything between two people who are enjoying a discussion. It is a tremendously important thing.

A: I was laughing at the irony of it. That inherent in the structure of that word there is a warning, and we just go right through the red light.

K: So what is immortality? Not the book, not the painting which I have done, not going to the moon and putting some idiotic flag up there. Not living a righteous life, or living an unrighteous life. So what is immortality? Cathedrals are marvellously beautiful, then an earthquake comes and they are gone. Michelangelo carved out of marble a marvellous thing, and a fire destroys it; or some lunatic comes along with a hammer and breaks it up. So it is in none of those.

A: Right.

K: Because that is capable of being destroyed. Every statue becomes a dead thing, every poem, every painting. So then one asks, what is immortality? It's not in the building – just see it, sir – it's not in the cathedral, it's not in the saviour which you have invented, which thought has invented, not in the gods that man has created out of his own image. Then what is immortality? Because that is related to consciousness and to death. Unless I find that out, death is a terror.

A: Of course.

K: I have tried to immortalize myself, become immortal by the thought that there is Brahman, there is a God, there is eternity, there is a nameless one, and I will do everything to approach him. Therefore I'll lead a righteous life, therefore I will pray, I will beg, I will obey, I will live a life of poverty, chastity and so on, in order to have that immortal reality with me. But I know all that is born of thought. Right, sir?

A: Yes.

K: So I see thought and its products are the children of barren women.

A: Precisely.

K: See what takes place. Then what is immortality? The beauty in the church – not I built the church – the beauty in the cathedral, the beauty in the poem, the beauty in the sculpture, the beauty, not the object of beauty.

A: The beauty itself.

K: Itself. That is immortal. And I cannot grasp that, the mind cannot grasp it because beauty is not in the field of consciousness.

A: Yes. You see what you have said again stands it all on its head. We think that when something beautiful dies which we have cherished that beauty dies in some sense with that which has passed away.

K: Passed away, yes.

A: Actually it's the feeling of being bereft of that beauty that I regarded as my privilege to have personal access to. The belief that that has perished, not simply been lost, because what is lost is by its nature predisposed to be found. But to perish is to be wiped out utterly, isn't it? And so the belief is deep.

K: Oh, very.

A: Extremely deep with respect to what we mean by perish. In fact the word isn't used very often, because it's a very frightening one. We always talk about losing things, hardly ever do we say something perishes. Now back to what I mentioned about standing it on its head. The image came to my mind as a metaphor – I hope not one of those images we've been talking about – that beauty, rather than being imprisoned and therefore utterly nullified when a thing perishes, has simply let it go. In some sense beauty has let this expression of it go. That is the contrary of what is usually thought.

K: I know, I know.

A: And it has probably let it go precisely on time.

K: That's right.

A: That is what is so marvellous.

K: So immortality is thought to be within the field of time; and death is also then within the field of time. Because I have created, through thought, the things of time. And death is the ending, or the beginning of a state which is timeless. Of that I am frightened. So I want everything preserved in the field of time. And that is what we call immortal – the statue, the poem, the church, the cathedral, and I see also that all that is corruptible, is destroyed by one accident or by an earthquake, everything is gone. So immortality is not within the field of time; and time is thought.

A: Of course, yes, that follows.

K: So anything that thought creates must be within the field of time. And yet thought is trying to seek immortality, which is the immortality of itself and of the things it has created.

A: Yes.

K: So then the problem is: can the mind see all this, *see* it? Not imagine that it is seeing it.

A: No, actually see it.

K: Actually see it.

A: And see that the field of time is another fragment.

K: So the mind, perceiving all this, if it is alert, if it has been watchful all the time we have been discussing, must inevitably see the whole content exposed, without any effort. It's like reading a map. You spread it out and look. But if you want to go in a particular direction, then you don't look at the whole map. Then you say, I want to go from here to there, the direction is there, so many miles, and you don't look at the rest. What we are asking is: have no direction but just look. Look at the content of your consciousness without direction, without choice. Be aware of it without any exertion of discernment. Be choicelessly aware of this extraordinary map. Then that choiceless awareness gives you this tremendous energy to go beyond it. And you need energy to go beyond it.

A: This leads me to the notion of reincarnation that we began to touch on a little earlier: I see the demonic root in that.

K: Yes, sir: reincarnate next life. Nobody says, incarnate now.

A: Yes, exactly.

K: You can only incarnate now when you die to the content of consciousness. You can be reborn, regenerated totally if you die to the content.

A: Yes. And there is a terrible truth on the dark side, the demonic side, to this doctrine of reincarnation, because if that content of consciousness is not emptied out then it must prevail.

K: It prevails. So what happens? I do not know, as a human being, how to empty this thing. I'm not even interested, I'm only frightened.

A: Only scared to death.

K: Scared to death. And so I preserve something, and I die, am burned or buried under ground. The content goes on. As we said, the content of 'me' is your content also, it's not so very different.

A: No.

K: Slightly modified, slightly exaggerated, given certain tendencies which depend on your environmental conditioning and so on, but it is essentially the same consciousness. Unless a human being empties that consciousness, that consciousness goes on like a river – collecting, accumulating, all that goes on. And out of that river comes the expression or the manifestation of the one that is lost. When the mediums at séances say, your brother, your uncle, your wife is here, what has happened is that they have manifested themselves out of that stream which is the continuous consciousness of struggle, pain, unhappiness, all that. And a man who has observed and looked at consciousness and empties it doesn't belong to that stream at all. Then he is living each moment anew because he is dying each moment. You understand, sir?

A: Oh, yes I do.

K: There is no accumulation of the 'me' which has to be expressed. He is dying every minute, living every minute, and dying every minute. Therefore in that there is – what shall I say – there is no content. You follow, sir?

A: Yes.

K: It is like a tremendous energy in action.

A: This gives a totally different understanding of what we mean by the phrase, in the afterlife. On the one hand there is this continuity of disordered content of consciousness . . .

K: It is totally disordered, that's right.

A: . . . whose nature is not radically affected qualitatively simply because somebody has stopped breathing for good. No. It's on its way.

K: On its way.

A: And therefore the attempt that is often made by people to contact this stream of consciousness after the death of a person, when made within the same quality of consciousness, achieves nothing but a reinforcement within their own personal life.

K: That's right.

A: And it does a terrible thing to that content of consciousness which has gone on, since it also feeds that some more.

K: That's right.

A: Yes, I do see that.

K: A person came to see me whose wife had died. And he really thought he loved her. So he said, 'I must see my wife again. Can you help me?' I said, 'Which wife do you want to see? The one that cooked? The one that bore the children? The one that gave you sex? The one that quarrelled with you? The one that dominated you, frightened you?' He said, 'I don't want to meet any of those. I want to meet the goodness of her.' You follow, sir?

A: Yes.

K: The image of the good he had built out of her. None of the ugly things, or what he considered ugly things, but the idea of the good which he had culled out of her, and that is the image he wants to meet. I said, 'Don't be infantile, you are so utterly immature, when you have slept with her, and got angry with her, all that you don't want, you want just the image which you have about her goodness.' And you know, sir, he began to cry, really cry for the first time. He said, afterwards, 'I cried when she died, but the tears were self-pity, my loneliness, my sense of lack of things. Now I am crying because I see what I have done.' You understand, sir?

A: Yes, I do.

K: So to understand death there must be no fear. The fear and the terror of death exist only when the content of consciousness is not understood; and the content is the 'me'; and the 'me' is the chair!

A: Yes.

K: Any thing which I am attached to! It is so stupid. And I am frightened of that, losing the bank account, the family, you follow?

A: Yes I do.

K: So unless one is really, deeply serious in this matter, you can't incarnate now in the deep sense of that word; and therefore immortality is in the book, in the statue, in the cathedral, in the things I have put together, the things I have put together by thought. That's all the field of time.

A: Right. It just occurred to me what a terrible thing we have been doing so often to Plato by this perennial attempt at academic analysis of the text, when he plainly said that the business of the philosopher – namely one who is concerned with a radical change and rebirth, which he associated with wisdom – is to practise dying. I don't think he meant routine or repetition, I think he puts it with an 'ing', because he doesn't want to fall out of act. I know I use this phrase all the time but it seems to say what I want to say. It's possible to fall out of act into the terror and the demonic stream of time, but when one is in act the whole thing is an ongoing movement.

K: So, sir, time has a stop.

A: Precisely.

K: See the beauty of it. And it is that beauty which is immortal, not the things which thought has created.

A: Right.

K: So living is dying.

A: Right.

K: And love is essentially dying to the 'me'. Not the things which thought has said is love – love-sex, love-pleasure. Dying to time is love. So living, love and death are one thing, not divisive, not separated, not divorced, not in the field of time but completely a living, moving, indivisible thing. And *that* is immortal.

A: Yes.

K: Now, most of us are educated wrongly.

A: How true that is.

K: From childhood we are never taught to be serious. From childhood we are taught the cultivation of thought, the expression and the marvels of thought. All our philosophies, books, everything is based on that. And when you say, die to all that, you really awaken the terror of not knowing. That gives me security in knowing.

A: Yes.

K: Then knowledge becomes the field of my safety. And you ask me to give all that up, to die to all that. And I say, you are insane. How can I die to that, that's part of me!

A: There's a very beautiful Zen saying that seems to relate to this when it's understood correctly. It speaks of jumping off the cliff with hands free. The hands are always grasping the past or reaching out towards the future, and we never get off that horizontal track.

K: So then comes the question, what is living in the present? Death is the future. And I've lived for forty years, with all the accumulation. So what is the present? The present is the death of the content of consciousness. You follow, sir?

A: Yes.

K: That has immense beauty. Because that means no conflict, you follow sir, no tomorrow. But if you tell someone who loves, who is going to enjoy a partner tomorrow, there is no tomorrow, he will say, what are you talking about?

A: Yes, I know. As you sometimes say, it sounds absurd.

K: Of course.

A: And, of course, in relation to the way we have been taught it does sound absurd.

K: Therefore, sir, can we educate children, students, to live totally differently? To live and understand and act with this sense of understanding the content of consciousness and the beauty of it all?

A: If I've understood you correctly there's only one answer to that question: yes. I see now what you mean about death and birth as intemporally related in terms of the question that we raised about their relation earlier, because when you say there is this incarnation now, upon the instant . . .

K: Yes, sir. If you see the beauty of it, the thing takes place.

A: Then it's happened.

K: It is not the result of mentation.

A: No.

K: It is not the result of man's thinking, thinking, thinking. This is actual perception of 'what is'.

A: And what is amazing is that it is the same energy at root.

K: Yes, sir.

A: It doesn't involve something over there that's a different energy called God.

K: No, that's bringing in an outside agency.

A: No.

K: It is the same wasted and dissipated energy which is no longer wasted and dissipated.

A: Exactly.

K: Therefore, it is . . .

A: There is a total change. And the transformation of each individual is a total one.

K: Which is not within the field of time and knowledge.

A: It is not within the field of time and knowledge.

K: You see how they are related.

A: And if I may add just one other thing here because it seems to me that it isn't the responsibility of one over against the other to do something. We begin together . . .

K: Yes, sir. Share together.

A: . . . to have a look.

K: Learn together.

A: Just quietly having a look. And that activity is not planned – one of the amazing things about this conversation is that it, to use your beautiful word, flowers.

K: It flowers, yes.

A: It doesn't require an extended imposition, contrivance or management.

K: Quite.

A: Somehow it grows out of itself.

This has been a wonderful revelation, the whole thing about death, living and love. I do hope when we have our next conversation that we could begin to pursue this even further in relation to education.

K: Yes, sir.

26 February 1974

DIALOGUE XV

Religion, Authority and Education – Part I

DR ANDERSON: We were talking last time about death in relation to living and love; and we thought it would be good to pursue this further with regard to education, what really goes on between teacher and student when they begin looking together, what traps immediately appear and shock. You mentioned the terror of death, not simply externally but internally in relation to thought; and it seemed to me it would be a splendid thing if we went deeper into that.

KRISHNAMURTI: I would like to ask again why we are educated at all? What is the meaning of this education that people receive? Apparently they don't understand a thing about life, they don't understand fear, pleasure, the whole thing that we have discussed, and the ultimate fear of death and the terror of not being. Is it that we have become so utterly materialistic that we are concerned only with good jobs, money, pleasure and superficial entertainment, whether it be of a religious nature or football? Is it that our whole nature and structure has become so utterly meaningless? And when we are educated in that way, to suddenly face something real is terrifying.

As we have already said, we are not educated to look at ourselves, we are not educated to understand the whole business of living, we are not educated to look and see what happens if we face death. Religion has become not only a divisive process but also utterly meaningless. After maybe 2,000 years of Christianity or 5,000, 3,000 years of Hinduism or Buddhism and so on, it has lost its substance. And we never inquire into what religion is, what education is, what living is, what dying is, the whole business of it. We never ask: what is it all about? And when we do ask we say, well, life has very little meaning; and it has very little meaning as we live it, and so we escape into all kinds of fantastic, romantic nonsense, which we can't discuss or logically inquire into, but which is mere escape from this utter emptiness of the life that one leads. I don't know if you saw the other day on television, a group of people adoring a human being and doing the most fantastic things and that's what they call religion, that's what they call God. They seem to have lost all reason. Reason apparently has no meaning any more, either.

A: I did see a documentary that was actually put on by this station in which the whole encounter was shown between the public and this young fifteen-year-old guru. It was extraordinary.

K: Disgusting.

A: It was in many respects revolting.

K: And that's what they call religion. So shall we begin with religion and go on? You know, man has always wanted and tried to find out something beyond everyday living, everyday routine, everyday pleasures, every activity of thought, he has wanted something much more. I don't know whether you have been to villages in India. They put a little stone under a tree, put some marking on it, the next day they bring flowers and of course to the people there it has become divinity, it has become something religious. That same principle is continued in the cathedrals. The mass and all the rituals in India are exactly the same thing and that is where it begins: the desire the human being has to find something more than what thought has put together. Not being able to find it, they romanticize it, they create symbols, or somebody who has got a little bit of this, they worship. And round that they do all kinds of rituals, Indian puja, you know all that business that goes on. And that is called religion; which has absolutely nothing to do with behaviour, with our daily life.

So both in the West and the East, in Islam, in Buddhism and the other religions, it is the same principle going on: worshipping an image which they have created; whether it is the Buddha or Christ, it is the human mind that has created the image.

A: Oh yes, certainly.

K: And they worship the image which is their own. In other words they are worshipping themselves.

A: And the division, the split between them, grows wider.

K: Yes. So when one asks what is religion, obviously one must negate, not in the sense of brutally cut off but understand all this. And so negate all the religions: negate the religion of India with its multiple gods and goddesses and here the religion of Christianity, which is an image which people have created, which is idolatry; they might not like to call it idolatry but it is. It is an idolatry of the mind, the mind has created the ideal and the mind through the hand has created the statue, the cross and so on. So to find out what religion is one must really put all that aside, if one can, the belief, the superstition, the worship of the person, the worship of an idea, and the rituals and the tradition, all that.

A: Exactly. There is a point of terror here that is many-faceted, it seems to me, it has so many different mirrors that it holds up to one's own dysfunction. To begin at the point where one makes this negation in order to find out, he thinks very often that he is being required to assume something in advance in order to make the negation.

K: Of course.

A: Therefore he balks at that and won't do it.

K: No, because the brain needs security, otherwise it can't function.

A: That's right.

K: So it finds security in a belief, in an image, in rituals, in the propaganda of 2,000 or 5,000 years. And in that there is a sense of safety, comfort, security, well-being, somebody is looking after me, the image of somebody greater than me who is looking after me, inwardly *He* is responsible. All that. When you ask a human being to negate all that, he is faced with an immense sense of danger – panic.

A: Exactly.

K: So to see all that, to see the absurdity of all the present religions, the utter meaninglessness of it all, and to face being totally insecure and not be frightened.

A: I sense a trick that one can play on oneself right here. Again I am very grateful to you that we are exploring together the various facets of this pathology. One can begin with the notion that he is going to make this negation in order to attain to something better.

K: Oh no, that's not negation.

A: And that's not negation at all.

K: No, negation is to deny what is false not knowing what is truth. To see the false in the false and to see the truth in the false, and it is the truth that denies the false. You see what is false, and the very seeing of what is false is the truth.

A: Yes, of course.

K: And that denies, that sweeps away all this.

Negation can only take place when the mind sees the false, the very perception of the false *is* the negation of the false. And when you see the religions based on miracles, based on personal worship, based on fear that you, your own life, is so shoddy, empty, meaningless, and that you are so transient you will be gone in a few years, then the mind creates the image which is eternal, marvellous, beautiful, heaven, and identifies with it and worships it. Because it deeply needs a sense of security, it has created all this superficial nonsense, this circus – it is a circus.

A: Oh yes.

K: So can the mind observe this phenomenon and see its own demand for security, comfort, safety, permanency and deny all that? Deny in the sense of seeing how the brain, thought, creates the sense of permanency, the eternal, or whatever you like to call it. To see all that. Therefore one has to go much more deeply, I think, into the question of thought because both in the West and the East thought has become the most important movement in life.

A: Oh yes.

K: Thought, which has created this marvellous world of technology, the marvellous world of science, all that, and thought which has created the religions, the marvellous chants, both the Gregorian and Sanskrit chants, thought which has built beautiful cathedrals, thought which has made images of the saviours, the masters, the gurus, the father image. Unless one really understands thought, what thinking is, we will still play the same game in a different field.

A: Exactly.

K: Look what is happening in this country. These gurus come from

India, they shave their heads, put on Indian dress, with a little tuft of hair hanging down, and repeat endlessly what somebody has said. The new gurus. They have had gurus in the past, the priests.

A: Oh yes.

K: The Catholics, the Protestants, and they have denied them but accept the others! You follow?

A: Yes.

K: The new are as dead as the old ones because they are just repeating tradition: repeating how to sit, how to meditate, how to hold your head, breathe. Finally you obey what the old guru says or the young guru says. Which is exactly what took place in the Catholic world and in the Protestant world. They deny that and yet accept the other. Because they want security, they want somebody to tell them what to do, what to think, never *how* to think.

A: This raises an issue that I hope we can explore concerning the word 'experience'. It's amazing how often in these times this word is used to refer to something that I desperately need, which somehow lies outside myself. I need the experience of an awakening. It isn't an awakening that I need, apparently, it's an experience of this awakening. The whole idea of religion as experience seems to me to need very careful investigation.

K: Quite. So, if I may ask, why do we demand, why is there this craving for experience? We have sexual experience, experiences of every kind as we live: insults, flattery, happenings, incidents, influences, what people say, don't say, we read a book, and so on. We have experiences all the time. But we are bored with that. So we say we will go to somebody who will give me the experience of God.

A: Yes, that's precisely what is claimed.

K: Now what is involved in that? What is involved in the demand for experience and the experiencing of that demand? I experience what that guru or master or somebody tells me. How do I know it is real? And I say, I recognize it. Look, I experience something, and I can know that I have experienced it only when I have recognized it. Right?

A: Right.

K: Recognition implies: I have already known.

A: Re-cognize.

K: So I am experiencing what I have already known, therefore it is nothing new. All they are doing is self-deception.

A: It is actually lusted after.

K: Oh, lord, yes.

A: The drive for it is extraordinary. I have seen it in many students who will go to extraordinary lengths of austerities. We sometimes think that young people today are very loose in their behaviour, well some are, but that has been going on since time out of mind. I think what is rarely seen is that many young persons today are extremely serious about acquiring something that someone possesses which they don't have, and if someone claims to have it, they are full of naive enthusiasm to get it.

K: Oh, yes, I have seen all that.

A: Which is called an experience.

K: That's why one has to be very careful, as you pointed out, to explore this word and to see why the human mind, a human being, demands more experience, when his whole life is a vast experience with which he is so bored. He thinks this is a new experience, but to experience the new how can the mind recognize it as the new, unless it has already known it?

A: Yes, and there is something very remarkable here in terms of what you have said in our previous conversations: in the recognition of what is called the new, the linkage with old thought, old image, establishes the notion that there is something gradual in the transition. That there really is some kind of genuine link here with where I am now and where I was before. Now I become the next guru who goes out and teaches others how gradually to undertake this discipline!

K: Yes, sir.

A: And it never stops. Driving down in the car this morning I was thinking about the whole business and beauty of chant and since this is related to experience, I thought maybe we could examine the aesthetics in terms of where the trap lies in it for the self. I thought of that beautiful Sanskrit invocation that introduces the *Īs'ā Upanishad*. And I said to myself, if one attended to those words there is the echo of the abiding throughout the whole thing, throughout that whole glorious cadence, and yet within it there's a perfect occasion for falling into euphoria.

K: Yes, sir.

A: And somnolence takes over. And I said to myself, well, maybe Mr Krishnamurti would say a word about one's own relation to the beautiful, when that relation is not seen for what it is. Since there is a narcosis present that I myself can generate. It isn't in the words themselves — and yet we think that the language must be at fault, that there must be something demonically hypnotic about it. And at times religious groups will separate themselves totally from all this. We had a period in Europe when Protestants, Calvinists, wouldn't allow an organ, any music, because music was seductive. I am not the self-seducer, it is the music's fault!

K: That's just it, sir. As we were saying the other day, beauty can only be when there is the total abandonment of the self. Complete emptying of the consciousness of its content, which is the 'me'. Then there is a beauty which is something entirely different from the pictures, chants, all that. And probably most of these young people, and also the older people, seek beauty in that sense through the trappings of the church, through chants, through reading the Old Testament with all its beautiful words and images, and that gives them a sense of deep satisfaction. In other words, what they are seeking is really gratification through beauty — beauty of words, beauty of chant, beauty of all the robes and the incense, and the light coming through those marvellous stained glass windows. You have seen it all in the cathedrals, Notre Dame and Chartres — marvellous. It gives them a sense of sacredness, a sense of feeling happy, relieved, at last here is a place where I can go and meditate, be quiet, get into contact with something. And then you come along and say, look, that's all rubbish, it has no meaning! What has meaning is how you *live* in your daily life!

A: Yes.

K: Then they throw a brick at you.

A: It is like taking food away from a starving dog.

K: So this is the whole point: experience is a trap, and everyone wants this strange experience which the gurus think they have.

A: Which it is interesting to note is always called the knowledge.

K: Very interesting.

A: Isn't it? Of course I was thinking about previous conversations, about this self-transformation that is not dependent on knowledge.

K: Of course not.

A: Not dependent on time and eminently requires responsibility.

K: And also, we don't want to work. We work very strenuously at earning a livelihood. Look what we do, year after year, day after day, the brutality, the ugliness of all that. But here, inwardly, psychologically, we don't want to work. We are too lazy. Let the other fellow work, perhaps he has worked, and perhaps he will give me something. But I don't say I am going to find out, I'll deny the whole thing and find out.

A: No, the assumption is that it is the priest's business to have worked in order to know so that I am relieved of that task; or if I didn't come into the world with enough marbles then all I need to do is simply follow his instructions and it's his fault if he messes it up.

K: We never ask the man who says, 'I know, I have experienced', what do you know?

A: Exactly.

K: What have you experienced? What do you know? When you say, I know, you only know something that is dead, which is gone, which is finished, which is the past. You can't know something that is living.

A: Yes.

K: A living thing you can never know, it's moving, it is never the same. And so I can never say, I know my wife or my husband, children, because they are living human beings. But these fellows come along, from India specially, and they say: I know, I have experienced, I have knowledge, I will give it to you. And I say, what impudence!

A: Yes.

K: What callous indifference to say that you know and I don't know. And what do you know?

A: It's amazing what has been going on here in terms of the relation between man and woman because a whole mythology has grown up about this. For instance our sex says, woman is mysterious, and never is this understood in terms of the freshness of life, which includes everything, not just woman. We have an idea that woman is mysterious. So we are talking about something in terms of an essence, which has nothing to be with existence. Isn't that so?

K: Exactly.

A: Goodness me! And as you said earlier we are actually taught this in books, in the conversations that go on in classrooms.

K: So that is why, sir, I feel that education – as it is now – is destroying people. It has become a tragedy. If I had a son – which I haven't, thank God – I would say, where am I to educate him? What am I to do with him? Make him like the rest of the group, like the rest of the community? Taught memories, accept, obey? You follow, sir, all the things that are going on. And since many people are now faced with this problem, we have said, look, let's start a school, which we have in India, and which I am going to do in California at Ojai. Let's start a school where we think totally differently, where we are taught differently. Not just routine, routine, routine, accept, deny, react, you know, the whole thing.

From that arises another question: why does the mind obey? I obey the laws of the country, I obey in keeping to the left side of the road or the right side of the road. I obey what the doctor tells me – personally I don't go near doctors, if I do I am very careful of what they have to say, I am watchful, I don't accept immediately this or that. But politically in the so-called democratic world people won't accept a tyrant.

A: No.

K: They say no authority, but freedom! But spiritually, inwardly, they accept every Tom, Dick and Harry – especially when they come from India.

A: Oh yes.

K: The other day I turned on BBC television and there was a man interviewing a group of people. And a boy and girl said, 'We obey entirely what our guru says.' And the interviewer said: 'Will he tell you to marry?' 'If he tells me I will marry. If he tells me I must fast, I will fast'. Just a slave. You understand sir? And yet the very same person will object to political tyranny!

A: It is absurd.

K: He will accept the tyranny of a petty little guru, with his fanciful ideas, and he will reject politically a tyranny or a dictatorship. So why does the mind divide life into accepting authority in one direction and denying it in another? And what is the importance of authority? The word authority means the one who originates.

A: The author.

K: And these priests, gurus, leaders, spiritual preachers, what have they originated? They are repeating tradition, aren't they?

A: Oh, yes, precisely.

K: And tradition, whether it is Zen tradition, Chinese or Hindu, is a dead thing. And these people are perpetuating this dead thing. The other day I saw a man, he was explaining how to meditate – put your hands here, close your eyes.

A: Yes, that's the one I saw. It was appalling.

K: Do this, that and the other, and people accept it.

A: And on the same programme there was a woman who had run out of money and every blessed thing, and she had nowhere to sleep and so forth, and she was saying hysterically, 'I'm in line, I've got all these people ahead of me, but I must have this knowledge.' There was desperation there.

K: That's why one must ask: what is behind this acceptance of authority? The authority of law, the authority of the policeman, the authority of the priests, the authority of these gurus, what is behind the acceptance of authority? Is it fear? Fear of going wrong spiritually, of not doing the right thing in order to gain enlightenment, knowledge, super-consciousness, whatever it is? Is it fear? Or is it a sense of despair, a sense of utter loneliness, of utter ignorance? I am using the word 'ignorance' in the deeper sense.

A: Yes, I follow.

K: Which makes me say, well, there is a man who says he knows, I'll accept him. I don't reason. I don't say, what do you know? What are you bringing, giving to me, your own tradition from India? Who cares? You are bringing something dead, nothing original, nothing real, but repeating, repeating, repeating what others have done – which in India they themselves are throwing out.

A: Yes. I was just thinking of Tennyson's lines, though written in a different context: 'Theirs not to reason why, theirs but to do and die'.

K: That's what the gurus say. So what is behind this acceptance of authority?

A: It is interesting that the root of the word 'authority' is related to the self – *autos*, the self. There is this sensed gaping void, through the division.

K: Sir, that's just it.

A: And that immediately opens up a hunger, doesn't it? And I run madly to my projection of my meal.

K: When you see this, you want to cry.

A: Yes.

K: All these young people going to these gurus, shaving their heads, dressing in Indian dress, dancing in the streets, doing all sorts of fantastic things. All in a tradition which is dead. All tradition is dead. And when you see that you say, my God, what has happened? So I go back and ask, why do we accept? Why are we influenced by these people? Why are we influenced when there is constant repetition as in a commercial, 'buy this, buy this'? It is the same thing. You follow sir?

A: Yes.

K: Why do we accept? The child accepts, I can understand that. Poor thing, he or she doesn't know anything, but needs security, a mother, care, protection, to sit on your lap and be given affection, kindness, gentleness. The child needs that. Is it that people think the guru gives them all this? Through his words, through the rituals, through their repetition, through their absurd disciplines? You follow? A sense of acceptance as I accepted my mother when a child, I accept that in order to be comfortable, in order to feel at last that something, somebody is looking after me.

A: This relates to what you said in a previous conversation when we looked into fear. The reaction of the infant is a reaction with no kind of intermediary of his own contrivance. He simply recognizes that he has a need, and this is not imagined, it is a radical need. He needs to feed, he needs to be held affectionately.

K: Of course, sir.

A: Then there is a transition from that to the point where as he gets older he begins to think about the source of the meeting of that need. He emerges as the image that is interposed between the sense of danger and the immediate action. And I've done that myself. It isn't because of anything I was told that actually coerced me to do it, even though what you say is true, we are continually invited, it's a kind of siren-like call that comes to us throughout our entire culture, in all cultures, to start that stuff.

K: You see sir, that's what I want to get at. Why is it that we accept authority? In a democratic world, we shun any political dictator. But religiously they are all dictators. And why do we accept it? Why do I accept the priest as an intermediary to something which he says he knows? It shows, sir, that we stop reasoning. Politically we reason, we see how important it is to be free, to have free speech, everything free, as much as possible. But spiritually we never feel the necessity of freedom. And therefore we accept authority – any Tom, Dick or Harry. It is horrifying! I've seen intellectuals, professors, scientists, falling for all this trash. Because they have reasoned in their scientific world, and they are weary of reasoning, and they say, at last I can sit back and not reason but be told, be comforted, be happy, he'll do all the work for me, I don't have to do anything, he'll take me over the river. You follow?

A: Oh, yes.

K: And I'm delighted. So we accept out of ignorance, where reason doesn't function, where intelligence is in abeyance, and you need all that: freedom, intelligence, reasoning, for real spiritual matters. Otherwise what? Some guru comes along and tells you what to do and you repeat what he says. You see how destructive, how degenerate it is? That is what is happening. I don't think these gurus realize what they are doing. They are encouraging degeneracy.

A: Well, they represent a chain of the same.

K: Exactly. So this brings up a very important question: can there be education in which there is no authority whatsoever?

A: I must say 'yes' to that in view of the experience that I had in class yesterday. It was a tremendous shock to the students when they suspended their disbelief for a moment, just to see whether I meant it when I said, now we must do this together, not your doing what I tell you to do.

K: You have to work together.

A: We will do this together.

K: Share it together.

A: Right. You will question, and I will question, and we'll try to grasp as we go along – without trying. And I went into the business about let's not have this shoddy little thing 'trying'. That took a little while and increased the shock because students who have been to their own great satisfaction what you would call devoted, who do their work, who make an effort, suddenly find out that this man has come into the room and is giving 'trying' a bad press. This does seem to turn things upside down. But they showed courage in that they gave it a little attention before beginning the true act of attention. I've quite followed you when you discussed the relation of courage to the pure act of attention. It seems to me that is not where it belongs.

K: No.

A: But they did summon it up for this preliminary step. But then we ran into what I called dropping a stitch – where they really saw this abyss, they were alert enough to stand over the precipice, and that caused them to freeze. And it's that moment that seems to me absolutely decisive. It is almost like seeing in terms of objective events. The Spanish philosopher Ortega y Gasset spoke of events that tremble back and forth before the thing actually tumbles into itself. That was happening in the room. It was like water that moved up to the lip of the cup and couldn't quite spill over.

K: You know, sir, I have been connected with many schools for forty years and more, and when one talks to the students about freedom and authority and acceptance they are completely lost.

A: Yes.

K: They want to be slaves: 'My father says this, so I must do this.' Or, 'My father says that, so I won't do that.' It is the same.

A: Exactly. Do you think in our next conversation we could look at that moment of hesitation?

K: Yes, sir.

A: It seems to me terribly critical for education itself.

27 February 1974

DIALOGUE XVI

Religion, Authority and Education – Part II

DR ANDERSON: It seems to me that we have reached in our series of conversations an especially critical place. In our last discussion we touched on the question of authority, not only in relation to what we project to be out there and what is actually out there, but also at the deeper level within oneself. And in going deeply into myself, in self-examination, there is a point of great hesitation where there is real fear and trembling. I think at the conclusion of our former conversation you were moving toward discussing the role of that hesitation in the religious life.

KRISHNAMURTI: Sir, why do we hesitate? That's what it comes down to, what you are saying. Why do we not take the plunge? Why is it always coming to the brink and withdrawing, running away? Why don't we see the thing as it is and act? Is it that part of our education has cultivated function, given tremendous importance to function – as an engineer, as a professor, as a doctor, and so on – functioning in a particular technique? And we have never cultivated or encouraged inquiry into what is intelligence? Where there is intelligence there won't be this hesitation: there is *action*. When one is very sensitive, you *act*: that sensitivity *is* intelligence. Now, education, as I have observed it both here and in India and other parts of the world, is merely training the mind to function to the dictates of society. So many engineers, so many doctors are wanted. And if you get into a profession where there are only a few you might make more money.

A: You watch out for the glut!

K: Yes, don't become a scientist, there are enough scientists, or whatever it is. So we are encouraged and trained to function in our careers. And now we hesitate to enter or plunge into something that demands not fragmentary attention but all our attention, because we don't have a measure. We know how to measure function: here we have no measure; therefore I depend, therefore here I won't reason because I don't know how to reason. To a man who says: 'I know,' I don't say: 'What do you know? You only know something that's gone, finished, dead. You can't say: I know something that's living'. And so gradually, as I see it, the mind becomes dull, restless, its curiosity is only in the direction of functioning. And it has no capacity to inquire. To inquire you must have freedom first. Otherwise I can't inquire. If I have prejudices I can't inquire. If I have conclusions about something I can't inquire into it. Therefore there must be freedom to inquire. And that is denied, because I've laid, society and culture have laid, tremendous importance on function; and function has its own status.

A: Yes, it's exalted ultimately.

K: So that status matters much more than function.

A: Yes.

K: And so I live in that field, in that structure, and if I want to inquire into religion, what is God, what is immortality, what is beauty – I can't do it. I depend on an authority. And I have no basis for reasoning – you follow, sir – in this vast field of religion. So it is partly the fault of our education, partly our incapacity to look at anything objectively, to look at a tree without all the rigmarole, knowledge, screen, blocks that prevent me from looking at the tree. I never look at my wife, if I have a wife, or girl-friend, or whatever, I never look. I look at her or him through the image I have about her or him. And the image is a dead thing. So I never look at a living thing. I never look at nature, with all the marvel, the beauty, the shape, the loveliness of it: but I am always translating it, trying to paint, write about or enjoy it, you follow?

A: Yes.

K: So from that arises the question, why do I, why do human beings accept authority? Why do they obey? Is it because they have been trained in the field of function where you must obey in order to learn, where you can't do anything else?

A: Yes, it has its own built-in laws.

K: It has its own disciplines, its own laws, its own ways. Because I have been trained that way I bring that over here into the field of religion, into the field of something that demands freedom. Freedom not at the end, but right from the beginning. The mind must be free from authority from the beginning. Say that I want to find out what God is, not I believe in God, that has no meaning, but whether there is God or no God. I really want to find out. I am terribly serious about this. And if I am really serious, if I am really concerned about understanding, learning about God, whether there is God, I must push aside completely all the beliefs, all the structure, all the churches, all the priests, all the books, all the things that thought has put together about religion. You follow?

A: Yes, I do. I've been thinking very hard about your word 'intelligence' and the word 'truth' in relation to what you have been saying. And two passages from St. John's Gospel came to my mind which would end up with a very different exegesis if one applied to them what you've been pointing to. 'When He, the spirit of truth is come He will guide you into all truth', and 'The truth shall make you free.' The truth is called a spirit here. And in the very same St. John's Gospel, God is also called spirit: radical act, not this spirit over there, out there somewhere that I have projected. The terrible thing is that this hasn't been taken seriously.

K: Because we are not allowed to be serious.

A: We can't even be serious about the thing that it is claimed we must be the most serious about!

K: That's just it. And, look, we are not serious about our children! We don't feel responsible for them, right through life; only till they are five or six; after that they can do what they want.

So freedom and authority cannot possibly exist together. Freedom and intelligence go together; and intelligence has its own innate, natural, easy discipline, discipline in the sense not of suppression, control, imitation and all that, but discipline which is the act of learning all the time.

A: In attention.

K: Yes, in attention.

A: This intelligence that you speak of is associated with splendour, isn't it? Its advent is immediate, not gradual.

K: Yes, of course. The perception *is* intelligence. And therefore acting.

A: Perception is the act.

K: Of course.

A: So the act, intelligence, beauty . . .

K: . . . all these . . .

A: . . . love, truth, freedom . . .

K: . . . death, all those are one.

A: . . . and order, they form a complete, total, integral movement in act.

K: That's right.

A: That once it's translated into a concept . . .

K: Oh, there is no longer that.

A: . . . becomes in itself an occasion for terror again.

K: Of course.

A: Because it seems that it runs away too fast from you.

K: Yes.

A: Isn't that marvellous. It's as though everything that you've mentioned, beauty, intelligence, love, freedom . . .

K: . . . and death.

A: . . . have, so to speak, secured themselves against all tomfoolery.

K: Absolutely, quite right.

A: They are so radically pure, secure from any foolery.

K: So that means can the mind put aside totally all the structure of thought with regard to religion? It can't put away the function of thought in the field of knowledge. That we have understood, that's very clear. But here there is something that I don't know, that we don't know. We pretend we know. When a man says: Jesus is the Saviour or whatever, it is a pretension. It is saying: 'I know and you don't know.' What do you know? In the name of heaven, you know nothing, you are just repeating what you have learned from somebody else! So can the mind put aside all the structure built around religion, because religion is, as we said at the beginning, the gathering of all energy in that quality of attention and it is that quality that regenerates, that brings about a real transformation of Man with regard to his conduct, his behaviour, his whole way of relationship, religion is that factor. Not all this foolery that is going on. So to inquire, the mind must put aside all the structure of thought built around that word. You follow, sir?

A: Yes I do.

K: Can one do it? If not, we are pretending, talking about God, whether we are saying there is no God or there is a God. All that nonsense that is going on. So that is the first question: can the mind be free of the authority of another, however great, however sublime, however divine or not divine?

A: And because an act is required in order to answer this question . . .

K: Absolutely.

A: . . . the individual must do this on his own.

K: Otherwise he continues merely to live in the routine of function and therefore he escapes into all these circuses which he calls religion.

A: This came home to me with great force yesterday in class. On the one hand we have textbooks which have survived the centuries because of their classical value. And the usual way in which this material is taught, is that one learns, let us say something about the Chinese vision of life, then about the Hindu vision of life and so we accumulate over a long period of time through school and then through graduate school, if you can stand it, and you come into possession of . . .

K: . . . what other people have said.

A: . . . what other people have said.

K: But you know nothing about it!

A: Exactly. You acquire certain skills in terms of function, as you have mentioned. Now the teacher has a problem. I am thinking of these schools that you have referred to in India and the one that will be in Ojai. There is a body of material here, clearly the teacher must be in possession of knowledge of a functional kind and so forth. And the child is going to read books in these schools that you mentioned.

K: Oh they do, they do.

A: And not all of these books have necessarily been written by somebody who is undertaking to do the sharing that goes on between the students and the teachers in these schools. Now the teacher must handle this written material in books in a way to indicate to both the younger student and the older student that it is possible to read this material without being self-divided in doing it.

K: And what would you do if there was no book?

A: You'd be in the same position.

K: No, if there were no book, nobody passing on tradition, you would have to find out for yourself.

A: But that's what we are asking him to do with his book, aren't we?

K: Are we?

A: No, not usually: but in this new approach we must somehow . . .

K: . . . bring the book and freedom together.

A: Bring the book and freedom together. Yes, this is what hit me with such a shock yesterday in class. And I immediately felt radically responsible for doing this, in so far as I could. And I was surprised to see that though the students were extremely hesitant – there was a lot of anxiety there, real fear and trembling – what they possessed of health did assert itself and there was tremendous interest in the possibility. But then there was the hesitation that somehow wasn't passed.

K: Quite.

A: The hesitation is there. I have this feeling that this has happened through the centuries with people who have seriously studied scripture – since we were talking about religion. Sometimes you can detect it in their very commentaries, in their very writing. They come right up to it . . .

K: . . . and miss it.

A: They can't go beyond that point.

K: Yes, sir. It has been my fortune or misfortune to talk to a great many people: and everybody comes to that point. They say: 'Please what am I to do, I've reached that point and I can't go beyond.' Sir, look at it this way, if I may suggest. If I had a class, I wouldn't talk about the book first but about freedom. I'd say: 'You're secondhand people, don't pretend you're not, you're secondhand, sloppy, shoddy people, and you are trying to find something that is original – God is, reality is original.' It's not coloured by all the priests in the world, it's original. Therefore you must have an original mind, which means a free mind. Not original in painting a new picture or a new this, that's all tommyrot. But a free mind. A free mind that can function in the field of knowledge and a free mind that can look, observe, learn. Now, how do you help another, or is it not possible to help another to be free? You understand? Look, I never belonged to anything. I have no church, no belief, all that. A man who really wants to find out if there is the eternal, the nameless, something beyond all thought, must naturally set aside everything based on thought: the saviour, the masters, the gurus, the knowledge, all that. Are there people to do that? Will anybody undertake that journey? Or will they say: 'You tell me all about it, old boy, I'll sit here comfortably, and you can tell me.'?

A: Yes, that's what goes on.

K: I say, 'I won't describe it. I won't tell you a thing about it. To put it into words is to destroy it. So, let us see if you can be free. What are you frightened about, frightened of authority, frightened of going wrong? But you are completely wrong in the way you live, completely stupid in the way you are carrying on, it has no meaning.' You follow, sir? 'Deny spiritual authority of every kind. What are you frightened of, going wrong spiritually? *They* are wrong, not *you* are wrong because you are just learning. *They* are the established in unrighteousness.'

A: That's beautiful. Yes.

K: So, 'Why do you follow them, why do you accept them? They are degenerate. And can you be free from all that, so that your mind through meditation finds out what it means to be free, what it means to wipe away all the things that people have put on you. So that you are innocent, your mind is never hurt, is incapable of being hurt. That is what innocence means. And from that inquire – let's take a journey from there – from this sense of negation of everything that thought has put together. Because thought is time, thought is matter. And if you are living in the field of thought, there will never be freedom. You are living in the past. You may think you are living in the present, but actually you are living in the past when thought is in operation, because thought is memory, the response of memory, knowledge, experience stored up in the brain. Unless you understand that and know the limitation of thought you can't enter into the field of that which you call religion.' You follow, sir? Unless this is told, repeated, shown to them, they can talk endlessly about books. This comes first: then you can read the books.

A: Yes.

K: Sir, the Buddha never read a book. He listened, watched, looked, observed, fasted; said, all that's rubbish, and threw it out.

A: I was just struck by something you said: one must keep on repeating this.

K: In different ways.

A: In different ways. I'm speaking now about teaching. This point of hesitation is the point where something will or will not get born.

K: That's right.

A: You used a beautiful expression in an earlier conversation: incarnate now.

K: Now, yes.

A: So we're on the brink. In the words of Ortega that I mentioned earlier, we're rocking back and forth on the brink of a new event; and we're not over the line. There is nothing that any of us can do at that point with respect to the terror of the person who hears this, including my own, I'm not setting myself apart from the student, since I'm a student too in this activity, a student among students. And there is this fear and trembling, and nothing can be done other than simply encourage . . .

K: . . . and tell them, wait, *stay there*. It doesn't matter if you wobble, but keep on wobbling.

A: Don't bolt.

K: Don't run away.

A: And so this is said in different ways over and over again. Now I understand what you meant by saying, let's start the class with ten minutes . . .

K: . . . of this.

A: . . . of this. We don't open the book, we start with this. And then when the book is opened perhaps the word, for a change, will disclose itself.

K: That's right.

A: Because intelligence has broken out.

K: That's right. You see, students rush from one class to the other; because the period is short they run from mathematics to geography, from geography to history, chemistry, biology, run, run. And if I was one of the teachers I would say: 'Look, sit down, be quiet for five minutes, be quiet. Look out of the window if you want to. See the beauty of light on the water or the leaf and look at this or that, but be quiet.'

A: We teach in classes that don't have windows now. That's a horror.

K: It is a horror. You are trained to be functional. Don't look at anything else but be monkeys. And my child is brought up that way. It is appalling.

A: The classroom is a tomb. Yes.

K: So, I say: 'Sit quietly.' Then after sitting quietly I talk about this first. I have done this in schools. Talk about this, freedom, authority, beauty, love, you know, all that we have been discussing. Then pick up your book. But you have learned much more here than in the book.

A: Oh, sure.

K: The book becomes a secondhand thing.

A: Yes. It's seen with a clean eye.

K: That's why, sir, I personally have never read a single book about all this, neither the Gita, the Upanishads, all that, nor what the Buddha has said. It somehow bored me – sorry – it meant nothing to me. What has meant something was to observe: observe the very poor in India, observe the rich, the dictators, the Mussolinis, the Hitlers, the Krushchevs, Brezhnevs, all that. I have watched the politicians. And you learn an awful lot. Because the real book is you. If you can read your book which is yourself you have learned everything, except the functional knowledge. So when there is self-knowing, authority has no meaning. I won't accept it. Why should I accept these people who 'bring truth' from India? They are not bringing truth, they are bringing a tradition, what they believe. So can the mind put away everything that man has taught or invented, imagined about religion, God, this and that? That means, can this mind, which is the mind of the world, which is the mind of common consciousness, can that consciousness empty itself of all the things that man has said about religion? Otherwise I can't . . .

A: . . . can't begin.

K: Not only begin, what do I discover? What other people have said? What Buddha, Christ have said, why should I accept that?

A: Well, the terrible thing is, I'm not in a position to grasp whatever they said that was worthwhile until this occurs.

K: So freedom, sir, is an absolute necessity.

A: Oh, yes, absolutely.

K: But none of them *say* this. On the contrary they say, 'Freedom will come to you much later. Be in the prison for the rest of your life and when you die you'll have freedom.' That's what they are preaching, essentially. So can the mind, the heart, and the whole storehouse in the brain be free of the things that man has said about religion? Sir, that's a marvellous question. You understand, sir?

A: Oh I do, I do. One of the things that seems to me of remarkable cogency in our conversations has been how continually you have returned to a question. The return has been presented as a movement to an answer. But that is not a return.

K: No, of course not.

A: No, because the return is toward that original that you mentioned. Therefore it is to the question, not to the answer at all.

K: Quite right, sir. You know I was staying once in Kashmir right among the mountains. And a group of monks came to see me, freshly bathed and everything, having done all their ceremonies, and all that. And they told me they had just come from a group of unworldly people, 'supermonks', who were very high up in the mountains. And they said they were totally unworldly. I said: 'What do you mean by that word, sirs?' They said: 'They have just left the world, they are no longer tempted by the world, they have this great knowledge of the world.' And I said: 'When they have left the world, have they left the memory of the world, the memory, the knowledge which the world has made, which the gurus have put together to teach us?' He said: 'That's wisdom. How can you leave wisdom?' I said: 'You mean wisdom is bought through a book, a teacher, from another, through sacrifice, torture, renunciation?' You follow, sir, their idea: wisdom is something you can buy from somebody else!

A: They went up the mountain with all this baggage.

K: Baggage, that's right. That's exactly what I said. You have put away all the baggage of the world, but you carry their baggage.

So that is really an important thing if a mind is really very serious to find out what religion means. Not all this rubbish. I keep on repeating this because the rubbish seems to be mounting. But to free the mind from all the growth, accretions and which therefore means: see the accretions, see all the absurdities.

A: This throws a very different cast on our word 'worldly'.

K: Yes, that's just it.

A: They are going up the mountain in order to leave the world, but they are taking immense pains to take it with them.

K: That's right and that's what they are doing when they go into the monastery.

A: Of course, accretions, incrustations.

K: So now, come back: can the mind be completely alone? Not isolated, not withdrawn, not build a wall around itself, but say: I'm alone. But alone in the sense of the aloneness that comes when you put away all this, all the things of thought. Because thought is so clever, cunning. It can build a marvellous structure and call that reality. But thought is the response of the past, so it is of time. Thought being of time, it cannot create something which has no time. Thought can function in that field of knowledge. It is necessary, but not in the other. And this doesn't need bravery, it doesn't need sacrifice, it doesn't need torture: just perception of the false. To see the false is to see the truth in the false.

A: To see the false is to see the truth in the false.

K: Of course. And see what is considered truth as the false.

A: Yes, yes.

K: So my eyes are stripped of all the false, so that there is no inward deception whatsoever because there is no desire to see something, to achieve something. Because the moment there is a desire to experience, to achieve, to arrive at enlightenment and all that, there is going to be illusion, something that desire has created. Therefore the mind must be free of this pursuit of desire and its fulfilment, which we discussed previously. Understand what the structure of desire is. We talked a great deal about that. So it comes to this point: can the mind be free and free of all the things which are born of fear, and of desire and pleasure? That means one has to understand oneself at great depth.

A: The thing that keeps popping up is that one can repeat those questions . . .

K: Yes, sir.

A: . . . and start to think that he has grasped them.

K: You grasp the words.

A: Exactly. There is something you have to come out the other side of.

K: Quite right.

A: But the repetition of the question does have a functional value.

K: Yes, sir, it does. That is if the person is willing to listen.

A: If he is willing to listen, because thought is incredibly deceitful.

K: Very.

A: As you have pointed out. I was just thinking of poor old Jeremiah's words: 'The heart is desperately wicked and deceitful above all things.' Surely he must have . . .

K: . . . tasted something.

Sir, I think that after coming to this point we ought to go very deeply into the question of meditation.

A: Yes.

K: Because religion, in the sense that we are talking about, and meditation go together. That means religion isn't just an idea but is actual conduct in daily life. Your thoughts, your speech, your behaviour are the very essence of religion. If they are not, religion can't exist.

A: Exactly.

K: It's just words, you can go around spinning a lot of words, go to various circus tents. But that's not religion. So after establishing that deeply in oneself, and understanding inwardly what religion is, the next thing is: what is meditation? That is of tremendous importance, because meditation is something which, if it is understood properly, is really the most extraordinary thing that man can have. Meditation is not divorced from daily life.

A: If I'm not mistaken, the root of the word goes back to *medesthai, medeo.*

K: *Medeo* meaning to think, to ponder, to go into.

A: In Homer, it actually carries the beautiful idea of providing for in the sense of to care for, which brings up the question that you raised earlier of true care: that one is not meditating unless one is careful and caring.

K: Caring rather than careful.

A: Yes, it's all there in the word, but we don't see it.

K: You see when we have divorced conduct from religion, which we have, divorced relationship from religion, which we have, divorced death from religion, which we have, divorced love from religion, when we have made love into something sensuous, something that is pleasurable, then religion, which is the factor of regeneration, disappears in Man. And that's why we are so degenerate. Unless you have this quality of a mind that is really religious, degeneracy is inevitable.

Look at the politicians who are supposed to be the rulers, the guides, the helpers of the people: they are degenerate. You see what is happening in this country and everywhere. They are so corrupt:

and they want to bring order. They are so irreligious, they may go to church or a temple or whatever, and yet they are really irreligious, because they don't behave religiously. And so man is becoming more and more degenerate. Because religion is the factor that brings a new quality of energy. It is the same old energy but it has taken on a new quality. Otherwise the brain doesn't regenerate and as we get older we tend to degenerate. But it won't if there is freedom from every kind of security of the 'me'.

A: I noticed this in class yesterday with regard to the energy that you are talking about. A quickening took place at the end of the class and it was strenuous because of this terrible hesitation. But even so there was a release of energy which had nothing to do with entertainment at all, there was an empirical demonstration of what you are saying. Something that is out there, it's to be seen, it's observable.

K: You see, sir, that's why the priests throughout the world have made religion into something profitable, both for the worshipper and the intermediary. It has become a business affair, intellectual business, or it has become really commercial, not only physically but inwardly, deeply: do this and you will reach that.

A: Utilitarian to the core.

K: Which is commercial.

A: Yes.

K: And so unless this is put an end to we are going to degenerate more and more and more. And that's why, personally, I feel so immensely responsible, tremendously responsible to the audience that I talk to. When I go to the various schools in India, I feel I am responsible for those children. You follow, sir?

A: Yes, I certainly do.

K: I say: 'For God's sake, be different, don't grow up like that, look!' I go into it very deeply, talk a great deal. And they begin to see: but the world is too strong for them. They have to earn a livelihood, they have to resist their parents who want them to settle down and have a good job and marry, a house. You know, all that business. And public opinion is much too strong.

A: The tremendous weight of that tradition of the four stages of life.

K: So I say, let us find out if a few, an élite – in quotes the word 'élite', if I may use that word without any snobbery – let's create a few who really are concerned, a few teachers, a few students. Even that becomes very difficult because most teachers are not good at other things and therefore become teachers.

A: Oh dear, yes.

K: So everything is against you. Everything. The gurus are against you, the priests are against you, the businessmen, the teachers, the politicians, everybody is against you. Take that for granted. They won't help you an inch. They want you to go their way. They've got their vested interests and all that.

A: Yes, I see that very clearly. In our next conversation do you think we could explore the activity of meditation within the context of all this horror that we have described?

K: Yes, sir, we will.

27 February 1974

DIALOGUE XVII

Meditation, a Quality of Attention that Pervades All of One's Life

DR ANDERSON: At the end of our last conversation we came almost to the point where we were about to begin another, on the subject of meditation.

KRISHNAMURTI: Sir, I don't know if you are aware of the many schools of meditation, for example in India, in Japan, in China, Zen, and the various Christian contemplative orders, those who pray endlessly, keep going on day after day, and those who wait to receive the grace of God – or whatever they call it. I think, if I may suggest, we should begin, not with what is the right kind of meditation, but what is meditation.

A: Yes.

K: Then we can proceed and investigate together and share together this question of what is meditation. The word itself means to ponder, hold together, embrace, consider very, very deeply; all those meanings are involved in that one word 'meditation'. But could we start by saying that we really do not know what meditation is.

A: Very well.

K: If we accept the orthodox, traditional Christian, Hindu or Buddhist meditation, and there is also, of course, the Sufi meditation among the Muslims, if we accept that, then it is all based on tradition.

A: Yes.

K: What some others have experienced and they lay down the method or the system to practise what they have achieved. So there are probably thousands of schools of meditation and they are proliferating in this country: meditate three times a day; think on a word, a slogan, a mantra. And for that you pay thirty-five or a hundred dollars and get some Sanskrit or Greek word and you repeat, repeat, repeat. Then there are all the people who practise various forms of breathing or who practise Zen. And all that is a form of establishing a routine and a practice that will essentially make the mind dull. Because if you practise, practise, practise, you will become a mechanical mind. So I have never done any of those things, because personally, if I may talk a little about myself, I have watched, attended groups of various kinds just to look. And I said: 'This isn't it.' I discarded it instantly. So if we could discard all that: the Hindu, the Buddhist, the Christian, and the various importations of meditation by the gurus from India, and the contemplative practices, all that as a continuance of a tradition which is the carrying over of what others have said, others' experiences, others' enlightenment, and so on. If we could totally discard all that, their methods, their systems, their practices, their disciplines. Because they are all saying, truth, or God, or whatever they like to call it, is something *over there*. You practise in order to *get there*. That is a fixed thing – according to them. Of course, it must be fixed. If I keep practising in order to get there, that must be static.

A: Yes, of course.

K: But truth isn't static. It isn't a dead thing.

A: No, I quite see that.

K: So, if we could honestly put away all that and ask: What is meditation?

A: Good.

K: Not how to meditate. In asking that question: what is meditation, we'll begin to find out, begin to meditate ourselves. I don't know if I make myself clear.

A: Yes, we're back again to the distinction between an activity the goal of which lies outside the activity, in contrast to the activity the end of which is intrinsic to itself.

K: Yes, sir. So, could we start with saying I do not know what meditation is?

A: Yes, I'm willing to start there.

K: It's really marvellous if you start from there, it brings a great sense of humility.

A: Also one intuits even from afar a freedom.

K: Yes, that's right. To say: 'I don't know' is a tremendous acknowledgment of freedom from the established known, the established traditions, the established methods, the established schools and practices.

A: Exactly.

K: I start with something I don't know. That, for me, has great beauty. Then I am free to move.

A: Exactly.

K: I'm free to flow or swim with the inquiry. So, I don't know. Then from that we can start. First of all, is meditation divorced from daily living? From daily conduct, the daily desires of fulfilment, ambition, greed, envy, the daily competitive, imitative, conforming spirit, the daily appetites, sensuous, sexual, other forms, intellectual appetite and so on? Is meditation divorced from all that? Or does meditation flow through all that, cover all that, include all that? Otherwise meditation has no meaning. You follow?

A: Yes, I do. This raises an interesting question I'd like to ask you. I've never personally undertaken meditation of the ritual character it has in some traditions or the monastic and radically methodical approach. I've read rather deeply in the literatures that have emanated from those practices and I'm thinking for instance of what I've understood from my study of what is called the Hesychast tradition, where what is called the Jesus prayer is uttered by the monks, particularly on Mount Athos, 'Lord, Jesus Christ, have mercy upon me a sinner.' This is repeated over and over with the hope that someday it will become so automatic that, as a modern-day depth psychologist might say, the unconscious comes into possession of it, so that whatever I am doing is focused entirely on that prayer. The claim being that when this is achieved, when I no longer have to utter the prayer in the ordinary sense, the prayer is uttering itself in me.

K: The same thing, sir, is expressed in India in a different way, through mantram. Repetition of a sentence or a word, and the repeating loudly first, then silently. Then it has entered into your being and the very sound of it is going on and from that sound you act, you live. But it's all self-imposed in order to arrive at a certain point. For instance in the prayer which you just repeated, you referred to sin — I don't accept sin. I don't know what sin is.

A: I can imagine the horror on the faces of some whose ears catch those words!

K: Which means they are conditioned to a belief that there is a Jesus, that there is sin, that they must be forgiven — all that is just carrying on a tradition.

A: This speaks to me very personally. The basis for the decision that I made years ago not to do any of these things was embodied in your statement a little earlier that it is expected that out of these words . . .

K: . . . out of breathing, all that.

A: . . . will somehow come this permeation of my total being. And the question that arose in my mind was that that statement itself, whether the mantram or the Jesus prayer, is a finite expression.

K: Absolutely.

A: Therefore, aren't I doing something strange here?

K: Yes.

A: And if I somehow attain to anything that's worth attaining to, it would probably be in spite of that rather than because of it.

K: Quite.

A: And therefore I simply wouldn't go ahead.

K: Quite right, sir. You see all that implies that there is a path to truth — the Christian path, the Hindu path, the Zen, the various gurus and systems, there is a path to enlightenment or to truth or to that immeasurable something or other. And it is there, all you have to do is keep on walking, walking, walking towards it. That means that thing is established, fixed, static, is not moving, is not living.

A: There flashes into my mind here the Blblical text in which God is described as the lamp unto my feet and the light unto my path. It doesn't say he is the path. But rather he is the lamp . . .

K: . . . to the path, quite.

A: Right. As a lamp to the feet and a light to the path. But it doesn't say that God is the path. That's very interesting.

K: Very.

A: But maybe nobody really looks at those words closely enough.

K: You see, sir, how you are looking at it already. You see the truth of that statement, the feeling of it.

A: Yes, yes.

K: So, that's one thing. Does meditation cover the whole field of existence? Or is it something totally apart from life? Life being business, politics, sex, pleasure, ambition, greed, envy, anxiety, death, fear, all that is my life, life, living. Is meditation apart from that or does it embrace all that? If it doesn't embrace all that, meditation has no meaning.

A: Something just came to me that I'm sure would be regarded as very heretical. But the words of Jesus himself: 'I am the way, the truth, and the life', when understood in the context of what has been revealed through these discussions, takes on, in relation to something else he said, an incredibly different meaning from what we've been taught. For instance, when he asks Peter who he is: 'Who am I, Jesus?', and Peter says: 'Thou art the Christ, the son of the living God', he immediately turns to him and says: 'Flesh and blood has not revealed this to you.' Not flesh and blood: 'But my Father which is in heaven', which he says, elsewhere, is One with him. And he's One with the Father. And then he prays that the disciples be One with him as he and his Father are One. That they all may be One. I'm aware that what I am about to say would, theologically speaking, be looked on as fantastical but when he says: 'I am the way, the truth and the life', if it's seen in the context of that One as act, then the whole business is utterly transformed.

K: Quite.

A: I'm going to be swallowing hard about that for a long time.

K: So if meditation is divorced from life then meditation has no meaning. It's just an escape from life, escape from all our travail and miseries, sorrows, confusions; and therefore it's not even worth touching.

A: Right.

K: If it is not, and it is not for me, then what is meditation? Is it an achievement, an attainment of a goal? Or is it a perfume, a beauty that pervades all my activities and therefore it has tremendous significance? Meditation *has* tremendous significance.

Then the next question is: is it the result of a search? Joining a Zen group, then another group, one after the other, practise this, practise that, don't practise, take a vow of celibacy, poverty, or don't speak at all, fast, in order to *get there*. For me all those are totally unnecessary. Because what is important is seeing, as we said yesterday, the false, not I judge the false as true or false, but the very perception reveals the truth or the falseness of it. I must look at it, my eyes must look at it without any prejudices, without any reactions. Then I can say this is false, I won't touch it. That's what happens. I won't. People have come to me and said: 'Oh, you have no idea of all the things one can do', they have said: 'You must do this or that', I have said: 'Nothing doing.' To me this is false because it doesn't include your life.

A: Yes.

K: You haven't changed. You may say: 'I'm full of love, I'm full of truth, I'm full of knowledge, I'm full of wisdom.' I say: 'That's all nonsense. Do you behave? Are you free of fear? Are you free of ambition, greed, envy and the desire to achieve success in every field? If not, you are just playing a game. You are not serious.' So, from that we can proceed.

A: Yes.

K: Meditation includes the whole field of existence, whether in the artistic or the business field. Because, to me, the division as the artist, the businessman, the politician, the priest, the scholar, and the scientist, the way we have fragmented all these as careers is the expression of the fragmentation of human beings.

A: Yes, yes, I'm thinking of what goes on in the university with respect to this. We are always saying to each other: 'For heaven's sake let's find an ordering principle by which to bring all this into some kind of integration so the student can really feel that he's doing something meaningful, not just adding another freight car to the long train of what he hasn't even seen.'

K: Quite. And meditation must be, or is, when you deny all this – systems, methods, gurus, authorities – a religious question.

A: Yes, profoundly religious.

K: Profoundly religious. Now, what place has an artist not only in the social structure but in the expression of the religious? You understand? What is an artist? Is he something apart from our daily living, the beauty of living, the quality of the mind that is really religious? You follow? Is he part of that? Or is he a freak, outside that? Because he has certain talents? And the expression of those talents becomes extraordinarily important to him and to people.

A: In our culture it often seems that the expression of that talent brings him into conflict with certain conventions.

K: And it also expresses that conflict in himself.

A: Of course. Yes, we have a long tradition in Western civilization of the artist as an outsider.

K: Yes, something outside. But he is much more sensitive, much more alert to beauty, to Nature, but apart from that he is just an ordinary man.

A: Yes, of course.

K: To me, that is a contradiction. First be a total human being and then whatever you create, whatever you do will be beautiful.

A: Of course.

K: Whether you paint or whatever you do. Don't let us divide the artist into something extraordinary or the businessman into something ugly. Let's call it just living in the world of the intellect or the scientist in the world of physics, and so on. But first there must be human being. You follow, sir? Human being in the sense, the total understanding of life, death, love, beauty, relationship, responsibility, not to kill. All that's implied in living, which establishes a relationship with Nature. And the expression of that relationship, if it is whole, healthy, is creative.

A: This is very, very different from what many artists conceive of as their task. Especially in modern times artists have the notion that they are in some sense reflectors of the fragmentation of their times.

K: Absolutely.

A: And so they make a statement which holds up the fragmentation as a mirror to us, and what this does is simply reinforce the fragmentation!

K: Absolutely.

A: Yes, I quite understand what you are saying.

K: You see, meditation covers the whole field of existence. Meditation implies freedom from the method, the system; because I don't know what meditation is, I start from that.

A: Yes.

K: Therefore I start with freedom, not with their burden.

A: That's marvellous. Start with freedom and not with their burden. This business of holding up fragmentation to us from that perspective is really nothing more than a species of journalism.

K: Journalism, absolutely. Propaganda.

A: Of course, yes.

K: Therefore, a lie. So I discard all that. So I have no burden. Therefore the mind is free to inquire: What is meditation?

A: Marvellous.

K: I have done this. You follow, sir? These are not verbal expressions. I don't say anything which I haven't lived.

A: That's very obvious to me as one sitting here conversing with you.

K: I won't. That is hypocrisy, I am not interested in all that. I'm really interested in seeing what is meditation. One starts with this freedom. And freedom means freeing the mind, emptying itself of the burdens of others, their methods, their systems, their acceptance of authority, their beliefs, their hopes, because all that is part of me. Therefore I discard all that. And now I start by saying, 'I don't know what meditation is.' That means the mind is free, has this sense of great humility. Not knowing and I'm not asking – then somebody else will fill it.

A: Exactly.

K: Some book, some scholar, some professor, some psychologist will come along and say: 'You don't know. Here, I know. I'll give it to you.' I say: 'Please don't. I know nothing. You know nothing either. Because you are repeating what others have said.' So I discard all that. Now I begin to inquire. I'm in a position to inquire. Not to achieve a result, not to arrive at what they call enlightenment, or anything. I don't know if there is enlightenment or not. I start with this feeling of great humility – not knowing – therefore my mind, the mind is capable of real inquiry. So I inquire. First of all I look at my life, because I said in the beginning meditation implies covering the whole field of life. My life, our life, is first the daily conscious living. I've examined, I've looked at it. There is contradiction and so on – we've talked about that. And also there is the question of sleep. I go to sleep for eight, nine, ten hours. What is sleep? I start not knowing. Not accepting what others have said. You follow, sir?

A: Yes, I do.

K: I'm inquiring in relation to meditation which is the real spirit of religion. That is: gathering all the energy to move from one dimension to a totally different dimension; which doesn't mean divorce from this dimension. So what is sleep? And what is waking? Am I awake? Or, I am only awake when there is a crisis, when there is a shock, when there is a challenge, when there is an incident, death, discord, failure. You follow? Or am I awake all the time, throughout the day? So what is it to be awake? You follow, sir?

A: Yes, I do. Since you are saying that meditation must permeate, obviously to be awake cannot be episodic.

K: That's it, cannot be episodic, cannot be something stimulated.

A: Cannot be described as peak experiences.

K: No. Any form of stimulation, external or internal only implies that you are asleep and you need a stimulant, whether it is coffee, sex or a tranquillizer. All to keep you awake.

A: Have a shot to go to sleep and have a shot to wake up.

K: So in my inquiry I am asking, am I awake? What does it mean to be awake? Not awake to what is happening politically, economically, socially, that is obvious. But awake. What does it mean? I am not awake if I have any burden. There is no sense of being awake when there is any kind of fear. If I live with an illusion, if my actions are neurotic, there is no state of being awake. So I'm inquiring and I can only inquire by becoming very sensitive to what is happening in me, outside me. So is the mind aware completely during the day of what is happening inside and outside me?

A: Upon every instant.

K: That's it, otherwise I am not awake.

A: At home we have some birds and also a cat. The birds don't run around in the room with the cat, but when the birds are put to bed in the evening the cat goes into the room and stays with them, maybe an hour or two, and watches. Just seems to have the feeling that it must look after the birds. And in the daytime, I've often watched the cat sit and look at the birds with an immense intensity and the ordinary reaction is: 'Well, for heaven's sake, haven't you seen them before? What is this everlasting intensity?' But she's looking.

K: That's right, sir.

A: And her eyes always have that jewel-like . . .

K: . . . clarity.

A: . . . intensity and clarity, cleaner than flame. And it never stops. And when she sleeps, she really sleeps. When you asked me what is sleep, there must be a relation between the cat's ability completely to sleep and to be completely awake.

K: That's right, sir. So in asking and inquiring what is sleep, I must also ask what it is to be awake.

A: Of course.

K: Am I awake or is the past so alive that it is dictating my life in the present? Therefore I am asleep.

A: Would you say that again? That's very important.

K: I'll put it differently. Am I awake? Is my mind burdened with the past? And therefore bearing a burden, I'm not awake in the present.

A: Not awake in the present, exactly.

K: Not awake as I am talking.

A: That's right.

K: Because I'm talking from the background of my past, of my experience, of my failures, my hurts, my depressions, therefore the past is dominating and putting me to sleep now.

A: It's a narcotic.

K: A narcotic. Therefore what am I to do with the past? You follow, sir?

A: Yes, I do.

K: The past is necessary.

A: Of course, yes, the whole field of knowledge.

K: Knowledge. The past is necessary. But when the past covers the present, then I am asleep. So is it possible to know what the past is and not let it overflow into the present? That question and the reality of it brings its own discipline. Therefore I say, yes, I know what it means. I can live, I can keep awake totally and widely and yet operate in the field of knowledge. So there is no contradiction. I don't know if I am conveying this?

A: Oh, you are.

K: So both are moving in harmony. One doesn't lag behind the other, one doesn't contradict the other. There's balance.

A: Well, what I am seeing here, if I am following correctly, is on the one hand we have knowledge and the grasp of its necessity with respect to know-how in practical affairs . . .

K: Of course.

A: . . . on the other hand we have seeing, understanding. And the act of meditation is the nexus between them so that there is no interruption of flow in the activity . . .

K: That's right.

A: . . . of understanding and knowing.

K: That is part of meditation.

A: Of course.

K: See what is taking place. Then what is sleep? I have understood now what it means to be awake. That means I am watching. I am aware. I am aware without any choice, choiceless awareness, watching, looking, observing, hearing, what is going on and what is going on outside, what people tell me, whether they flatter me or they insult me. I am watching. So I am very aware. Now, what is sleep? I know what is sleep: resting, shutting your eyes, going to bed at nine or ten or later. What is sleep? And in sleep, dreams. What are dreams? I don't know what the others say, I am not interested in what the others say. You follow, sir? Because my inquiry is to find out whether meditation covers the whole field of life, not just one segment.

A: Again my inquiry is from the point where I say I don't know.

K: That is right. So I'll proceed. I dream. Why should I dream? So I have to find out why I dream. What are dreams? Dreams are the continuation of my daily sleep. Which is, I haven't understood – see what is taking place, sir – I have not understood my daily life. I watch my daily life. My daily life is in disorder; so I go to sleep and the disorder continues; and the brain says, I must have order otherwise I can't function. So if the mind doesn't put order during the day, the brain tries to bring order during the night.

A: Through the dream.

K: Through dreams, through intimations. When I awake I say, yes I have a certain feeling this must be done. So see what takes place. When the mind is awake during the day it has order, it establishes order, in the sense we have discussed previously, order which comes out of the understanding of disorder. The negation of disorder is order, not the following of a blueprint or a pattern, all that's disorder. So during the day, the mind, the brain has established order. So when I sleep the brain isn't working out how to establish order in itself in order to be secure. Therefore the brain becomes rested.

A: I see.

K: Therefore the brain becomes quiet, sleeps without dreams. It may have superficial dreams when you eat wrongly, all that kind of thing. But I am not talking about that. So sleep means regeneration of the brain.

A: I wonder if I could ask you a question about dreams here, that might introduce a distinction between dreams in terms of their nature. Sometimes we report that we've had a dream which points to a future event.

K: That's another thing.

A: That's entirely different from what you are talking about.

K: Yes.

A: So we could say that . . .

K: Sir, I think we can understand that very simply. The other day we were walking high up in the hills in India and there was a river flowing down below. And two boats were coming in opposite directions and you knew where they were going to meet.

A: Of course.

K: When you go high enough you see the boats coming together at a precise point.

A: But that's very objective. That has nothing to do with my subjective, unfinished business.

K: No.

A: Which is the other thing you were talking about.

K: That's right.

A: Yes, I quite see. What an amazing thing it would be to have all your business done and go to sleep. And if order should present you with . . .

K: Yes, sir.

A: . . . an understanding.

K: Of course.

A: Then the understanding never stops from waking through sleeping.

K: That's right.

A: Yes. Of course, marvellous.

K: So you see, that way the brain is regenerated, keeps young, with no conflict. Conflict wears out the brain.

A: Yes.

K: So sleep means not only order, rejuvenation, innocence, but also in sleep there are states in which there is absolute freedom to inquire, to see into something which you have never seen with your eyes, physical eyes.

A: Yes.

K: So we have described that, I see that. So do I, does the mind, live that kind of life during the day?

A: That would be rare.

K: Otherwise it is not meditation.

A: Otherwise it is not meditation, of course.

K: And I don't want to play a game, a hypocritical game, because I am deceiving nobody. I am deceiving myself and I don't want to deceive myself. I don't see the point of deceiving myself because I don't want to be a great man, a big success and so on. That's all too infantile. So I say, am I living that? If not, what is happening? And it gives me energy to live that way because I have no burden of the others.

A: This reminds me of a story that is told about a swordsman and his three sons in old Japan. The swordsman was getting old and he wanted to pass on the responsibility for his art to his sons so he asked the sons each to come into his room and he would speak to them. He was a man of knowledge in terms of the sword but he also was a man of understanding. And unbeknownst to them he put a ball on top of the lintel above the door. The youngest was called in first and when the ball dropped, the son, in a flash, cut it in two with his sword as it fell. And his father said: 'Please wait in the other room.' The second son came in, the ball fell down but precisely as it touched his head he reached up and took it in his hands. And the father said: 'Please wait in the other room.' Then the eldest son came in and as he opened the door he reached up and took the ball. And the father called them in, and he read out the youngest son. He said: 'Very brilliant. You've mastered the technique, but you don't understand anything.' He said to the second one: 'Well, you're almost there. Just keep on, keep on.' And to the eldest son he said: 'Well, now you can begin.' It's like the word 'prajna' which means 'pra' – ahead, 'jna' – to know, to know beforehand in the sense not of some work of prediction that we do based on the study of rats in the lab or something but understanding is ahead and behind in the total movement of that one act.

K: Yes, sir. So I see this, because I do not separate meditation from daily living. Otherwise it has no meaning. So I see the importance of order during the waking hours. And therefore freeing the mind, the brain from conflict, all that, during sleep, so there is total rest for the brain. That's one thing. Then, what is control? Why should I control? They have all said 'control'. All religions have said 'control'. Control, be without desire, don't think about yourself. You follow? All that. I say to myself: 'Can I live without control?' You follow, sir?

A: Oh yes, one has to start that question too at the very beginning.

K: I am doing it, that's what we are doing.

A: Yes, my statement is a reflection, just a mirror to that.

K: Is it possible to live without control? Because what is control? And who is the controller? The controller *is* the controlled. When I say I must control my thought, the controller is the creation of thought. And thought controls thought. It has no meaning. One fragment controls another fragment, and they therefore remain fragments. So I say, is there a way of living without control? Therefore no conflict, no opposites. Not one desire against another desire, one thought opposed to another thought, one achievement opposed to another achievement. So, no control. Is that possible? Because I must find out. You follow, sir? It's not just asking a question, then just leaving it alone. I've got energy now because I am not carrying their burden anymore. Nor am I carrying my own burden, because their burden is my burden. When I have discarded that I have discarded this. So I have got energy when I say: 'Is it possible to live without control?' And it is a tremendous thing, I must find out. Because the people who have control, they have said through control you arrive at Nirvana, heaven – to me that's wrong, totally absurd. So I say: 'Can I live a life of meditation in which there is no control?'

A: When intelligence breaks out, as we saw before, then with it comes order and that order ...

K: That's it. Intelligence is order.

A: And intelligence is that order, the seeing is the doing.

K: The doing, yes.

A: Therefore there is no conflict at all.

K: So do I live a life without control, not only is it possible, do I live it? I've got desires: I see a car, a woman, a house, a lovely garden, beautiful clothes, or whatever it is, and instantly all the desires arise. And not to have a conflict. And yet not yield. If I have the money I go and buy it. Which is obvious. That's no answer. If I have no money I say: 'Well, I'm sorry, I have no money, and I will get some sometime. Then I'll come back and buy it.' It's the same problem. But desire is aroused. The seeing, contact, sensation and desire. Now that desire is there, to cut it off is to suppress it. To control it is to suppress it. To yield to it is another form of fragmenting life into getting and losing. I don't know if I am conveying this?

A: Yes, yes.

K: So to allow for the flowering of desire without control. You understand, sir?

A: Yes, I do.

K: So the very flowering is the ending of that desire. But if you chop it off, it'll come back again. I don't know if this is clear?

A: Yes, it's the difference between a terminus and a consummation.

K: Quite, yes. So I let the desire come, flower, watch it. Watch it, not yield or resist. Just let it flower, and be fully aware of what is happening. Then there is no control.

A: And no disorder.

K: No, of course. The moment you control there is disorder. Because you are suppressing or accepting — you know, all the rest of it. So that is disorder. But when you allow the thing to flower and watch it, watch it in the sense be totally aware of it – the petals, the subtle forms of desire to possess, not to possess, to possess is a pleasure, not to possess is a pleasure, you follow? – the whole of that movement of desire.

A: Exactly.

K: And for that you have to have very sensitive watchfulness, very sensitive, choiceless watching.

A: This image of the plant that you have referred to metaphorically, could we pursue that in our next conversation and look further into meditation?

K: We haven't finished meditation, there's lots more involved.

A: Good, good.

28 February 1974

DIALOGUE XVIII

Meditation and the Sacred Mind

DR ANDERSON: Mr Krishnamurti, in our last conversation we discussed meditation. And just as we concluded you brought up the very beautiful analogy of the flowering of a plant, and it struck me that the order intrinsic to the plant as it flowers is revelatory of the order that you have been discussing. And we were talking also about the relation of meditation to understanding on the one hand and to knowledge on the other, a distinction that's very rarely made.

KRISHNAMURTI: Yes.

A: Though in ordinary language we make the distinction perhaps unwittingly. It's there, we have the two words.

K: Quite.

A: But then to go into what the distinction is was something you were beginning to do. So perhaps . . .

K: We could go on from there. Sir, we were talking about control and we said the controller is the controlled; and we went into that sufficiently. When there is control there is direction. Direction implies will, control implies will. And in the desire to control there is established a goal and a direction: which means to carry out the decision made by will, and the carrying out is the duration of time; and therefore direction means time, control, will, and an end. All that's implied in the word 'control'.

A: Yes.

K: So what place has will in meditation and therefore in life? Or it has no place at all? That means there is no place for decision at all. Only seeing, doing. And that doesn't demand will or direction. You follow?

A: Yes, I do.

K: See the beauty of this, sir, how it works out: when the mind sees the futility of control because it has understood that the controller is the controlled, one fragment trying to dominate other fragments, and the dominant fragment is a part of other fragments, and therefore it is like going around in circles, a vicious circle, never getting out of it. So can there be living without control? Just listen to it, sir. Without will, and without direction? There must be direction in the field of knowledge, agreed. Otherwise I couldn't get home, to the place I live. I would lose the capacity to drive a car, ride a cycle, speak a language, to do all the technological things necessary in life. There, direction, calculation, decision in that field is necessary. Choice is necessary between this and that. Here, where there is choice there is confusion, because there is no perception. Where there is perception there is no choice. Choice exists because the mind is confused between this and that. So can a life be led without control, without will, without direction that means time? And that is meditation. Not just a question, an interesting, perhaps a stimulating question: a question however stimulating has no meaning by itself; it has a meaning in living.

A: I was thinking about ordinary usage again, as you were speaking. It's interesting that when somebody has performed an action that we call wilful we regard this as an action undertaken without understanding.

K: Of course.

A: So in the very distinction between will as a word and wilful as an adjective, we have a hint of this distinction. But I'd like to ask you, if I may, about the relationship of will; even though we are talking about meditation, we did consider that knowledge, in its own right, has a proper career.

K: Of course.

A: And we say that decision is referred to that, choice is referred to that and therefore will is operative there.

K: And a direction and everything.

A: And a direction and so on. And so we are making a distinction here between will and its role in relation to the whole field of what we loosely call know-how.

K: Know-how, knowledge.

A: Yes. And the confusion that occurs when that activity, so necessary in its own right, is brought over into this.

K: That's right.

A: And then we can't do either of them, really.

K: That's just it, therefore we become inefficient.

A: Yes.

K: Personal.

A: But you see we don't think that. What we think is that we can be terribly efficient in knowledge and be what is called unspiritual. And be a success here and not be a success there. Whereas, if I understand you correctly, you don't fail in one or the other, you just fail – period. There is a total failure if this confusion is made. You simply can't even operate well here no matter what it might look like in the short run.

K: As long as you are not completely in order inside yourself.

A: Right. Exactly. So the very division that we make between inner and outer is itself a symptom of this terrible . . .

K: . . . a symptom of thought which has divided the outer and the inner.

A: Yes, I hope you'll bear with me in going through that because I know in religious thought, my academic discipline, this confusion, well, the weight of it.

K: Yes, I know, you are quite right.

A: You feel . . .

K: . . . oppressed.

A: And as soon as you begin to make a comment of any kind about it that is simply raising the question, the extreme rigidity and nervousness that occurs is dramatic.

K: Quite. So meditation covers the whole field of living, not one segment of it. Therefore living a life without control, without the action of will, decision, direction, achievement. Is that possible? If it is not possible it is not meditation. Therefore life becomes superficial, meaningless. And to escape from that meaningless life we chase all the gurus, the religious entertainment, circuses, you follow? All the practices of meditation. It has no meaning.

A: In the classical tradition we have a definition of will. We say that it's desire made reasonable.

K: Desire made reasonable.

A: Desire made reasonable. Now, of course, we've long since lost the idea of what the ancients meant, against their contemplative background, by the word 'reason'. We think it means calculation. But of course that's not what the classical tradition means when it says reasonable. It points rather to that order which isn't defined. And it occurs to me that if we understood that statement correctly we'd be saying will is the focus of desire without my focusing self-consciously.

K: Yes, that's right. And watching desire flower.

A: Yes.

K: And therefore watching the will in operation and letting it flower and as it flowers, as you are watching, it dies, it withers away. After all, it's like a flower: you allow it to bloom and it withers.

A: It comes to be and passes away in its own time.

K: Therefore if you are choicelessly aware of this movement of desire, control, will, focusing that will in action, and so on, let it flower, watch it. And as you watch it you will see how it loses its vitality. So there is no control. So from that arises the next question which is: can there be space with a direction?

A: Yes, of course.

K: It's very interesting. What is space? Space which thought has created is one thing. Space that exists in heaven, in our universe. There must be space for a mountain to exist, for a tree to grow, for a flower to bloom. So what is space? And have we space? Or are we all so limited physically to living in a little apartment, a little house, no space at all outwardly, and therefore having no space we become more and more violent.

A: Yes.

K: I don't know if you have watched of an evening when all the swallows are lined up on a wire and how exact the spaces are they have in between them.

A: Yes, I have.

K: It's marvellous to see this space. And space is necessary. And we have no space physically, with more and more population and all the rest of it. And therefore there is more and more violence, more and more living together in a small flat, thousands of people crowded together, breathing the same air, thinking the same thing, seeing the same television, reading the same book, going to the same church, believing the same thing, having the same sorrow, the same anxiety, the same fears. My country – all that. So mind, and thus the brain, has very little space. And space is necessary, otherwise I stifle. So can the mind have space? And there will be no space if there is a direction.

A: Of course.

K: There is no space if direction means time. When the mind is occupied with the family, with business, with God, with drink, with sex, with experience, occupied, filled, there is no space.

A: That's right. Exactly.

K: So when knowledge occupies the whole field of the mind as thought, there is no space. And thought creates a space around itself as the 'me' enclosed and 'you' enclosed, 'we' and 'they'. So the self, the 'me', which is the very essence of thought, has its own little space and to move out of that space is terror, is fear, is anxiety – because I am only used to that little space.

A: Yes, exactly. That brings us back to an earlier conversation when we touched on the point of terror.

K: Yes, that's right. Not being and being is in the little space which thought has created. So thought can never give space.

A: Of course not.

K: So meditation is the freeing of the mind of its content as consciousness which creates its own little space. You follow, sir?

A: Yes, I do.

K: So from that one asks: 'Is that possible?' Because I'm occupied with my wife, my children, my responsibilities, I care for the tree, I care for the cat, I care for this and that and I'm occupied, occupied, occupied.

A: This throws a marvellous light on that saying of Jesus which people have pondered and thought very strange: 'Foxes have holes and birds of the air have nests but the Son of Man hath not where to lay his head.' Man as such who understands is not inventing a space for himself. It fits perfectly.

K: I don't know what . . .

A: No, I understand. This just flashed over me. Our conversations have been such a revelation to me with respect to the literatures that I've soaked myself in for so many years. It's a demonstration to me of what you've said: for instance, in so far as I ask these questions of myself personally, precisely as they become answered so all these things out here become answered. And what could be more empirically demonstrable to an individual that 'I am the world and the world is me' than that!

K: That's right. So, sir, look. The world is getting more and more overpopulated, cities are growing more and more, spreading, spreading, spreading, suburbs, and so on. Man is getting less and less space and therefore driving out animals, killing. You follow? And, having no space out there, outwardly, except on occasions when I go off into the country and say to myself: my God, I wish I could live here. But I can't because I've got responsibilities and so on.

So, can there be space inwardly? When there is space inwardly there is space outwardly.

A: Exactly.

K: But the outward space is not going to give the inner space. The inner space of mind that is free from occupation, though it is occupied for the moment with what it has to do, the moment it is finished it is over with, it is free. I don't carry the office to my home. It is over with. So space in the mind means the emptying of consciousness of all its content and therefore the consciousness which thought as the 'me' has created ends and therefore there is space. And that space isn't yours or mine, it is space.

A: Yes, I was thinking of the creation story in Genesis. The appearance of space occurs when the waters are separated from the waters and we have the vault over which the birds fly and this space is called heaven.

K: It is heaven. That's right.

A: Of course, of course. But then we read that, you see, we don't ...

K: Fortunately I don't read any of those things! So space, direction, time, will, choice, control. Now, all that has importance in my living, in the daily living of my life, in the life of every human being. If he doesn't know what the meaning of meditation is, he merely lives in the field of knowledge and therefore that becomes a prison. And therefore being in prison he says, I must escape through entertainment, through God, through this and through that, through amusement. You know, that is what is actually taking place.

A: The word 'vacation' says it all, doesn't it.

K: Yes, absolutely.

A: To vacate is to exit into space, but then we go from one hole to another!

K: To another hole. So if that is clearly established, perceived in myself, I see the thing operating in my daily life, then what takes place? Space means silence. If there is no silence there is direction, it is the operation of will, I must do, I must not do, I must practise this, I must get this, you follow? The should be, should not be, what has been, what should not be, regrets. All that operates. Therefore space means silence inwardly.

A: That's very deep, very, very deep. Archetypally, we associate manifestation, as over against latency, with sound.

K: Yes, sound.

A: And what you have said puts the whole thing into astonishing ...

K: Silence isn't the space between two noises, silence isn't the cessation of noise, silence isn't something that thought has created. It comes naturally, inevitably as you open, as you observe, as you examine, as you investigate. So then the question arises, silence without a movement, whether of direction, movement of thought or movement of time, can that silence operate in my daily life? I live in the field of noise as knowledge. That I have to do. And is there a living with silence and at the same time with the other? The two moving together, two rivers flowing in balance. No division. In harmony. There is no division. Is that possible? Because otherwise, if that's not possible, to be deeply honest, I can only live there, in the field of knowledge. I don't know if you see this?

A: Oh yes.

K: For me it is possible. I am not saying this out of vanity, I say this in great humility. I think that is possible, it is so. Then what takes place? Then what is creation? Is creation something to be expressed – in paint, in a poem, in a statue, in writing, in bringing about a baby? Is that creation? Must creation be expressed? To us it must be expressed – to most people. Otherwise one feels frustrated, anxious, I am not living. All that business. So what is creation? One can only answer that if one has really gone through all this. Otherwise creation becomes a rather cheap thing.

A: Yes, it becomes, in terms of the word expressed, simply something pressed out.

K: Pressed out, of course.

A: That's all.

K: That's all. Like the life of literary people who – some of them – are everlastingly in battle in themselves, with tension and all that, and out of that they write a book, become famous.

A: Yes, the psychological theory that works of art are based on neurosis, which means I am driven.

K: Yes, so what is creation? Is it something, a flowering in which the flower does not know that it is flowering?

A: Exactly, exactly.

K: Yes, sir. So, sir, see what takes place. Creation in my living. You follow, sir? Not expressing, creating a beautiful chair, this or that may come, will come, but in living. And from that arises another question which is really much more important: thought is measure. And as long as we cultivate thought, and all our actions are based on thought as is the case now, the search for the immeasurable has no meaning. I can give a meaning to it, say there is the immeasurable, there is the unnameable, there is the eternal, don't let's talk

A WHOLLY DIFFERENT WAY OF LIVING

about it, it is there. That has no meaning, that is just a supposition, a speculation, or the assertion of a few who think they know. One has discarded all that. Therefore one asks, when the mind is utterly silent, what is the immeasurable, what is the everlasting, what is the eternal? Not in terms of God and all the things Man has invented. Actually to *be that*. Now silence in that deep sense of the word opens the door. Because there you've got all your energy, not a thing is wasted, there is no dissipation of energy at all. Therefore in that silence there is the summation of energy.

A: Precisely.

K: Not stimulated energy, not self-projected energy, and so on, that's all too childish. Because there is no conflict, no control, no reaching out or not reaching, searching, asking, questioning, demanding, waiting, praying, none of that. Therefore all that energy which has been wasted is now gathered in that silence. You follow? That silence has become sacred.

A: Of course it has.

K: Not the sacred thing which thought has invented.

A: Not the sacred over against the profane.

K: No, not all that. So it is only such a sacred mind that can see this, the most supreme sacred, the essence of all that is sacred, which is beauty. You follow, sir?

A: I do.

K: So there it is. God isn't something that man has invented, or created out of his image and longing and failure. But when the mind itself becomes sacred, then it opens the door to something that is immeasurably sacred. That is religion. And that affects the daily living, the way I talk, the way I treat people, the conduct, behaviour – all that. That is the religious life. If that doesn't exist then every other kind of mischief will exist, however clever, however intelligent, however – all that.

A: And meditation does not occur where there is disorder.

K: That is the most profound religious way of living. You see, sir, another thing takes place. As this thing is happening, because your energy is being gathered – energy is being gathered, not yours – you have other kinds of power, extra-sensory power, you can do miracles, all of this has happened to me, exorcism, all that kind of stuff, and healing. But they become totally irrelevant. Not that you don't love people. On the contrary religion is the essence of that. But they are all secondary issues: and people get caught in the secondary issues. I mean, look at what has happened, a man who can really heal becomes someone people worship – because of a little healing.

A: It reminds me of a story you told me once about an old man sitting on the bank of a river and a young man came to see him, after the older man had sent him away to learn what he needed to learn. And he came back with the marvellous announcement that he could now walk on water. The older man looked at him and said: 'So you can walk on water. You have taken all these years to learn how to walk on water. Didn't you see there was a boat over there?'

K: You see, sir, that's very important. Religion, as we have said, is the gathering of all energy, which is attention. In that attention many things happen. Some of them have this gift of healing, miracles. I've had it and I know what I'm speaking about; and the religious man never touches it. He may say occasionally: 'Do this or that' but it is a thing to be put away, like a gift, like a talent. It is to be put away because it is a danger.

A: Exactly.

K: The more you are talented, the more 'me', 'I' am important, 'I' have this talent, worship 'me'. With that talent I'll get money, position, power. So this too is a most dangerous thing. So a mind that is religious is aware of all this and lives a life . . .

A: . . . in this space, in this marvellous space. This reminds me of your earlier remark that energy, when it patterns itself – I've forgotten how you described the nature of the patterned energy, but I suspect it's what we call matter . . .

K: Matter, yes.

A: . . . right. In terms of this pointing to act that you have mentioned, it throws a very different light on the character of patterned energy and draws our gaze away from the pattern and reminds us that the substantive element that we point to is not the pattern but the energy.

K: Energy, quite. You see sir, that is love, isn't it?

A: Precisely.

K: And when there is this sense of a religious summation of energy that is love, that is compassion and care. That operates in daily life.

A: In love the pattern never resists change.

K: So, you see, sir, with that love you can do what you like, it will still be love. But there the love becomes sensation. You follow?

A: Yes, the whole track of knowledge.

K: And therefore there is no love there.

A: Yes, that image of the toy train that goes round and round and round.

K: You see, that means can the mind – I'm using the word 'mind' in the sense of mind, brain, body, the whole thing – can the mind be really silent? Not induced silence, not silence put together, not silence that thought imagines is silence. Not the silence of a church or temple. They have their own silence when you enter a temple or an old cathedral, they have an extraordinary sense of silence, thousands of people have chanted, talked, prayed and all that. But it is above all that, it is not that. So this silence isn't contrived and therefore it is real. It isn't a silence that I have brought about through practice.

A: No, it's not what you mentioned earlier, that space between two noises because that would become an interval and as an interval it simply becomes successive.

K: That's right.

A: This is extraordinary in terms of the continuing return to questioning. It seems to me that it's only in the attitude of the question that there's any possibility of even intuiting from afar the possibility of the silence, since already the answer is a noise.

K: Yes. So, sir – just a minute, there is something very interesting – does this come about through questioning?

A: No, I didn't mean to suggest that questioning generates it. I meant that simply to take a step back from the enthralment and enchantment with answers is in itself a necessary step.

K: Of course.

A: And that in itself has its own terror.

K: Of course. But I'm asking, does silence, does the sense of the immeasurable, come about by my questioning?

A: No.

K: No. Perception sees the false and discards the false. There is no question, it sees, and it's finished. But if I keep on questioning I keep on doubting; doubt has its place but it must be kept on a leash.

A: Now, let me ask you a question here, if I may. The act of perceiving is, as you have said, the doing, there's absolutely no interval.

K: I see danger and I act.

A: Exactly. Now, in this perceiving, the act is totally free and then every energy pattern is free to become changed.

K: Yes, quite, sir.

A: No more hoarding to itself . . .

K: No regrets.

A: . . . all that it has worked for all its life. And amazingly though, it seems to me, there is a corollary to this. Not only is the pattern free to be changed but the energy is free to pattern itself.

K: Or not to pattern.

A: Or not to pattern.

K: There it patterns. In knowledge it has to pattern.

A: Of course.

K: But here it can't pattern, pattern for what? If it patterns it has become thought again. And therefore thought, if it is divisive, is superficial. Somebody was telling me the other day that in the Eskimo language 'thought' means the outside. Very interesting. When they say, go outside, the word is 'thought'. So thought has created the outer and the inner. If thought is not, then there is neither the outer nor the inner: that is space. It isn't that I've got inner space.

A: No. We've been talking about meditation in relation to religion and I feel I must ask you to speak about the relationship of prayer to meditation, because eventually we always refer to both.

K: To repeat a prayer has no place in meditation. To whom am I praying? Whom am I supplicating, begging, asking?

A: A prayer as petition has no place in it. But is there any use of the word 'prayer' that would be consonant with what we've been talking about?

K: If there is no petition, deeply, inwardly . . .

A: No grabbing, grasping . . .

K: . . . because the grabber is the grabbed.

A: Exactly.

K: If there is no petition what takes place? I petition only when I don't understand, when I'm in conflict, when I'm in sorrow, when I say: 'Oh, God, I've lost everything, I'm finished, I can't arrive, I can't achieve.'

A: When there's no petition I can look. Yes. Exactly.

K: A woman came to see me some time ago. She said: 'I have prayed enormously for years. I have prayed for a refrigerator. And I have got it.' Yes, sir! I pray for peace, and I live a life of violence all the time. I have divided my country from another country and I pray for *my* country. It becomes so childish.

A: In conventional prayers there is usually both petition and praise.

K: Of course, praising and receiving. You must know how in a Sanskrit chant it always begins, some parts of it, praising and then begging. There is a marvellous chant which asks for the protection of the gods, and it says: 'May you protect my steps.' Praising God, then saying: 'Please protect my steps'. So if there is no petition, because the petitioner is the petition, the beggar is the begged, is the receiver, then what takes place in the mind? No asking.

A: An immense quietude, immense quietude. The proper sense of whatever the word 'tranquillity' points to.

K: That's right, sir. That is real peace, not the phoney peace they are all talking about – politicians and the religious people. There is no asking a thing.

A: There is a very beautiful Biblical phrase: 'The peace which passeth all understanding.'

K: I heard that phrase when I was a small boy.

A: I've always asked myself since childhood how there can be so much talk about such a thing and so little evidence of it.

K: Sir, you know books have become tremendously important. What 'they' have written, what 'they' have said. And so the human mind has become secondhand; or the mind that has acquired so much knowledge about what other people have experienced about reality, how can such a mind experience or find or come upon that which is original?

A: Not by that route.

K: No. And can the mind empty itself of its content? If it cannot, it cannot acquire, then reject, then receive. You follow?

A: Yes.

K: Why should I go through all those things? Why can't I say, 'I'll look. There is no book in the world that is going to teach me, there is no teacher who is going to teach me.'? Because the teacher is the taught, the disciple is the teacher.

A: As we said in an earlier conversation on the subject of looking, if one holds that statement: 'I am the world and the world is me', it is an occasion for healing.

K: Yes, sir.

A: But that very statement: 'I am the world and the world is me' sounds, as you have said so often, so absurd that one starts to bolt again.

K: I know.

A: To panic again.

K: That means one has to be very, very serious. It isn't a thing that you play with.

A: No, it's not what's called these days a 'fun thing'.

K: No sir!

A: In no sense. The discussion that you have undertaken concerning meditation is so total. It isn't a thing that you do among other things.

K: Meditation means attention, care. That's part of it, care for my children, for my neighbour, for my country, for the Earth, for the trees, for the animals. Don't kill animals, don't kill them to eat, it's so unnecessary: it's part of the tradition which says you must eat meat. Therefore, sir, all of this comes down to a sense of deep, inward seriousness, and that seriousness itself brings about attention, care and responsibility, and everything that we have discussed. It isn't that one has gone through all this, one sees it; and the very perception is action which is wisdom, because wisdom is the ending of suffering. It isn't callousness, but the ending of suffering. And the ending of suffering means the observation, the seeing of suffering. Not to go beyond it, refuse it, rationalize it or run away from it, just to see it. Let it flower. And as you are choicelessly aware of this flowering, it comes naturally to wither away. I don't have to do something about it.

A: Marvellous how energy can be free to pattern itself or not pattern itself.

K: Yes, sir. It covers the whole of Man's endeavour, his thoughts, his anxieties, everything.

A: So, in our conversations, we have reached the point of consummation here. I wonder if Shakespeare had some intimation of this when he said: 'Ripeness is all.'

K: Sir, time comes to an end, time stops. In silence, time stops.

A: In silence, time stops. Immensely beautiful. I must express to you my gratitude from the bottom of my heart. I hope you will let me, because throughout our discussions I have been undergoing a transformation.

K: Because you are willing enough to listen, good enough to listen. Most people are not, they won't listen. You took the time, the trouble, the care to listen.

A: I've already seen, in relation to my classes, in the activity my students and I share, the beginning of a flowering. Again, thank you so much.

28 February 1974